#189

Gwendolyn,

your brother
In Christ

Terry

#184 6 of 7-61-9

Gwendolyn

your brother

In Christ!

Jim

𝔍𝔢𝔰𝔲𝔰 𝔠𝔥𝔯𝔦𝔰𝔱𝔲𝔰 𝔤𝔢𝔰𝔱𝔢𝔯𝔫 𝔲𝔫𝔡 𝔥𝔢𝔲𝔱𝔢
𝔲𝔫𝔡 𝔡𝔢𝔯 𝔰𝔢𝔩𝔟𝔢 𝔞𝔲𝔠𝔥 𝔦𝔫 𝔈𝔴𝔦𝔤𝔨𝔢𝔦𝔱

בראשית ברא אלהים
את השמים ואת הארץ

CAIN'S WIFE

and other

Biblical Conundrums

𝔍𝔢𝔰𝔲𝔰 𝔠𝔥𝔯𝔦𝔰𝔱 𝔱𝔥𝔢 𝔰𝔞𝔪𝔢
𝔶𝔢𝔰𝔱𝔢𝔯𝔡𝔞𝔶 𝔞𝔫𝔡 𝔱𝔬 𝔡𝔞𝔶 𝔞𝔫𝔡 𝔣𝔬𝔯 𝔢𝔳𝔢𝔯

Ιησους Χριστος εχθες και
σημερον ο αυτος και εις τους αιωας

Terry A. Roberts

Jesus Christ is the same
yesterday today and forever

IESVS CHRISTVS HERI ET
HODIE IPSE ET IN SAECVLA

WESTBOW
PRESS®
A DIVISION OF THOMAS NELSON
& ZONDERVAN

Copyright © 2018 Terry A. Roberts.

All rights reserved. No part of this book may be used or reproduced by any means, graphic, electronic, or mechanical, including photocopying, recording, taping or by any information storage retrieval system without the written permission of the author except in the case of brief quotations embodied in critical articles and reviews.

Unless otherwise stated, scripture taken from the New King James Version®. Copyright © 1982 by Thomas Nelson. Used by permission. All rights reserved.
Scripture taken from the King James Version of the Bible.
Scripture texts in this work are taken from the New American Bible, revised edition © 2010, 1991, 1986, 1970 Confraternity of Christian Doctrine, Washington, D.C. and are used by permission of the copyright owner. All Rights Reserved. No part of the New American Bible may be reproduced in any form without permission in writing from the copyright owner.
Scripture quotations marked (NIV) are taken from the Holy Bible, New International Version®, NIV®. Copyright © 1973, 1978, 1984, 2011 by Biblica, Inc.™ Used by permission of Zondervan. All rights reserved worldwide. www.zondervan.com The "NIV" and "New International Version" are trademarks registered in the United States Patent and Trademark Office by Biblica, Inc.™

WestBow Press books may be ordered through booksellers or by contacting:

WestBow Press
A Division of Thomas Nelson & Zondervan
1663 Liberty Drive
Bloomington, IN 47403
www.westbowpress.com
1 (866) 928-1240

Because of the dynamic nature of the Internet, any web addresses or links contained in this book may have changed since publication and may no longer be valid. The views expressed in this work are solely those of the author and do not necessarily reflect the views of the publisher, and the publisher hereby disclaims any responsibility for them.

ISBN: 978-1-9736-1320-6 (sc)
ISBN: 978-1-9736-1322-0 (hc)
ISBN: 978-1-9736-1321-3 (e)

Library of Congress Control Number: 2018900190

Print information available on the last page.

WestBow Press rev. date: 3/1/2018

Contents

Author's Note ix
Acknowledgments and Art Credits xix
Dedication xxxi
Foreword xxxiii

Chapter 1	How we got the Bible	1
Chapter 2	Time	21
Chapter 3	Genesis: The Creation Stories	31
Chapter 4	Cain's Wife	61
Chapter 5	Noah's Ark and the Flood	75
Chapter 6	The Tower of Babel	107
Chapter 7	I will go down now and see	119
Chapter 8	Angels, Aliens, Ghosts & Giants	131
Chapter 9	Jonah	157
Chapter 10	Mary	169
Chapter 11	Merry Christmas	189
Chapter 12	INRI	213
Chapter 13	"That's in the Bible Somewhere – I Think?"	223
Chapter 14	List	231

    Genealogies 232
    The Ten Commandments 238
    Comparison Of Old Testament Book Orders 240
    The Twelve Sons And Twelve Tribes 243
    Twelve Disciples 247
    The Women Of The Cross 255

Appendix: of American Christian Holidays 265
Post Script 293
Heaven's Junk Yard 296
Plan of Salvation-My Commitment to Jesus Christ 299

UNBROKEN CIRCLE BOOKS, A division of REVTAR Productions, by Terry A. Roberts are:

You've Got to Be Somewhere, An American Odyssey WestBow Press, a Division of Thomas Nelson and Zondervan, 2015. (originally published by CrossBooks, a Division of LifeWay, 2014.)

LETTERS HOME: One Man, Three Wars, A Patriot Odyssey WestBow Press, a Division of Thomas Nelson and Zondervan, 2015.

Cain's Wife and other Biblical Conundrums
WestBow Press, a Division of Thomas Nelson and Zondervan, 2018.

Author's Note

"In the beginning, God." In the end, that is enough said, and that is really all we need to know.

For those with more inquiring minds, I will attempt to pen these pages for the purposes of deepening faith in Jesus Christ through the Holy Spirit, while spurring spiritual discussion, and to challenge long, and deep held personal thoughts, beliefs, and opinions. This is a discussion book. Read this book as if I am speaking directly to you, and your discussion group friends. The goal for all who turn these pages is to have more Biblically-rooted spiritual insight, and academic clarity with good solid Biblically-based notions and concepts. Because some issues are beyond the scope and purpose of this work, some topics are treated with a "broad-brush," while others receive the "fine-tooth comb" treatment.

THE BIBLE IS NOT A PUZZLE TO BE SOLVED, BUT A TREASURE TO BE DISCOVERED.

I will be approaching this work from the perspective of a conservative Christian in the year of our Lord 2018, who is most particularly an "over fifty" white male Southern Baptist. I was brought into the saving grace of Jesus Christ as a seven-year-old first-grader. I have grown in faith, and knowledge, as well as, hopefully wisdom since then, and it is my eternal hope that all who turn these pages will do the same. After I somehow graduated from the Walter E. Stebbins High School, in Dayton, Ohio in 1984, I received my Bachelor of Arts in Religion and History from Cumberland College in Williamsburg, Kentucky in 1989 (now the University of the Cumberlands). Additionally, I received my Master of

Divinity Degree from The Southern Baptist Theological Seminary in Louisville, Kentucky in 1993.

From here, I pastored and served in churches in Ohio, Kentucky, West Virginia, and Alabama. I also retired from the military, being a disabled triple war combat veteran of the Persian Gulf War 1990-91, Iraq Invasion 2003, and Afghanistan 2009 respectively. I first served as an enlisted Marine in the Persian Gulf War, and later as a Navy and Marine Corps Chaplain with Marines, and various "green-side Sailors." Also, I am currently a cancer survivor. I have been fighting this diabolical plague since 2010. Additionally, I have a practical grasp of the humanities, math and science, with a fine mix of life experience, and world travels, marbled with worldly wisdom, all of which the Apostle Paul calls foolishness. "For the wisdom of this world is foolishness with God..." (I Corinthians 3:19a).

While I am "conservative," I would not consider myself "ultra-conservative." Although, those with heretical and/or left leaning views may disagree. On the other hand, those who are ultra-conservative, may indeed think me a heretic. While you, your friends, and acquaintances enjoy Sunday night after church parking lot debates, or those mystic middle-of-the-night camp fire discussions; I would encourage you, and your group discussion friends to explore the well weathered and feathered pages of your Bibles so that you can know what you know and why you believe it. As an additional note, I still use my well weathered, black leather, tattered and torn, and many times taped, New King James Version of the Bible, I received for my 1993 ordination. Most Biblical references will be taken from the same unless otherwise noted. Some key thoughts to remember while surveying this text:

WHAT DOES THE SCRIPTURE SAY?
WHAT DOES THE SCRIPTURE NOT SAY?

We all read the scripture through the lens of our own education and experience, as well as, our individual family and church traditions. Throughout the book, I challenge you the individual, or group readers to: Dig-Discover-Discuss. This is a discussion book. You can draw your own conclusions – enjoy.

Saying *I don't know ... but I just think,* is usually not a great discussion tool for debate.

The target audience of this book is anyone who is trying to better understand his or her Bible, and their faith; whether they are a new Christian, or someone who has been in Christ for many years. Although, this work may also be of interest to most anyone who is merely curious about the Bible and Christianity. A certain level and amount of academic acumen has been used to produce this volume. However, for those who are looking for a more high-brow, and high-minded distant, dusty, dull, dry, drab doctoral dissertation for use at Harvard, Yale, Oxford, or Cambridge ... you may want to look elsewhere for your Biblical enlightenment. Hopefully, you will find this book to be interesting, intriguing, engaging, poetic, and many times humorous, but always challenging.

What is my inspiration for writing? During my last military deployment in 2009, I was with the Marines. I was the Command Chaplain for the Second Battalion, Eighth Infantry Regiment of the Second Marine Division of Camp Lejeune, North Carolina. We were in mortal combat against the Taliban in the Garmser District of the Helmand Province in southwestern Afghanistan. Here, we sadly lost fourteen courageous young men with scores of others being wounded in various degrees. I mostly slept on the ground along with my faithful body guard, Petty Officer Timothy W. Ross of Simi Valley, California. One sultry morning while I was arising from the dust and sandman dreams of being at home in my own bed, far away from this most dreadful and desolate places; one of my staff sergeants, Staff Sergeant Bowles, walked by and said to me, "Sir, you should write a book." Shortly upon returning home, and in short course of being diagnosed with cancer, I began penning my first book, *You've Got to Be Somewhere, An American Odyssey,* which was published in 2014. This was quickly followed by the companion book in 2015, *LETTERS HOME: One Man, Three Wars, A Patriot Odyssey.* The nature of these first two books, was my spiritual journey, through the kaleidoscope of my life in the ministry and military. Whereas, the nature of this *Cain's Wife* book, is to be primarily based upon the Biblical record. In places it is colored by my own human experience.

My writing inspiration is strongly influenced by several sources. First of these would be, my ancestor, John Filson. John was a cousin to my Great-great-great Grandfather, Samuel Filson. These men were of Scots-Irish extraction and American Revolutionary stock. Among many talents, John Filson was an author, college professor, school teacher, explorer, Indian fighter, frontiersman, friend of Daniel Boone, land agent, map maker, a co-founder of what would be the city of Cincinnati, Ohio, and was the first historian of Kentucky. His legendary and groundbreaking work was published in 1784, *The Discovery, Settlement and present State of Kentucke*, which bounded Daniel Boone onto the world stage as an American frontier legend. However, John's first commercial map of Kentucky was rejected by George Washington. Another source of inspiration was the legendary American Civil War authority, writer, and historian, the late great Shelby Foote, as well as, the American frontier writer, Allan W. Eckert, who has also recently passed on to the angels and the ages. This "angels or ages" issue depends on how one wants to interpret, or remember what was said at the bedside when President Abraham Lincoln passed on into eternity. Many of my youthful hours were wished away as I turned the pages these men wrote, envisioning that I was participating in the stories alongside the American heroes of whom they wrote about; and hoping one day to only be at least half the writers they were.

The poetic side of my writing along with the strong use of alliteration, acrostics, and other similar literary, and verbal vehicles, was somewhat influenced by the drummer and lyric writer, Neil Peart, of the Canadian musical rock group, Rush. However, our spiritual views on Jesus Christ and Christianity are diametrically opposed.

My series of books fall under the banner of *Unbroken Circle Books*. Those familiar with gospel music will recognize the "unbroken circle" theme. The other side of this double-entendre is the thirteen stars which were supposedly laid out in a circle pattern on our nation's first flag by Betsy Ross under the direction and request of General George Washington. Upon leaving for Afghanistan in 2009, my friend, Lieutenant Commander and Navy Dentist, Andrew Varga, of Bradenton, Florida, gave me a Betsy Ross Flag to carry into combat. After the deployment, at our memorial service at Camp Lejeune, I referenced the thirteen fallen Marines, and compared them to the unbroken circle of stars on my flag. Later, my friend, Dr. Andy Varga asserted that he was glad he did not give me a flag with fifty stars. Sadly, a few days after the memorial service, we lost a fourteenth fallen hero.

Even though the book is entitled *Cain's Wife, and other Biblical Conundrums*, the Cain's Wife part is only a short portion of the volume. This title is mostly for the purposes of my own self indulgence and enjoyment. Although, the much discussed and debated topic of Cain's wife is, in fact, the genesis of why I put quill pen to parchment to produce this work, with all the other topics being the progeny and off-shoots of this original idea. The concept of a "conundrum" is a discussion river which shall never run dry.

I have used a "shingled," or a layered approach to the topics covered in this work. In places it will appear that the same topic is covered, or touched upon in multiple places. This approach shows that the whole Bible is interrelated, intra-woven, and connected on many levels. The issue of the *War in Heaven,* with the fall of Lucifer, and one third of his angels out of Heaven, is one of these issues as, it is the central tap-root to the *Problem of Evil,* which we all have struggled with since the dawn of time. The Bible is not a monolithic work, nor is it a set of non-connected, pigeon-holed topics, but rather a series of many interrelated topics with a single goal – the salvation of God's people through the saving grace of Jesus Christ through the working hand of the Holy Spirit.

As a special note to the reader: where Hebrew font is inserted into the text, remember that the written Hebrew language is read "right-to-left." Greek font is also used to a lesser degree, and is read in the conventional "left-to-right" mode as is English. For the purposes of print clarity and simplicity, I have chosen not to use the Hebrew vowel point system, or the *daghesh lene* for the Beth, Gimel, Daleth, Kaph, Pe, and Tau consonants.

A special note of gratitude to Dr. Robert C. Dunston, "Dr. Bob," for my Hebrew instruction at Cumberland College so long ago. My many apologies beforehand to the aforesaid Dr. Bob for any such malfeasance, difficulties, or troubles with translation which may have occurred during the production of this work with regards to the Hebrew language.

Also, a special note of thanks to my many talented artists: Ariane L. Brown of Cincinnati, Ohio, Connie S. Gifford of Kettering, Ohio, and Jennifer L. Martin of Centerville, Ohio. They have brought to life and vision what I have tried to convey in mere words. It is said, "A picture is worth a thousand words." No truer words have ever been spoken.

My original thoughts expressed in this work are based upon my faith in Jesus Christ through the Holy Spirit. These original thoughts are underpinned by the bedrock of my faith, my aforementioned education, ministry experience, sermon preparation for thousands of sermons, and decades of Biblical study. While I am not using a strict bibliographical format, I must give academic credit to those who have studied, written, and published before me, for all those allusive micro details such as: times, dates, numbers, titles, spellings, and other such public domain minutia particulars. The following is a list of published academic credit in no particular order:

The Believer's Study Bible, New King James Version, Thomas Nelson Publishers, Nashville, Tennessee 1991

The Holy Bible 1611 Edition King James Version, Thomas Nelson Publishers, Nashville, Tennessee. (London, England, 1611)

The Thompson Chain Reference Bible, King James Version, B.B. Kirkbridge Bible Company, Indianapolis, Indiana, 1964

New International Version, International Bible Society, Colorado Springs, Colorado, 1984

The New American Bible, Catholic Book Publishing Corporation, New Jersey, 1992

Biblia Hebraica Stuttgartensia, Deutsche Bibelgesellschaft, Stuttgart, Federal Republic of Germany, 1967

The Greek New Testament, United Bible Society, Third edition, Stuttgart, Federal Republic of Germany, 1983

Strong's Exhaustive Concordance of the Bible, James Strong, Thomas Nelson Publishers, Nashville, Tennessee, 1996

The Broadman Bible Commentary series, Broadman Press, Nashville, Tennessee, 1970

All of the Men of the Bible, Herbert Lockyer, Zondervan Publishing House, Grand Rapids, Michigan, 1958

Mercer Dictionary of the Bible, Watson E. Mills – General Editor, Mercer University Press, Macon, Georgia, 1990

Pictorial Bible Dictionary, Merrill C. Tenney – General Editor, Zondervan Publishing House, Grand Rapids, Michigan, 1976

The Timechart of Biblical History, compilation by Samuel T. Jordan - Chartwell Books Inc., New York 2010 edition

Noah's Ark Pocket Guide, Dr. Ken Ham & Tim Lovett, Answers In Genesis, Petersburg, Kentucky, 2016 edition

The Global Flood Pocket Guide, Dr. Ken Ham & Tim Lovett, Answers In Genesis, Petersburg, Kentucky 2016 edition

The Origin of Species, Sixth Edition, Charles Darwin, Barnes & Nobles Classics, New York, 2004

Chariots of the GODS, Fourth Edition, Erich von Daniken, Berkley Books, New York, 1999

The Declaration of Independence, Thomas Jefferson, Philadelphia, July 4, 1776, reproduced by: Applewood Books, Bedford, Massachusetts,

The Discovery, Settlement and Present State of Kentucke, John Filson, Corinth Books, New York 1962 (originally published in 1784)

The Historical Atlas of the Celtic World, Dr, Ian Barnes, Chartwell Books, Inc, New York, 2010

The Historical Atlas of Native Americans, Dr. Ian Barnes Chartwell Books, Inc, New York, 2010

The American Heritage Dictionary of the English Language, American Heritage Publishing Company Houghton Mifflin Company, Boston, 1973

Langenscheidt's German-English English-German Dictionary, Pocket Books sixth edition, New York, 1973

Google, various public domain articles

Glossary Of Technical Terms

Antediluvian – "Before the Deluge," or the period before the Noah flood.

Apocrypha – Various intertestimental writing. The Roman Catholic Church accepts some books as Canon, whereas these writings are largely rejected as Canon by Protestant groups.

Canon – The thirty-nine Old Testament and twenty-seven New Testament books of the Bible officially recognized by the Church.

Christophany – An Old Testament or pre-nativity physical human appeareance of God, most specifically Jesus Christ.

Conundrum – A problem admitting to no satisfactory solution.

El or Elohim – An ancient Hebrew name for God.

Pangaea – The concept that all the continental land masses were originally of one semi-contiguous land mass.

Theophany – An Old Testament physical human appearance of God. (see Christophany)

YHWH – Or Yaweh, - The TO BE name of God as revealed to Moses in the Burning Bush on Mount Sinai.

Acknowledgments and Art Credits

SPECIAL THANKS AND GRATITUDE TO DR. BOB DUNSTON FOR DOING THE FORWARD FOR THIS WORK.

Dr. Robert C. Dunston, Williamsburg, Kentucky:
Doctor of Philosophy in Old Testament-
The Southern Baptist Theological Seminary, Louisville, Kentucky.
Master of Theology-
Union Theological Seminary, Richmond, Virginia.
Master of Divinity-
Midwestern Baptist Theological Seminary, Kansas City, Missouri.
Bachelor of Science in Mathematics-
Virginia Polytechic Institute and State University (Virginia Tech), Blacksburg, Virginia.

Department Chair and Professor of the Missions and Ministry Department, University of the Cumberlands (Cumberland College), Williamsburg, Kentucky. Ad Hoc Interim Pastor for churches in the Appalachian region of Kentucky and Tennessee.

Doctor Robert C. Dunston has been affectionally known as "Dr. Bob" by his students at Cumberland College/University of the Cumberlands since 1983. I began my tutelage under Dr. Bob in the fall of 1984 and have considered him as an academic inspiration, but even more so as a friend ever since.

Editor-in-Chief

Kevin L. Wilson: Fairborn, Ohio:
Master of Arts in Music Education-
Wright State University, Fairborn, Ohio.
Bachelor of Arts in Music Education-
Wright State University, Fairborn, Ohio.

Minister of Music and Worship
University Baptist Church, Middletown, Ohio.
Choir Director/Music Instructor/Stage Production.
Vandalia-Bulter High School, Vandalia, Ohio.

Kevin was my Editor-in-Chief for this
"Cain's Wife" book as well as my second book,
"LETTERS HOME: One Man, Three Wars, A Patriot Odyssey."
Kevin has served as a bi-vocational minister of music in various
Southern Baptist churches in the Dayton, Ohio area since 1987.
Additionally, Kevin has been a music instructor at Vandalia-Bulter High School
since 1990. Kevin and I have been best friends of the first order since 1973.

Concept & Content Editorial Team

Harrison M. Cyrus, Esquire, South Charleston, West Virginia,
Juris Doctor-
West Virginia University, Morgantown, West Virginia
Bachelor of Arts in History-
Marshall University, Huntington, West Virginia.

Associate at Bailey & Wyant, Attorneys at Law, Charleston, West Virginia

Harrison is licensed in, practicing insurance personal injury defense, constitutional law, and employment law attorney, in the states of West Virginia and Kentucky. I have known Harrison since he was born and regard him as a nephew.

Kellie M. Sweeney Cyrus, Prichard, West Virginia:
Master of Science in Adult and Technical Education-
Marshall University, Huntington, West Virginia.
Bachelor of Arts in Elememtary/Early Childhood Education-
Marshall University, Huntington, West Virginia.
Associate of Science in Nursing-
St. Mary's School of Nursing, Huntington, West Virginia.

Assistant Professor and Medical Assistant Program Director,

Mountwest Community and Technical College, Huntington, West Virginia.

Kellie has been a nurse as well as a youth and children's minister in

American Baptist Churches in West Virginia for over a decade. I have considered her as a sister for decades.

David H. Foster, Fairfield, Ohio:
Master of Education-
Xavier University, Cincinnati, Ohio.
Master of Theology-
Xavier University, Cincinnati, Ohio.
Master in Executive Leadership & Organizational Change-
Northern Kentucky University, Highland Heights, Kentucky.
Bachelor in Business Management-
Indiana Wesleyan University, Marion, Indiana.
(Doctor of Leadership Studies in process
at Xavier University, Cincinnati, Ohio).

Director of Facilities for the Sycamore Community Schools, Cincinnati, Ohio Adjunct Professor, Haile/U.S. Bank School of Business, Northern Kentucky University, Highland Heights, Kentucky.

David is a retired First Sergeant of the United States Marine Corps (1980-2003) with over thirty Combat and Service awards. David has worked in public schools
as a facilities administrator in the Cincinnaiti area for decades. David is a faithful
Luthern and my military mentor. We have been "battle buddies" since 1987.

Pamela D. Northern McIntosh, Riverside, Ohio:
Certified Medical Administrative Assistant-
Sawyers College of Business, Dayton, Ohio.
Lexis-Nexis Certified Six Sigma Green Belt, Dayton, Ohio.

Content Quality Consultant for Reed Elsevier-Lexis-Nexis, Dayton, Ohio.
Certified Community Services Chaplain. Montgomery County Volunteer Jail Chaplain.
Treasurer/Secretary for Montgomery County Volunteer Jail Chaplain Board. Licensed Church of God Minister (Cleveland, Tennessee).
Sunday School Superintendent – Evangel Church of God, Dayton, Ohio.

Pamela was the editor for my first book,
You've Got to Be Somewhere, An American Odyssey,"
For many years, Pam has had an extensive uplifting
ministry to women in detention and those with chemical addiction. Pamela and I have been faithful childhood friends since 1973.

Reverend Mark S. Moore, Gastonia, North Carolina:
Master of Divinity-
The Southern Baptist Theological Seminary, Louisville, Kentucky.
Bachelor of Arts-
Mars Hill College, Mars Hill, North Carolina.
Associate of Arts-
Gaston College, Gastonia, North Carolina.

Founder & Executive Director,
Louder Than Words Mission Adventures, Weaverville, North Carolina.
Gaston Christian School, Gastonia, North Carolina.
Spanish Language/Culture Instructor & World Religions Instructor.

Mark and his wife, Amy and their six children
have been leading many to Christ as part time
missionaries to Hondouras, as well as, various domestic missions for the last two decades.
Mark is my ministry mentor and we have been friends since our Seminary days in the early 1990's.

Reverend Bryan N. Sweeney, Beckley, West Virginia:
Master of Theology and Christian Education-
The Southern Baptist Theological Seminary, Louisville, Kentucky.
Bachelor of Arts in Sociology-
Marshall University, Huntington, West Virginia.

Founder and Director of the West Virginia Baptist Convention Bow Hunter Retreat,
Parchment Valley, West Virginia. National Chair for Christian Bow Hunters of America, Medina, New York.

Bryan has been a social worker and American Baptist Youth Minister throughout West Virginia for the last three decades.

Bryan and I have been "best-buds and hunting buddies" since 1989 with more adventures than pen & ink can allow.

Chief Petty Officer Timothy W. Ross, Simi Valley, California:
Bachelor of Arts in Biblical Studies,
-Azusa Pacific Universtiy, Azusa, California.

Religious Program Specialist, United States Navy.
State Department, Military Detachment, United States Embassy, Canberra, Australia.

Tim Ross earned the rank of Eagle Scout while a Boy Scout,
as did his twin brother, Spencer, who is also in the Navy.
Chief Ross joined the Navy in 2008 as a Religious Programer (Chaplain Assistant).
Tim is a combat veteran and has three deployments to include being a a two-time deployer to Afghanistan. Tim was my combat body guard in Afghanistan in 2009 and is a friend that sticks closer than a brother.

Paul James Winslow, Cookeville, Tennessee:
"Honorary Doctorate" from the "School of Hard Knocks."
"Honorary Masters" degree in "Jack of all Trades and Master of Most."
"Honerary Bachelor" degree of a "Man after God's own Heart."

PJ is a veteran of the Army and the quintessential salt of the earth man.
PJ is the guy you want living next door, when something hits the fan.
He can fix, make, build, or invent most anything, from computers, plumbing, electricity, carpentry, welding, boat building and so more.

PJ is my near-kinsman through the circumstances of life
which I have had the great honor to share life with since
we were rambunctious little boys in the mid-1970's.
(PJ also wanted me to mention that he is 8-foot tall and
has slain many other giants.)

Special Thanks To My Artist And Other Contributors And Supporters

Ariane L. Brown of Cincinnati, Ohio for
the original interior black & white ink art graphics.

Connie S. Gifford of Kettering, Ohio for
The original interior black & white pencil and ink art graphics.

Jennifer L. Martin of Centerville, Ohio for
the original interior black & white pencil art graphics.

Chestor Ricks of the New View Management Group of Cincinnati, Ohio for the backcover author photo.

Susan Kemme of the New View Management Group, of Cincinnati, Ohio for graphic assistance for back cover author photo.

Erika Burns at the Beavercreek, Ohio, Office Depot, for various printing and graphic assistance.

Christen N. Garrett of Gauntlet Awards, Vandalia, Ohio
for various promotional materials

Carla and Todd Anderson at the Faith Christian Bookstore, Fairborn, Ohio for being the first book store to shelve my books.

Rose-Marie Bradley at Country Blessings Gifts, Xenia, Ohio for also shelving my books and for various promotion.

A Very Special Eternal Thanks To

Skip, Dottie, Mike, Kellie, Harrison, and Lensie Cyrus for allowing me to hunt and climb all over Cyrus Mountain for decades. The "wrap-around" background book cover image is a photo I took in May 2017, of one of the large car-sized rocks which sits atop the mountain.

Ultimately, I must thank my mom, **Nancy Roberts**, to whom this *Cain's Wife* book is dedicated. For many years, while at the wheel of a green '72 Plymouth, she drove me back-and-forth to the First Baptist Church of Fairborn, Ohio. Many of these years, my life hero, my late great dad, Jackie A. Roberts, did not always attend church for reasons unknown to either Mom or myself. So, Mom bore this burden of the eighteen-mile round trip to church each Wednesday night, and multiple times on Sundays. Many of these trips were in the dark of the night, often with snow and ice covering the roads. It was for certain, we floated on the feathered wings of angels, as we never ended up in a ditch, or worse, as we careened down the Colonel Glenn Highway. Without her noble efforts as a deeply dedicated Christian mother, I would not have become the man of God that I am, and certainly, this book would have never been written. ***Thanks Mom!!!***

Dedication

for Mom

Foreword

Paul wrote that the cross was the primary stumbling block for people considering the Christian faith (I Corinthians 1:18-25). From a human standpoint the cross seems to be a stange and foolish way to provide salvation. But what seems a foolish thing to do from our standpoint was quite a wise thing from God's perspective. Paul was right, but his words also point out that even our greatest human wisdom fails to understand some of the puzzling aspects of faith and theology.

Biblical passages raise questions and cause struggles for both Christians and those examining the Christian faith. Some of those questions are important theological issues. How can Jesus have been both fully human and fully God? What exactly happened at the cross that brought atonement? How much does God know and how much does He predestine or does He predestine? Theologians have wrestled with those questions and others for centuries and will continue to do so.

Sometimes, however, it is not the big questions we struggle with. It's the smaller ones, the conumdrums, the ones that just pique our curiosity – ones that are not the great matters of faith but ones we would just like to know an answer to. Who did Cain marry? Did Jonah really live inside a fish for three days? Why do we celebrate Christmas on December 25?

If you have puzzled over those questions, then this book you now hold in your hands may be exactly what you are looking for.

Shortly after I began teaching at Cumberland College (now the University of the Cumberlands) I met a young man named Terry A. Roberts who was studing for the ministry. We hit it off immediately – both of us having a similar sense of humor, a weird streak, and a commitment to Christ. Terry introduced me to the group Rush and I play them sometimes on the weekly radio show I host on our university's radio station. When he served in the Armed Forces I prayed for him. When he has returned to campus to visit I have been delighted to see him. He is a friend whom I admire, appreciate, and love.

By the way, in addition to liking him, I like the book, *Cain's Wife and Other Biblical Conundrums*. I like the book for several reasons. First, not many people dare to answer these questions. They do not want to be put on the spot or accused of being liberal or conservative or wasting time on silly, inconsequential matters when they and we should be serving Christ in other ways. But people wonder about these questions and so often do not get thoughtful, reasonable answers. In *Cain's Wife and Other Biblical Conumdrums* you will find thoughtful and reasonable answers.

Second, after exploring the conundrums and suggesting answers, Terry invites the reader – us – to think further and develop our own answer or theory. For all the conundrums Terry discusses, we could easily imagine someone saying "but" and bringing up one or more objections. This book stimulates our thinking. Terry doesn't always provide answers that everyone will accept. You don't have to agree with every explaination, but think about them in the context of faithfully following Christ with an open and honest mind and spirit. In fact, each chapter concludes with questions to consider. You can use this book for your own edification or as a guide for a small group Bible study.

Last but not least, the book is readable. Terry writes in a conversational style. You feel you are visiting with a friend who has a great sense of humor and deep passion for God, the Bible, and people.

So, fix yourself a cup of coffee or a glass of tea, sit in a comfortable chair with your Bible at the ready, and explore the conumdrums. You'll be glad you did.

- Doctor Robert C. Dunston, Department Chair and Professor of Missions and Ministry, University of the Cumberlands, Williamsburg, Kentucky, April 2017

Chapter One

How we got the Bible

How Did We Get The Bible?

How did we get the Bible? How did we get the Bible in its current form complete with maps, red letters, and center-file concordances? For some wishful thinkers, perhaps the 1611 Authorized King James Version of the Holy Bible with red letters, fell straight out of Heaven, being dictated word for word, straight from the mouth of God. We will revisit the whole King James issue in the following pages. However, if you were a Muslim regarding the Koran, then this heavenly dictation would be an acceptable answer, as the Koran, or Quran, as it is also spelled, proclaims that it was dictated from the Angel Gabriel to Mohammed over a twenty-three-year period between AD 609 to 632. The Holy Bible that Christians use is, in fact, inspired by the breath of God. "Inspired" means to "breath in." God inspired the men and perhaps some women, to write what they wrote in the context of the world in which they lived.

The Bible began as oral traditions. Stories about God would be passed down from generation to generation from the elders to their children and grandchildren. Since Moses was brought up in the house of Pharaoh with the best education that the world could offer, who then better to do this epic task of gathering and writing the word of God?

MOSES

Oral traditions, in the process of time, became original manuscripts. By the leading hand of God, God used Moses to collect, edit, and write down these oral traditions. Over time, early copies were made and circulated. There is about a four-decade gap in time between Exodus 2:10 and 2:11. Here, one could conjecture that Moses, having grown up in the house of Pharaoh, would not have had much contact with these stories about the Hebrew God. This would soon change. After Moses killed the Egyptian, he fled to the land of Midian where he met his future wife, Zipporah, and his father-in-law, Jethro, or Reuel, as he is also called. The Midianites were close cousins to the Hebrews. There is some thought that Moses may have maintained some contact with his birth family through the years as Moses was nursed by his own mother for some time after his birth as told to us in Exodus 2. The length of this familial tie and time of nursing is unknown. Numbers 26 reveals to us Moses' family by name. His father and mother were Amram and Jochebed, who also gave birth to his brother Aaron and his sister Miriam.

Midian was the fourth of six sons born to Abraham's second wife Keturah, whom Abraham took as his second bride after the death of Sarah (Genesis 25:1). Joseph with his coat of many colors was sold by his elder brothers to his own cousins, which was the root cause of the whole four hundred and thirty years of slavery in Egypt. (Exodus 12:40) With all of this said, it is likely that Moses first hears of this YHWH יהוה or El אל God from Jethro while living in Midian as a shepherd in Jethro's tent for some forty years. Once with the many Israelites during their forty-year journey of walking in the Sinai wilderness, it is most likely that Moses became familiar with all the other oral traditions. In Exodus 34:27-28, "Then the LORD said to Moses, Write these words, for according to the tenor of these words I have made a covenant with you and with Israel. So he was there with the LORD forty days and forty nights; he neither ate bread nor drank water. And He wrote on the tablets the words of the covenant, the Ten Commandments." It is certain that during this wandering in the wilderness period on the Sinai Peninsula that Moses, gathered, edited, and wrote his first five books of the Bible as he died before crossing over into the Promised Land. "So Moses the servant of the LORD died there in the land of Moab, according to the word of the LORD. And He (God) buried him in a valley in the land of Moab, opposite Beth Peor; but no one knows his grave to this day. Moses was one hundred and twenty years old when he died. His eyes were not dim nor his natural vigor diminished." (Deuteronomy 34:5-7) However in the book of Jude we find Michael the Archangel contending with the Devil over the body Moses.

ORAL TRADITIONS

In classic Biblical scholarship, there is the JEPD concept of oral tradition. There is much debate, discussion, and personal interpretation about the JEPD theory first brought forth by Julius Wellhausen in 1877. Here is a brief description of this theory. The discussion will start with the 'D' tradition. This was the Deuteronomy tradition, or the second telling of the Law. The 'P' was the priestly tradition. This book will give more attention to the 'E' and 'J' traditions. The 'E' traditions were those stories which were told from the prospective which used the name "El," אל or "Elohim," אלהים for God. Muslims use the similar "Allah" name for God. The 'J' tradition is symbolic for the "Jehovah" oral traditions. Jehovah is a translation of the Hebrew name for God, or YHWH יהוה which is translated "I AM." In English, YHWH is often pronounced as "Yahweh."

THE NAME OF GOD

Out of either honor, or fear, or both, the followers of Judaism never wanted to pronounce the name of YHWH, or God, so they would speak the word Adonai (English = Lord) instead of YHWH when they would read the text. We first find YHWH Elohim אלהים יהוה "LORD God" in Genesis 2. When looking at an English text of the Old Testament, when the name of God YHWH appears, it is best, or properly printed as "LORD" in small print upper case. Here it is interesting to note, that this YHWH name for God was first used as early as Genesis 2. However, this name for God was not known to the Hebrews and children of Israel until God revealed this I AM name to Moses in the burning bush at Mount Sinai some thousands of years later. This is one of the confirming points that Moses was the collector/editor/writer of these early books. The word 'Lord,' which is similar to our English word 'master' or 'sir' is not to be confused with the YHWH/LORD/I AM name for God. The name for God, 'Elohim,' first appears in Genesis 1. This simply appears as 'God' in an English text. The name 'Elohim' is a Hebrew plural form of 'El,' often called the majestic plural. The 'im' ים ending to a Hebrew noun makes it plural much in the same way as adding an 's' to an English noun makes it plural. Is there more than one God? We will review this later, but the short answer is no. As we get into the first few chapters of Genesis, we will see how these oral traditions come into play.

When looking at the first eleven chapters of Genesis, it can become confusing and seemingly repetitive. Often the question may be asked by the reader, "Why does the text say the same thing at least twice?" In trying to stay faithful to the oral JEPD traditions, Moses did not want to edit out, omit, or cut away any of the ancient words or thoughts. Some things are repeated, but from the different oral traditions. This does not mean there were different events, but rather, different stories told from different perspectives of the same event. A New Testament parallel would be the four different gospels.

STORIES OF GOD

When thinking about the word "myth," our minds may wander to Grimm's fairy tales of the German Schwarzwald or the Greco-Roman myth stories. These were the Greek and Roman ancient writings about the great epic tales of Zeus and his court of lesser gods on Mount Olympus. Quite simply, the word "myth" means "stories about God or gods." When Christians hear the first few chapters of Genesis being called "myths," they should not be offended, as this is a technical term. The Scriptures are not being called fairy tales, but rather, stories about God, the one and only true God. What is remarkable about many of these early Biblical stories is that many other ancient traditions such as the Gilgamesh Epic, and other regional religions have similar stories, such as the flood story. For some, this only confirms that such events took place.

For Christians, which means any *born again* followers of Jesus Christ, the Bible is divided into two major sections. The Old Testament has thirty-nine books and was mostly written in Hebrew except where it is written in the very similar Aramaic language. The Aramaic mostly occurs in large fractions in the books of Daniel and Ezra. It also appears in small measure in scattered verses. The New Testament has twenty-seven books and was originally written in Greek which was the international business language of the Roman Empire, much in the same manner as English is used in the international business world today. We will discuss the New Testament at length after a fuller discussion of the Old Testament.

THE OLD TESTAMENT

What Christians call the Old Testament, the followers of Judaism divide into three parts: The Law, the Prophets and the Writings. These three parts are collectively called the Tanak, as Jews do not use the term "Old Testament." The Law is most specifically called the Torah, or the Pentateuch, as it is also called which means "five." These first five books of the Bible are also called the Books of Moses as Moses is thought by many scholars to be the major collector, editor, and writer of these first five books. Moses was the central figure in the four books following Genesis. As per above, in Exodus 34:27, God says to Moses, "Write these words." Moses did receive at least some direct dictation straight from the mouth of God in the presence of God's face on Mount Sinai.

The Writings were books of wisdom and poetry such as the Psalms and Proverbs. The Prophets are divided between the Major and Minor Prophets which were the voice of God to the children of Israel for hundreds of years. The Jewish combination of books is in a somewhat different, and more historically, and chronologically correct order than that of the Christian order. It only has thirty-six books as some books such as I & II Samuel, I & II Kings and I & II Chronicles are combined into three books instead of six books. See this comparison in the List Chapter.

PROPHETS POETS & PREACHERS

After Moses, the hand of God would inspire Biblical writers to record the rise of the nation of Israel. Much of the authorship of the Old Testament is unknown, however, this in no way diminishes the meaning or inspiration. Others to put quill pen to parchment were Joshua, possibly Samuel, Ezra, and Nehemiah. The authorship of Esther is unknown, but some would vote for someone like Mordecai who was close to the story in the house of King Ahasuerus. The Psalms were mostly authored by King David, but he had considerable help from his wise son, King Solomon, as well as, the sons of Korah, Asaph, and perhaps others. The book of Job is thought to be the oldest written book in the Bible. Even though its authorship is unknown, it is thought to be written by someone who was not Hebrew-Israelite-Jewish. The Proverbs were mostly written by the wise King Solomon along with some additions from such notables, as Agur, the son of Jakah, and King Lemuel. Solomon is also given credit for Ecclesiastes and the Song of Solomon. A special note here: Many pastors and preachers over the years have wanted to very coyly say this Song of Solomon book was exclusively about God's love for His people which is true on a symbolic level. However, a simple reading clearly shows it is also about sexual relations between a husband and his wife. Once again, what does the Scripture say?

The Prophets are divided into two groups based upon the size of the writing. The major prophets were Isaiah, Jeremiah, Ezekiel, and Daniel. Jeremiah is commonly thought to be the writer of Lamentations as well as his name sake book. Some scholars believe some other writers may have co-written portions of Isaiah's book. This is a high point of discussion for many Biblical scholars. However, regardless of the authorship, it does not diminish the impact of the book of Isaiah.

The minor prophet writers were Hosea, Joel, Amos, Obadiah, Jonah, Micah, Nahum, Habakkuk, Zephaniah, Haggai, Zechariah, and finally Malachi.

APOCRYPHA

Between the end of the Old Testament and the beginning of the New Testament is what is called the 400 years of silence. Here, the Roman Catholic Church adds in the Apocrypha. Many of these writing are considered by the Roman Catholic Church, as additions to existing books such as a second part of Esther. The Song of the Three Children, Susanna, and Bel & the Dragon are considered as additions to Daniel.

The Protestant version of the Apocrypha was originally included in the 1611 King James Version with fourteen books. These Apocrypha books are most exclusively used by the Roman Catholic Church. In Catholic Bibles, these seven books are integrated throughout the Old Testament. In Protestant Bibles, where they occur, they are segregated between the Old and New Testaments. See List Chapter.

THE NEW TESTAMENT
THE APOSTLE PAUL

The New Testament centers around the life and teachings of Jesus Christ, the foundational beginnings, and doctrine of the early Christian Church. In large part, the New Testament was written by the Apostle Paul, Παυλος, who was formally known as the Jewish Pharisee, Saul of Taurus, Σαυλος (Acts 13:9). He was a major persecutor of the early Christian Church before his Damascus Road conversion which was his super-natural close encounter with Jesus Christ, Himself, which caused Paul blindness for three days. "As he journeyed he came near Damascus, and suddenly a light shone around him from heaven. Then he fell to the ground and heard a voice saying to him. "Saul, Saul why are you persecuting Me?" ... And he was three days without sight and neither ate nor drank." " (Acts 9:3, 4 & 9).

It was after this blinding and enlightening experience that Saul of Taurus would soon be known as the Apostle Paul. Paul would go on to write thirteen letters or epistles as they are sometimes called, which were written to specific churches or regions for spiritual instruction. These letters are known for their foundational Christian doctrine. Paul traveled about the Mediterranean world in what we still call Greece and what was then called Asia Minor, which today is mostly known as Turkey. Paul eventually traveled to Rome, in what we now call modern Italy. Paul relates in Romans 15:24-28 that he even had thoughts of traveling to the far reaches of the Mediterranean Sea by going to Spain. Many ancient churches currently still in Spain and other locations in the Mediterranean region have traditions of Paul and other Biblical figures, visiting their church or town. Eventually, these letters would be circulated and passed around until finally reaching us today. Paul's letters to the Ephesians, Philippians, Colossians, and Philemon were written while he was in prison. "This salutation by my own hand--Paul. Remember my chains. Grace be with you. Amen" (Colossians 4:18). Paul's writings are sometimes referred to as "the Pauline letters."

Most of these letters were written about 50-70 years after the birth of Christ. Even though Paul's letters were written well before the Gospels, they appear after the Gospels in the printed Bible, likely because of the content of the text. Paul's letters appear in the Scripture in order according to their size, starting with the letter to the Romans, being the longest, which is bookended by Titus, being the shortest in length.

OTHER WRITERS

Others to write letters which appear in the New Testament were Peter, John, James, and Jude. These are sometimes called the "catholic" or "general" epistles. The authorship of Hebrews is unknown and often the topic of much debate. There is also some debate as to which "James" wrote the book bearing his name. Was it Jesus' half brother, or was it the brother of John, or otherwise? Most will vote for the half brother of Jesus. The same can be said for the authorship of Jude. Most of these letters were written about the same time as Paul's letters.

The letters of John to include The Revelation, were also thought to be written in the latter part of the first century. Some alternative thinkers believe the authorship of I, II, & III John may be a combination of different writers who wrote under the name of the beloved disciple. The writer of II & III John refers to himself as "The Elder." The writing of I John is most similar in style to the Gospel of John. As a note of interest, there is no book of "Revelations." There is no "s." It is just The Revelation.

THE GOSPELS

The four gospels appear first in the New Testament, even though they were written a short time after the Pauline letters. Even though Mark is the oldest and the shortest of the Gospels, it appears after Matthew. This is likely due to Matthew and Luke having two different lineage and birth narratives of Jesus. It is likely that Matthew appears first in the New Testament because it immediately begins with the apparent lineage of Joseph. It is extremely important to note that even with this lineage, Joseph *was not* Jesus' physical father, as Jesus was conceived in Mary through the Holy Spirit, thus, making Jesus divine. "And the Angel answered and said to her, the Holy Spirit will come upon you, and the power of the Highest will overshadow you; therefore, also, that Holy One who is to be born will be called the Son of God." (Luke 1:35) Also in Matthew 1:20 the Scripture says, "But while he thought about these things, behold, an angel of the

Lord appeared to him in a dream, saying, Joseph, son of David, do not be afraid to take to you Mary your wife, for that which is conceived in her is of the Holy Spirit." The Luke linage goes all the way back to Adam, created by the breath of God, as all current humans are descendant from Adam and Eve according to the Scripture. We will address these linage issues further with the Mary chapter as both lineages appear to run through Joseph – a conundrum.

Mark is the "fast-forward" gospel, as he gets straight to the point, beginning with the adult ministry of Jesus. Mark uses the word "immediately" seventeen times. Mark is also known as John Mark and was a co-worker with Paul. As a point of conjecture, what if the Gospel of Mark was our only Gospel? We may not have Christmas. Nor would we have the linage of Jesus. If we only had Mark, our perspective of Christianity would be different. This is why we have four gospels. The end of the book of Mark is also a source of much controversy. There is the school of thought that the last few verses of the book may have been added at a later time, and were not a part of the original text. A small group of churches use these verses for the foundation of their faith by engaging in "snake handling" and other related dangerous activities.

Luke is the writer of both the third gospel as well as the Acts of the Apostles, which is a detailed account of the early church. Both books are addressed to Theophilus, "the friend of God," θεοφιλε in Greek. This nebulous figure may have been most anybody. As with the "no Christmas" concept of the gospel of Mark, our Christmas narrative would also be quite different if we only had either Matthew or only Luke.

Sandwiched between the twin writings of Doctor Luke is the book of John, which is called the fourth gospel. This forth gospel is much different in approach than the first three synoptic gospels and shows the more divine side of Christ. John is called the "beloved disciple." He, and his brother James, were fishermen, as were their co-workers, Peter, and his brother, Andrew. They lived and cast their nets in the Sea of Galilee in the northern area of Israel before Jesus called them to be fishers of men. John and James were the sons of Zebedee and they were called the "sons of thunder."

The books of Matthew and Luke both appear to rely in part on the authorship of Mark. They may have used other sources as well, what some scholars call the "Q source". As a note of interest, Matthew and John were two of the actual twelve disciples, whereas Mark and Luke were not. However, Mark and Luke were co-workers with Paul.

COMPILATION

The accepted books of the Bible are called the Canon. The Canon was closed around about AD 400. Some books like Esther and James almost did not make the cut by those determining such things. The Old Testament book of Esther was almost discarded because the name of God did not appear in the text, but was retained due to the historical significance to the nation of Israel during the Babylonian/Persian Captivity.

The New Testament book of James almost did not become Scripture because at first, it appears to be in conflict with the *saved by grace* doctrine of the Apostle Paul. Upon further review, the book of James, appears to be a "how to book" for those who were already Christians – putting your Christian faith into action; not earning your salvation through your own works or deeds. Other so-called "lost books of the Bible" like the book of Enoch, the gospel Thomas, and others, were not canonized due to doctrinal inconsistencies and/or authorship issues.

Below is a short time line of how we got the Bible as we have it today. First, we will look at letters before we get into numbers. "B.C." does in fact mean "Before Christ." For those with political correctness leanings, the term "Before Common Era," or B.C.E. or C.E. is sometimes used in modern secular scholarship settings. On the other end of the time line, many believe that "A.D." means "After Death," but this is an urban legend. A.D. means "In the year of our LORD," "Anno Domini" in the Greek. In this time line, there is no year "zero" between the last BC year and the first AD year. In about AD 525, Dionysius Exiguus created this calendar which we use today in conjunction with the Julian calendar created by Julius Caesar in 46 BC, and the now reformed Gregorian calendar instituted by Pope Gregory XIII in 1582.

However, the commonly held scholarly belief is that the calculations of the year of Christ birth may have been off by a few years. Many scholars now believe that Jesus may have been born somewhere between 2-6 B.C. This is a subject of much debate. The time of year of Christ's birth is also a matter of debate. However, creating this calendar was a giant attempt in scholarship many years ago which still serves us well today.

EARLY CHURCH FATHERS & COUNCILS

400 BC = The Torah was soundly accepted as Scripture.

285 BC = The Greek Septuagint translated at least the Torah into Greek at Alexandria, Egypt. This is known as the LXX.

132 BC = The Prophets are considered as Scripture.

118 BC = The Writings were now included as Scripture at the Council of Jamnia. This could have been as late as 90 BC.

AD 140–200 = Early Church fathers such as Marcion, Irenaeus, Tertullian, and Clement of Alexander were key in pulling together what we have as the New Testament.

393 = Finally, the Synod of Hippo decided on what we have today as the New Testament.

400 = The Vulgate was the Old and New Testaments translated into Latin in Bethlehem, by the early Catholic Church father Jerome.

The Early Roman Catholic Church of Europe used this Latin Vulgate as their "official" Bible for hundreds of years in all places, regardless of the vernacular, or native language of the local people. However, times were changing with the coming of the Gutenberg Press and the Reformation. Before the time of the movable type printing press, all books, and other literature, were produced by actual hand writing. Ancient monks would dedicate their whole lives to writing and rewriting copies of the Bible by hand, one letter and one word at a time. These Bibles also often included intricate artwork in addition to the actual text. Each letter and word had to be counted, and every Bible had to be perfect by the number of the letters and words, or it would be destroyed.

Johann Gutenberg produced his first printed Bibles in the Latin language about 1455. A few years later, a young man in Wittenberg, Germany, named Martin Luther, nailed 95 theses on the local church door on Halloween of 1517 which started the Protestant Reformation.

1380 = John Wycliffe attempted to translate the New Testament into common English.

1525 = William Tyndale translated the New Testament into English and the five books of Moses, five years later.

1535 = Miles Coverdale translated another English version Bible.

1537 = The Matthews Bible was published.

1539 = The Great Bible was produced. And like the others, it relied on the Latin, and previous English translations which came before it.

1560 = The Geneva Bible was produced. Bible of the Mayflower Pilgrims.

1568 = The Bishop's Bible was printed.

1610 = The Catholic Church produces the Douay Bible, an English Language Bible.

KING JAMES

1611 = Who is King James? King James VI of Scotland (1566-1625) and King James I of England as such things are counted in British royalty; was the same person, and was of the house of Stewart, which was the Scottish spelling. Stuart would be the English spelling. He concurrently sat on the thrones of Scotland and England starting in 1603, through his death in 1625. By default, of his kingship, King James was the head of the Church of England. The Church of England is also known as the Anglican Church, and latter the Episcopal Church in the United States. King James wanted a standard or an authorized version of the Bible for use in the Church of England, as there were various versions in circulation at the time. This original King James Version included the Apocrypha. Forty-seven scholars were commissioned for this project for the Church of England. This work was based on existing English language text, as well as, available Hebrew and Greek text, which was completed in 1611, and has been a classic standard for English Bibles in various versions for over four hundred years.

1760 = The original 1611 King James Version text was upgraded at Cambridge.

1769 = The Cambridge KJV was once again upgraded at Oxford. This is the version of the King James Bible that most people in the twentieth century grew up with; the more readable classic which we have today. Somewhere in the process of time, as the original 1611 King James Bible was being produced, the printed letters "S" and "F" were sometimes difficult to distinguish. Additionally, the letters "U" and "V" were still used interchangeably. This can still be seen today in the engraving on some college and government buildings using all capital letters as the "U" may appear as a "V." When looking at the letter "Double-U" (W) it mostly appears as a Double-V. The letter "J" was still not in strong use during the first printing in 1611, as Jesus was sometimes spelled "Iesvs" in the original 1611.

1982 = The classic 1611 King James Version was revisited once again, as the New King James Version Bible was produced in both New and Old Testament. The New Testament was completed in 1979, with the Psalms to follow in 1980. Word for word, it sticks very close to its 1611 ancestor-cousin, however, the "thees & thous" and other such ancient verbiage were simply removed, and replaced with the more modern, and readable twentieth century English language. No longer were children going to ask if God were a "Ghost" as the Holy Ghost was now to become known as the Holy Spirit. The next time you pick up your (New) King James Version with red letters, know that much red blood was shed over many centuries, by many saints from years gone by, for you to have your modern English Bible.

In the DelMarVa area of the East Coast, Appalachia, and other isolated regions, there are churches known as King James Only Churches. Around the beginning of the twentieth century, these churches were born out of protest of all the many modern translations along with the charismatic movement which started in California with the Azusa Street Revival. This protest was for good cause. Some believed controversial academic work, and political agendas were at work with some of these new translations and paraphrases. However, there are many Christians, mostly of older generations, and ultra-conservatives, who as individuals, are "King James Only." In a conversation with a lady, I asked her if her Bible was a Thomas

Nelson Bible. She boldly proclaimed in response, "I only use King James!" Regardless, it is the most beautiful and poetic, as well as, the most quoted of English translations.

"For God so loued ye world, that he gaue his only begotten Sonne: that whosoeuer beleeueth in him, should not perish, but haue euerlasting life." - John 3:16 in the original 1611 King James Version.

MODERN TRANSLATIONS

Following the classic King James Version was the Revised Standard Version, the first American English version in 1884, which was followed by the American Standard Version in 1901. The New English Bible came about in 1946. The Good News for Modern Man came into production in 1966. Staying with the tumultuous times in which it was birthed, a very controversial version was produced. The Living Bible, also known by some, as the "Green Monster," was an American paraphrase produced in 1971. In 1976 The Good News Bible came off the press. This was closely followed in 1978 by the New International Version. 1989 brought forth both the New Revised Standard Version, as well as, the Revised English Version. With the turn of the new Millennium in 2001, the English Standard Version was begotten along with Holman translation in 2004. Finally, Today's New International Version in 2005, and many more not listed here.

Questions and Discussion for
Chapter One - How we got the Bible
Dig-Discover-Discuss

1. Do you believe that the Bible is the true and inspired word of God?

2. Do you trust your English language Bible which is translated from the Hebrew and Greek is still the true word of God?

3. Do you believe that all of the men (and perhaps women) who wrote the Bible were inspired by God?

4. Do you believe that Moses collected various "oral traditions" before editing and writing the first Five Books of the Bible?

5. Do you believe that God inspired people over the centuries to decide what was put into the Bible, as well as, what was left out of the text?

6. Do you believe there may be parts of the Bible which we may have lost over the years?

7. Do you believe the Bible, as we have it, is sufficient for our salvation through God's grace?

8. Do you believe that the version of the Bible which you use is the only real Bible?

9. Do you understand who King James was? Have you seen a copy of an actual 1611 King James Bible?
Google 1611 King James Bible, printer, Robert Barker.

10. Do you believe modern translations are inspired by God?

Chapter Two

Time

Time. What is time? What is Eternity? God is eternal. Even though God is eternal, we as mere physical human beings are not. Even though we are created in the image of God who is eternal; we as the clay pots created by God the Potter, do not have the mental capacity to comprehend eternity. We cannot fathom how God has existed forever, and then one "day" decided that He was going to create an endless universe which includes an endless number of suns, moons, stars, planets, comets, asteroids, and other such heavenly bodies. We cannot absorb this ocean of thought. Certainly, we all know that suns and stars are the same thing – hopefully we all learned that in elementary science class.

What is science? Is science contrary to God? No! science is merely man discovering what and how God created and designed His universe. In childhood thought, there is the idea that the universe might end. This is where the endless black sky of space in cartoon fashion suddenly stops, and then an endless void of white starts. We know that space is called space because there is nothing there, and it is dark because it is devoid of light, thus, the blackness and darkness. Our own mind, childhood or otherwise, cannot capture the vastness of God's creation of an endless universe and His everlasting eternity.

God is not bound by time, but we are. Time is a device by which we, as people, measure our lives. From the time we are born time is the train that drives our lives: when to get up, when to eat, when to work, when to sleep. "When" is a word that is not only a totally time driven word, but a question that also drives our lives from cradle to grave. Most every tomb stone has a date of birth, a dash, and a date of death engraved on it. The small dash is the time we spend on this earth. These mere numbers only record the time we were physically on the planet Earth, which God created. Does time stop for us at the grave? No, it does not. Our fleshly bodies are merely the earthly time machines which we occupy on this created earth. The Apostle Paul, who was also a tent maker by trade, calls our bodies, tents. "For we know that if our earthy house, this tent, is destroyed, we have a building from God, a house not made with hands, eternal in the heavens" (II Corinthians 5:1). At the time of our fleshly/earthly death, our eternal spirits are launched into a timeless and endless eternity. Followers of Christ, will spend this endless eternity with Jesus in Heaven. Those who are not followers of Christ, they will spend this endless eternity in separation from God in torment in Hell with the devil. "Then He will also say to those on the left hand, Depart from Me you cursed, into the everlasting fire prepared for the devil and his angels" (Matthew 25:41). I have always liked to say, "Go looking for Jesus before He comes looking for you." From a pointed theological stand point, God certainly draws us and loves us first. However, we all need to become Christians before we die. Almost boggles the mind, time without end. That is how it is with God. God is without beginning or end. God is not bound by time.

The Apostle Peter says in II Peter 3:8, "But beloved, do not forget this one thing, that with the Lord one day is as a thousand years, and a thousand years as one day." King David records a prayer of Moses in Psalm 90:4, "For a thousand years in Your sight are like yesterday when it is past, and like a watch in the night." In just these two verses, we can see the eternity and the unbound timelessness of God.

Genesis 1:1 simply states, "In the beginning God created the heavens and earth." When did this happen and how long did it take? How long did God wait in eternity before He started to create the Earth? This question can never be answered, because our frail human minds and math are not capable of doing the formula for Eternal Math 101. Some may even ask the incomprehensible question of, "Who created God?" Of course, for Christians and Jews, this question is beyond the pale of faith and the scope of logic.

"Yom," יוֹם is the Hebrew word for "day." Day in the Hebrew language can mean day, as in daytime, as in daylight, or a day as in a twenty-four-hour calendar day. The word Yom can also mean an epoch, era, or period of time. As a note here, the Biblical-Jewish day started at what modern westerners call six AM in the morning. This was the first hour of the day. Night or evening began at what modern westerners call six PM. 'Midnight' in Biblical-Jewish time keeping was indeed just that, the middle of the night. A Biblical example of this hourly time keeping can be seen in one of Jesus' parables in Matthew 20. Most of the modern world with our twenty-four global time zones, international dateline, daylight savings time, start the morning just after midnight. With this said, which method seems to make more sense?

In our modern western world, we measure a day as a twenty-four-hour period of time. This twenty-four-hour period of time is determined by how long it takes the planet Earth to make one rotation on its axis while orbiting around the sun. In the meantime, our moon moves around the Earth about every twenty-nine and a half days, or a Hebrew lunar month. As a point of interest, the moon does not spin as the earth does. The same surface of the moon consistently faces the earth.

In modern English idiom, some use the terminology in such phrases as; "Back in my day," or "And a day will come," as expressions of a period of time; not an actual twenty-four-hour day. Even within conservative Christian circles, there is much debate on when, and how long it took God to create the Earth. What does the Scripture say? What does the Scripture not say? The Scripture says it took God six days to create the whole universe and one day to rest. The how long part depends on how we interpret the Hebrew word 'Yom' for 'Day' as it can mean several different things as discussed above. First thing out of the box; did God, or could have God, created the whole universe in one hundred and forty-four "working-man" hours? The answer is an absolute YES! But *did* God, as God is not bound or operate within the bounds of our human time keeping?

We will break down the day-by-day creation in the "Genesis: Creation Stories" chapter. But here, we are still working with the issue of time and eternity. In DAY ONE: God is pre-supposed since God is eternal. The Scripture also pre-supposes a deep, and watery abyss, and a shapeless earth. The Spirit of God is said to be hovering over the waters. At this point, God speaks into being "light" and so it was, there was light and it was good. The first day is complete by God calling light day and the darkness night. The words morning and evening are used as if it was a twenty-four-hour day. Strangely, the word evening comes before morning in the Scripture. Light is a symbol for God throughout the scripture. In Revelation 21:23, God is the light in Heaven, as there is no need for a sun or moon to light Heaven just as in John 8:12, Jesus says I am the Light of the World.

The strange part of the Light is, there is still no sun or moon. God is the light. For human time keeping purposes, we still do not have a time keeping device, as in the earth rotating and revolving around the sun. It is not until DAY FOUR that the Scripture says God created the "two great lights" and the stars. It is not until DAY FOUR that we have something to record time as human beings understand time. With DAY FOUR, we now can begin calculating twenty-four-hour days. Once again, could have God created everything in one hundred and forty-four man hours? Once again, the answer is an absolute yes. On the converse, once again, did God, as God is eternal, and not trapped by the contraption of our human time?

Could the Hebrew word yom for day have a different shade of meaning in the first part of the chapter than what it does in the later part of the chapter? This would be a literary inconsistency, yet very possible. Is it possible that some of the days were twenty-four-hour periods of time, while some days were epochs, eras, or realms of time? Is it possible that there may have been an undetermined amount of time *between* the days whether they were twenty-four hours, or epochs of time? Once again, what does the Scripture say? What does the Scripture not say?

With all of this said, how old is the earth? In classic conservative creation the Bishop Ussher says the Earth is 4,004 years old as of about 1654 in his exhaustive work, *The Annals of the Old Testament*. In this work the good Bishop even goes on to say that the creation of the earth began on Sunday morning on the 23rd of October 4004 BC. According to this calculation, the earth is now roughly 4,367 years old if you are still counting. This calculation is based primarily on the years of the genealogies in Genesis. One of several problems here is, we don't know how much time elapsed in the Garden of Eden before the Fall and how much time elapsed from the time the first family was expelled until the birth of Cain, and then eventually Abel. Genesis 4:3 uses the phrase "And in the process of time." This half of a verse, and others like it, throws a monkey wrench into being able to have a strict and detailed account of time. However, Genesis 5:5 says that Adam lived 930 years.

Some conservative creationist scholars and thinkers speculate that the universe to be 10,000-15,000 years old. This is about when common science says the so-called "Ice Age" happened. It is difficult to find human written records which go much beyond this time span. According to some, Chinese written records go back to about 1,600 – 1,700 BC. Asian Indian written records are thought by some to start about 2,600 – 2,500 BC. Depending on whom one reads, some "science" will say that the universe and/or the earth are perhaps billions of years old. This may be true, however, true science does not have either a test case, or bench mark, on which to base such a premise. This kind of thinking and theory is speculation at best with no true scientific repeatable test cases. How do we know something is a million years old unless we absolutely have something without a shadow of a doubt that is verified to be a million years old? And we don't.

What about carbon dating? Carbon dating is concerned with C14 and is reliable in scientific thought, up to about 50,000 years. Here again, do we have anything that is documented to be 50,000 years old as a solid test case? This is a discussion for another format other than here.

The number forty is used over one hundred and fifty times throughout the Scripture. This seems to be a central number for God and the Scripture. Forty days and forty nights is the time frame for Noah's flood saga. Moses had three forty-year divisions to his life. The first forty years were spent in the house of Pharoah as "the prince of Egypt." The second forty years were spent in the tent of his father-in-law, Jethro, as a shepherd in the land of Midian. The third part of Moses' life was spent leading the children of Israel while wandering in the Siani Wilderness before entering the Promised Land. However, after this forty-year trek, Moses died in Moab and did not enter the Promised Land. Another use of the forty time frame is the forty days that Jesus spent in the wilderness, where He was tempted by the Devil. Some scholars will suggest that the word forty may even mean "a long time." Either way, this is a significant number in the scripture.

28 | Terry A. Roberts

{Editorial note: Editor Paul James Winslow sugguest that the War in Heaven was likely in the later part of the creation before Humans were created.}

{Editorial note: Editor Timothy Ross states: It is O.K. for the Christian academic to be a skeptic in both matters of faith and science. Science is not at war with religion. However, science stops at the door of faith.}

Questions and Discussion for
Chapter Two – Time
Dig-Discover-Discuss

1. How do you explain or describe eternity and an eternal God without beginning or end?

2. How long was God in eternity before He started Creation?

3. Is God controlled or hindered by our human understanding of time?

4. How old is the earth?

5. How do modern western humans calculate time? Points of interest to consider: a) earth rotation around sun b) Earth spinning on axis c) Moon traveling around earth

6. With regards to hourly time keeping; which makes more sense: a) the ancient Jewish system which starts "hour one" at 6AM. b) the modern western system of starting the day at 12:01 AM Discuss and explain.

7. I described the term "science" as: "Science is merely man discovering what God created and how He designed it." How would you describe the term "science?"
   The American Heritage Dictionary defines science this way: "The Observation, identification, description, experimental investigation, and theoretical explanation of natural phenomena." Is Science in conflict with God, creation or Christianity?

8. Discuss the significance of the number "40" and the Biblical stories using the number 40.

Chapter Three

Genesis:
The Creation Stories

GENESIS CHAPTER ONE AS COMPARED TO GENESIS CHAPTER TWO CREATION IN GENERAL POINTS

CHAPTER ONE	CHAPTER TWO
1. Elohim אלהים name used for God	YHWH Elohim יהוה אלהים name used for LORD God
2. Six/seven day יום account of creation	One day יום account of creation
3. "Wet" creation	"Dry" creation
4. General account of creation	Detailed account of creation
5. "Male & female" creation of humanity	Adam & Eve created and named as individuals
6. Humanity created last in creation	Adam created first in creation from the dust. Eve created from Adam's rib.

GENESIS CHAPTER ONE ORDER OF CREATION AS COMPARED TO GENESIS CHAPTER TWO

CHAPTER ONE	CHAPTER TWO
God and watery abyss assumed	God and dry earth assumed.
Day One: Light	A mist waters the earth and man is made from the dust and God breaths into his nostrils.

Day Two: the "firmament" (Sky)	God plants a garden in Eden and puts the man in it.
Day Three: Land with vegetation	God creates trees to include the Tree of Life and The Tree of Knowledge of Good and Evil.
Day Four: Sun, moon, and stars	Mention of the four-headed rivers, gold, and other precious stones.
Day Five: Sea creatures and birds	God puts the man in the garden to tend it.
Day Six: Mammals and finally humans	God creates animals and the man names them.
Day Seven: God rests from His Creation	God makes the woman from Adam's rib.

Below are three different possible examples of collected, edited, and written oral traditions by Moses of the creation story:

Genesis Chapter One: "In the beginning, God created the heavens and the earth."

Genesis Chapter Two: "This is the history of the heavens and the earth when they were created, in the day that the LORD God made the heavens and the Earth."

Genesis Chapter Five: "This is the book of the genealogy of Adam. In the day that God created man. He made him in the likeness of God."

Face Of The Waters

"In the beginning, God created the earth" is how we begin the Word of God begins in Genesis 1. The Genesis 1 account tells us that God created the earth in six "Yom" יוֹם days and rested on the seventh day. This is the classic Judeo-Christian story many know and adore because it is true according to what the scripture says. But, what does chapter two say?

One of the oddities or conundrums about the creation is how it started and what was already there. The given here is that God was there. But, what else was already there at the beginning of the creation? Apparently, in Genesis 1:2, there was already a watery and shapeless earth abiding with the eternal creator God. This is an often skimmed over issue. Was this just a writing style form from Moses? Why was this shapeless and watery earth not listed as the first thing formed by God's hand? Is it possible that God had already created a heaven and/or an earth, and then destroyed them, and He was starting all over again? God destroyed the earth with a flood with Noah. Who is to say that God did not flood the earth before, and did not have a Noah figure of redemption to come through the back side of this possible first flood? This could be a viable argument for the dinosaur dilemma. This may at first seem like a non-traditional view, *unless* the reader considers the fall of Satan and a third of the angels from heaven not listed in this early part of creation. When did Satan and the angels fall? We will get back to this point in following chapters.

In Genesis 1, God ends the first and second days with the phrase, "So the evening and morning were the "X" day. The third, fourth, and fifth days add in the phrases "And God saw that it was good." The sixth day ends with the enhanced phrase "and indeed, it was very good." God blesses and sanctifies the seventh day, making it different from all the rest, making it a day of rest.

TRINITY - ETERNITY & THE IMAGE OF GOD

In Genesis 1:2, we first see the Spirit of God hovering over the face of the earth. Christians believe in the Trinity. Trinity means God in three persons, or expressions. God the Father, Jesus the Son, and the Holy Spirit, formerly known as the Holy Ghost. Here is the first mention of the Holy Spirit in scripture hovering over the face of the waters. For many Christians, it is easy to grasp the concept of God the Father in Heaven. Additionally, it is an easy jump to recognize Jesus the Son of God in human form. What about the Holy Spirit? As a child in Sunday School, we may have been told that God is everywhere, and He is. The Spirit of God is everywhere, except one created place. God is everywhere except Hell.

Genesis 1:26 highlights the Trinity of God with the bold pronouncement of "Let Us make man in Our image." Who is "Us" and "Our?" This is the full Trinity of God. Jesus the Christ, and the Holy Spirit, were present with God the Father, before and at the Creation. In the New Testament, the Gospel of John relays to us a brief creation story in John 1, with Jesus being the prime mover in creation. "In the beginning was the Word, and Word was with God and the Word was God. He was in the beginning with God. All things were made through Him, and without Him nothing was made that was made... and the Word became flesh and dwelt among us."

Is there more than one god? The Muslims and others accuse Christians of worshipping more than one god. There is only one God. The one and only true God. God is able to express Himself in more than one form. We as humans cannot fully understand an eternal God, nor can we in any totality understand a Trinity of God. These issues must be a matter of faith. If we have faith, then we can believe in the trinity of an eternal God. If God can create an entire eternal universe, then He can certainly express Himself in three different forms. Not only are the issues of the eternity of God and the trinity of God two of the greatest discussed conundrums in all of Christianity, but also in all of religion and human philosophical thought.

Genesis 1 uses the Elohim name for God. Elohim is the plural form of El, or a simple name for God. Once again, is there more than one god? Once again, no! In Biblical Hebrew, this is called the majestic plural. Another point of Genesis 1:26 is, that we, as humans are made in the image of God. Above all the other creation, we are set above and apart. A different class of creation with an eternal spirit and soul, making us unique in all of creation. We are made in the image of God, *not* evolved from monkeys and apes through a process of evolution. To be sure, we are in the scientific classification of animals, then mammals, and eventually primates. This is a part of what creation scientists call "common design" of God. To be sure, a set apart creation of God.

Strangely enough, Adam and Eve are not mentioned anywhere by name, or as individuals in Genesis 1. In Genesis 1:26 & 27, the scripture simply states, "So God created man in His own image; in the image of God He created him; male and female He created them." These two verses simply state that God created "people." This will be important to remember when we get into the "Cain's Wife" chapter.

With this uniqueness of creation, comes responsibility. God gave humans dominion over all the creation. We are commanded to be caretakers of the earth. This not only includes the animals, but also the environment, and the natural resources of which we were commanded to subdue.

HAVE DOMINION & SUBDUE

For various religious and/or dietary reasons, some people are vegetarians because they think and believe this was God's original plan. This Biblical thinking could be based on Genesis 2:16 which says, "Of every tree of the garden you may freely eat." However, Genesis 1:28 says the following: "…fill the earth and subdue it; have dominion over the fish of the sea, over the birds of the air, and over every living thing that moves on the earth." Genesis 1:28 possibly suggests that not only was the herb and seed to be food for us, but also everything that creeps on the earth in which there is life. Do the words "subdue" and "dominion" suggest "to eat?" This dietary point is clarified to Noah after the flood. God tells Noah in Genesis 9:3, "Every moving thing that lives shall be food for you. I have given you all things, even as the green herbs." It is also important to note that "cattle" are emphasized in several different passages before and during the flood epic. Apparently, cattle were an important aspect of the life of Noah. One could conclude that Noah and his family were already eating beef and/or at least using diary products before the flood. Additionally, in Acts 10 and 11, God reveals a miracle to Peter in which God says, "Rise, Peter; kill and eat." "What God has cleansed you must not call common." Also the Apostle Paul instructs his son in Christ, Timothy in I Timothy 4:3-5 " ... and commanding to abstain from foods which God created to be received with thanksgiving by those who believe and know the truth. For every creature of God is good and nothing is to be refused if it is received with thanksgiving; for it is sanctified by the word of God and prayer."

Many people who are vegetarian, or even vegan, often do it for the benefit of the animals because they do not want to kill, or harm any animals for the purposes of feeding themselves. This is indeed a noble and valid point. However, this train of thought taken to its full fruition, and extant is not beneficial to the animal kingdom. Of the many millions of livestock, cattle, hogs, and various poultry, would all eventually die because they would no longer have a human purpose. The millions of world-wide farmers and ranchers in theory are not going to maintain chicken, cow, and pig "zoos." Yes, some of these barn yard animals would be able to return to the wild and survive, but many would perish. As before, there is a known benefit to a vegetarian diet, but it is not entirely Biblical. Once again, what does the scripture say?

IN THE DAY

What does Genesis 2 say? Straight out of the starting blocks, we must note from a literary point of view, that Genesis 2 does not *actually* start until Genesis 2:4; as the first three verses of Genesis 2 are still rounding out the first week of creation ending with the seventh day of God's day of rest. Genesis 2 is a different account, or a different oral tradition of the creation story. Many readers will gloss over this point and will want to see Genesis

2 as merely a detailed continuation of Genesis 1, but it is more likely a concurrent account told from the perspective of a different oral tradition.

As from our previous discussion, Moses gathered different oral traditions. Genesis 1 is an example of the "E" oral tradition, using the Elohim name for God, whereas Genesis 2 is an example of the "J" tradition, using the Yahweh name for God. Here, we see Moses using the YHWH name for God (LORD God) for the first time in scripture which was first revealed to him at the burning bush at Mount Sinai. However, more significant in Genesis 2:4 is the phrase, … "in the day that the LORD God made the earth and heavens" ביום צשות יהוה אלהים ארץ ושמים. Here we have the scripture saying that God created the earth in one day. A conundrum.

The 1982 New King James Version introduces this Genesis 2 creation story by stating the scripture this way: "This is the history of the heavens and the earth when they were created, in the day that the LORD God made the earth and the heavens." The 1769 Oxford King James Version states it virtually the same way. As a comparison point, the New International Version says it this way, "This is the account of the heavens and the earth when they were created." The New American Bible, a Catholic version, translates Chapter 2:4 as, "Such is the story of the heavens and the earth at their creation." The Hebrew text uses the phrase, "in the day" ביום.

This takes the reader to the point of "How is the Hebrew word 'Yom' used?" Is yom being used as a twenty-four-hour day, or as an era/epoch realm of time day? This is extraordinarily important if you are concerned with how long creation took, and how old the earth is. If it is being used as a twenty-four-hour day, then this means that the whole world, or whole universe was created in one twenty-four-hour day according to Genesis 2. Is this possible? Yes, it is absolutely possible, as all things are possible with God. Or, is yom being used as an epoch, era, or realm of of time? "What does the Scripture say?"

Genesis 2 begins with the Creation of the man in a pre-existing assumed "dry earth." God creates the man by forming him from the dust and breathing into his nostrils, or "inspiring him." God goes on to create the herbs and plants of the fields by causing a mist to water the earth, as it had not rained on the earth. God planted the Garden of Eden with trees and put the man in it.

In Genesis 2, God commanded the man to eat of every tree in

the garden, but he is not to eat of the Tree of Knowledge of Good and Evil under penalty of death. It is important to note that the man is not prohibited from eating the fruit of the Tree of Life, as it was intended for man to live forever here in the Garden of Eden.

God recognized that the man was alone and announced His intention to make a *helper* for him. In Genesis 1, God made all the animals first and then finally people. In Genesis 2, God made the man first, then the beast of the field and the birds of the air towards the end of the creation. After God made all the animals, they were brought to the man to be named. At this point, God still acknowledged that He still has not created a helper comparable for the man.

ADAM & EVE = DIRT & LIFE

If a man is a farmer or a gardener, it may be appropriate to call him a man of the soil or a man of the dirt. In Hebrew, the words for "dirt and/ or soil, or dust" "Ah-Da-Ma" אדמה and the word for "man" אדם are closely related. In the various King James Versions, the man is not properly called "Adam" until Genesis 2:19. The Catholic New American Bible does not use the proper name Adam. As a comparison point, the NIV first names the man as Adam in Genesis 2:20. Genesis 2:7 tells us that the man was made from the dust of the ground and that God "inspired" or breathed into him the breath of life. In the Hebrew pronunciation, "The Man" would be pronounced as "Ha-Ah-Dahm." האדם The "Ha" is the definite article "the" ה in Hebrew.

Genesis 2:21 tells us that God caused a deep sleep to come upon Adam after he named all the animals, a daunting task indeed. This is the second nap mentioned in the Bible if one wants to consider God taking a whole day of rest after the week of creation. One of the great untrue Biblical-biological legends is that all men have one less rib than do women. Perhaps you heard this in the first-grade lunch line. Your doctor or science teacher will gladly tell you that both men and women, normally have the same amount of ribs. The final crowning glory of God's creation, was the woman. This first named woman was made from a rib taken from Adam's side as he took his first nap. Notice that God did not take the bone from Adam's head, that the woman should be over him; nor did God take the bone from his foot that Adam should trample over the woman. Rather, God took the bone from his side, that the woman would be forever at Adam's side as a co-equal to him in Eden.

After this first surgery, God awakens Adam and brings the woman to him. Adam says she is bone of my bones and flesh of my flesh and she shall be called "Ishshah" אשה or woman because she was taken out of the man or "Ish" איש. Now we have the first marriage with the man and the woman becoming one flesh and they were naked and everyone lived happily ever after...well, at least for a little while.

One of the several questions children or perhaps new Christians and/or Bible readers may ask. "Did Adam and the first woman have navels or "belly-buttons?" This question may at first sound like a silly question, but this thought is a most enlightened and thoughtful question. Most all humans have a navel, a scar from our physical birth from our umbilical cord. These first two people were not "born of woman," but created directly from God in the case of the man; and created from the rib of the man in the case of the woman. They likely would not naturally have had belly-buttons, unless God put them there. Did Adam have a "rib scar" from his rib extraction? Something to consider– a conundrum.

What did this first named and created couple look like? Were they picture-perfect muscularly cut, and sculpted beauties, as we see beauty today? What race and color were they? How long and what color was their hair? Did Adam have a beard? How tall were they? The only answers that we may have here is that they were made in the image of God.

FALLEN ANGEL - SERPENT - SATAN

"Now the serpent was more cunning than any beast of the field which the LORD God had made," is how Genesis 3 begins. This is where things start to get weird, or interesting. If God just created a perfect world, then how did this whole serpent-apple-thing happen? First of all, we don't know what the fruit was that was picked from the Tree of Knowledge of Good and Evil. It is doubtful if this fruit and fruit tree even still exist. However, the apple has often been given this unfortunate moniker and still bears this burden as the forbidden fruit. What we can rule out as the forbidden fruit is the fig. Figs come from the fig trees, not the Tree of Knowledge of

Good and Evil, unless one believes that the fig tree is the surviving Tree of Knowledge of Good and Evil? Not likely, and not probable. It was the fig tree that was the first thing that both Adam and the woman grabbed for to cover their newly found nakedness. Once again, a conundrum.

Who or what was the serpent which tempted Adam and the Woman? This is certainly one of the most difficult things to piece together, or understand in the Bible. Why was evil allowed to be introduced into this perfect world at such an early point in creation? This is certainly the ultimate Biblical conundrum, *a problem admitting of no satisfactory solution."* Here we may gravitate towards the Devil, Satan, Lucifer, The Tempter, or The Accuser. It is important to note, that even though the Devil is God's adversary of evil, he is not God's equal counterpart. God is the creator, the Devil is a creature, a creation of God.

In the ancient book of Job 2, Satan is said to present himself to God with the other "sons of God." The LORD asked Satan, "From where do you come?" And Satan answers back and says to God, "From going to and fro on the earth, and from walking back and forth on it." In I Peter 5:8 we find Peter saying, "Your adversary the devil walks about like a roaring lion seeking whom he may devour."

In the book of Job, Satan accuses Job before God. God says to Satan in Job 2:6-7, "Behold, he (Job) is in your hand, but spare his life. So, Satan went out from the presence of the LORD and struck Job." Perhaps this can account for evil in the world. God permits evil, yet again, a major conundrum. Jesus tells us in Matthew 5:45, "He makes His sun rise on the evil and on the good, and sends rain on the just and the unjust." It is up to us as individual people with our freewill, to choose God and good and not the Devil and evil. Apparently, Adam and the woman chose poorly, thus, allowing evil into the world.

Oddly enough, we have to go to the end of the Bible in the book of Revelation, to fill in this story from the beginning of the Bible. John records for us in Revelation 12:7 the following story: "And war broke out in heaven; Michael and his angels fought with the dragon and the dragon and his angels fought, but they did not prevail nor was a place found for them in heaven any longer. So that great dragon was cast out, that serpent of old called the Devil and Satan who deceives the whole world; he was cast to the earth and his angels were cast out with him." Revelation 12:4, it says; "His tail drew a third of the stars of heaven and threw them to the earth." Isaiah 14:12 also gives us another scripture picture of Lucifer, "The Day Star" falling from heaven. "How you are fallen from heaven O Lucifer son of the morning how you are cut down to the ground … yet you shall be brought down to Sheol to the depths of the Pit… Is this the man who made the earth to tremble? …who made the world as a wilderness…" Ezekiel 28 also gives us a similar example. "You were in Eden the garden of God; Every precious stone was your covering … You were the anointed Cherub … You were perfect in your ways from the day you were created till iniquity was found in you … You became filled with violence within and you sinned; therefore I cast you as a profane thing out of the mountain of God …I cast you to the ground." Notice here: the Serpent at the time of the fall before the cursing of God for the Serpent to crawl on his belly, was not a slimy, scaly snake, but rather a beautiful creature covered with precious stones … perfect in his ways. Jesus says the following in Luke 10:18, "I saw Satan fall like lightening from heaven." Two things here: Jesus was with God the Father in Heaven as a part of the Trinity, and was present at the fall of Satan from the very early eons of time.

MAJOR PREMISE POINTS AND QUESTIONS

When considering the serpent/Satan and the fallen angels, can we conflate the following chapters?
Genesis 3, Genesis 6, Isaiah 14, Ezekiel 28, Luke 10, and Revelation 12?

1.) Can we equate the Serpent in the Garden of Eden in Genesis 3 to the Devil, Luficer, or the Dragon in Revelation 12?
2.) If so, what happened to the one third of the fallen angels who fell to the earth?
3.) Were these fallen angels of Revelation 12, which fell to the earth, the same as the fallen ones, the Nephilim, the giants, "the sons of God," of Genesis 6?
4.) When going with the premise that the war in Heaven happening *before* the Garden of Eden, this would allow for the Serpent/Tempter/Devil to be in the Garden of Eden to tempt Eve. And, that the one third of the fallen angels would also be present and

wandering the earth, awaiting for Cain to leave his family and find his wife in the land of Nod.

5.) This pre-Eden realm of time of the war in Heaven could also parallel the era of the dinosaurs.

6.) Perhaps God destroyed this dinosaur filled earth with a flood and this is where we begin with the watery chaos of Genesis 1:2.

The sin of Lucifer caused the war in Heaven. Is this why we have a void, dark earth without form with evil existing and waiting in the wings for a new and naïve Eve in Genesis 1:2?

It is possible that the Nephilim story of Genesis 6 should be read as concurrent with the previous Genesis chapters.

Could it be that the descendants of Cain became more evil with each consecutive generation because they were intermingled with the fallen angels? If this is the case, this would account for their intelligence and talents. This fallen angel concept of bringing knowledge to humans would parallel other ancient stories and myths of the "gods" or angels and/or aliens bringing technology to the people of the earth.

THE TEMPTATION

The Temptation – Adam and Eve, had at their hands all the world had to offer. God had given them a perfect life and a perfect world in which to live it. They could eat anything they wanted in the Garden of Eden, including eating from the Tree of Life and they were to live with each other and God in perfect harmony forever. Um… ugh…ahh… Enter: stage left, the serpent. He is described as more cunning than any other beast of the field. Apparently, he was able to speak. If you don't count parrots, most other animals or birds can't speak, so this alone made him a bird of a different feather. Also at this point, he, the serpent, still apparently had legs and/or perhaps wings, as he was not crawling on his belly at this point. From this perspective, this serpent was not in the traditional snake form as we now think of serpents without legs. Apparently, he did have a "forked tongue." Temptation begins with trust, which may extend to teasing, which then stems to testing before giving birth to full-blown temptation. This is true now as it was at the beginning of time.

Eve had no reason to think she would be beguiled. In her innocence, and lack of experience, she had no concept of what temptation or sin was. She had all the reason in a very new world to trust the serpent. For after all, why should she not? She was in the perfection of the Garden of Eden, and this speaking serpentine creature was one of God's creations. She had no concept of a war in Heaven between Michael and Lucifer. All she knew at this point in time, was that she was naked and hungry. Actually, she didn't even know that she was naked.

This is the first question in time, which has had ramification all through eternity reaching down to us today. "Has God indeed said, 'You shall not eat of every tree in the garden?' Eve responds, "Yes, all… but." Eve knew that she was not to eat of the Tree of Knowledge of Good and Evil in the midst of the garden, because she knew the penalty was death. However, she had no concept of what death, or the sin leading to it was. She had never seen sin, or death, or any evidence of such in the shiny new perfection of Eden.

The Serpent continues in his beguiling ways. He, the serpent, knew what sin and death were, as he had already sinned against God by rebelling against Him. Then came the first lie, the first sin of Eden.

"You will not surely die, for God knows that in the day you eat of it your eyes will be opened, and you will be like God knowing both good and evil." This seemed like a good deal to the new naïve Eve. Eve may have thought, "If Eden is this great, how much greater it would it be, to know everything God knows, … evil, whatever that is." "If all the other fruit is as good as it is, then this really good-looking fruit, which is pleasant to the eyes, must be even better. I wonder what "wise" means?"

"She took of the fruit and ate and she also gave to her husband with her and he ate." Now, the party was over. No more frolicking around naked outside in the forest. "Their eyes were opened and they knew they were naked." Eve often bears the brunt of the blame here in the garden. If we look at the Scripture, we will see the phrase, "her husband with her." Adam was right there with her and did nothing to stop this train of temptation, the trusting of the serpent, the teasing of the serpent, the testing of the serpent, and the full-blown temptation of the serpent. Adam shares the blame of the fall. Paradise was lost on this earth forever.

THE FALL

Now Adam and Eve were newly naked and ashamed, they grabbed for some nearby fig leaves and stitched together their first suits of sin. This was the new "fig-o-flage" fig leaf camouflage, which may have covered them in the cool of the day, but not from the all-seeing gaze of God.

As a possible Theophany, or Christophany form of God, God walked among his newly tarnished trees. God called for Adam. As from the beginning, God is always calling us from our sins to redeem us with His forgiveness of grace and love. Even though God is a God of grace, love, and forgiveness, He is also a God of punishment and justice. Sin must be punished, and covered, as God cannot look upon sin.

God calls for Adam, "Where are you?" Notice God does not call for Eve, just Adam. Then Adam replies much as we all do when we sin, by trying to deflect, or justify, our sin within ourselves. Adam says, "I was naked and hid myself." We, as people are always trying to hide our sin from God, but the only solution for our sin, is to confess our sin to God. Then God ask two more questions: "Who told you that you were naked? Have you eaten from the tree of which I commanded you that you should not eat?" Then, as now, Adam wanted to blame someone else, namely Eve, for the sin, almost implying that if God had not made the woman, then he would not have sinned. "The woman whom You gave to be with me, she gave me of the tree and I ate."

The sin-shuffle continues as Eve answers back to God, "The serpent deceived me," or "The devil made me do it." From here, God pronounced judgment upon the serpent. At this point, we cannot say with any real certainty what this serpent/fallen angel/Lucifer looked like. Although, his appearance and manner were certainly convincing and beguiling to Eve. This most cunning of all the creatures is now going to be the most cursed of creation. A far cry from the cherub covered with every precious stone, perfect in his ways which fell from heaven. God condemns the serpent to crawl on his belly and to eat dust. This is the same dust that Adam, the man, "Ha-Ah-dam" האדם was taken from, and created through the inspiration of God, by God breathing into the man's nostrils. God was going to put "enmity" between the serpent and Eve, and all their offspring. Man was now and forever going to bruise the head of the serpent, and the serpent was now, and forevermore going to bruise the heel of the man. God goes on to pronounce judgment on the mother of all life.

God's judgment on Eve was going to be multi-layered. Eve and all mothers proceeding from her, were now going to have great sorrow and pain in their childbirth. Her desire was going to be for the man. Instead of being Adam's Rib of Equality, Eve, was now going to be ruled by Adam. This would be a burden for both for time and eternity on fallen planet earth. Many modern so-called feminist, and the like, may not like, or concur, with this judgment of God, but from history and reality, we can see that this is the way in which the world has gone.

And finally, to the man, Adam, the man of dirt, Ha-Ah-dam, the ground was going to be cursed and in toil he would eat and work from the dirt of the earth. The ground was now going to be cursed with thorns and thistles. He would now eat by the sweat of his brow. And because he was created from the dirt, to the dirt he would return in death. Ashes to ashes and dust to dust. These may seem like harsh pronouncements from God for their sin, but God was God and is God. And this is what God saw fit.

God is a God of love, forgiveness, and redemption. It is said, "you can't un-ring a bell," and this is a true thing. What is done is done, and there is no changing it. But how we go forward, with anything, is a choice. With freewill, we must choose, and we must choose wisely. Since God cannot look upon sin, it must be covered. Since Adam and Eve felt as though they needed to be covered, God covered both their sin and shame. In the wisdom of God, God chose that sin must be covered with blood. In Matthew 26:28, Jesus says, "For this is My blood of the new covenant which is shed for many for the remission of sins." God made the first blood sacrifice for Adam and Eve by killing some of His innocent creatures, and took their skin to cover Adam and Eve's naked skin. An animal hide, to hide human sin. A skin for sin.

A great schism had now occurred. A multitude of sins; lying, deception, and death. Since Adam and Eve had eaten from the tree of the Knowledge of Good and Evil, mankind could no longer live in the perfect Garden of Eden where the Tree of Life existed. Adam and Eve must be banished from the Garden of Eden. God sent them east out of the garden to till the earth. To guard the Tree of Life, God set an angel or angels, Cherubim, with flaming swords which turned in every direction to guard the path to the Tree of Life. Turn out the lights, the perfect party was now truly over.

As a note here, it is not until after the serpent temptation that Adam names the woman "Eve" "Cheveh" חוה in Genesis 3:20, which means "Life" or "Mother of all Life" אם כל חי.

CREATION VS. EVOLUTION

GENESIS CHAPTER ONE CREATION ORDER VERSES STANDARD EVOLUTION THEORY

CREATION

1. Created by God (watery abyss assumed)

2. Day one: light

3. Day two: "firmament" (sky)

4. Day three: land with vegetation

5. Day four: sun, moon, and stars

6. Day five: sea creatures and birds

EVOLUTION

Big Bang Theory – in short, cosmic chaos with explosions and fire resulting in molten lava morphing into water in which primitive germ life eventually emerged.

Primitive germ life randomly morphs into first biological forms; early plants and animals.

7. Day six: mammals and finally humans

    Male and female humans beings are created and given charge of the earth.

    In short, fish morph into amphibians, amphibians to reptiles, reptiles to birds, birds to mammals, with various mammal forms with the primates leading to various proto-types of humanoids with homo-sapiens finally arriving on the scene.

8. Day Seven: God rest from his creation

The general flaw with the basic tenants of the theory of evolution is that is does not follow the fundamentals of true science. In true science, there are to be known and provable baselines with repeatable test cases. True science is not random and not given to chance. True science runs parallel to basic mathematics. As an example; a male and female breeding pair of horses is always going to produce a colt horse. Horses are never going to produce a raccoon. Likewise, breeding pairs of apes of various sorts will always produce apes of their own kind, not human beings. In this same thought; if humans came from apes, then why are there still apes? Yes, the principals of the "strongest of the fittest" and isolation and separation of gene pools will produce certain results. As before, a certain species is not going to arise from another species. Yes, there are genetic mutations which can and do arise in nature. Mutations in general, do not thrive, and rarely are able to reproduce in consecutive generations. Horses and donkeys are very similar species and can breed and produce mules. However, mules are not able to reproduce as they are always sterile. In fresh water fish, Striped Bass can reproduce with the very similar White Bass, but as with the horses and donkeys, the hybrid off-spring are sterile. With canines, there are a vast variety of dogs. In the end, dogs are still only dogs. There is more to this conversation, but it is beyond the point and scope of this work. It is important to remember that the Bible is first of all, a book of faith, and not intended to be a book of science. However, the Bible in not anti-science. Science is merely man discovering what God created and how He designed it.

In short, the theory of evolution, in some points follows the basic pattern of Biblical creation as set forth in the Genesis 1 Creation. The major point of opposition is that this theory does not acknowledge a prime mover of creation or "God." Evolution is based on random chance and circumstances and is not true science. It is merely a contrived theory versus the creation of God. In short, some may say that evolution in its various forms is a religion and/or faith in, and of, its self. From the perspective of the Judeo-Christian faiths, it would appear that it takes more faith to believe in this theory of chance than of a God of Creation.

DINOSAURS & DRAGONS

Before we go any further, we must address the 500-pound gorilla in the room, or the two-ton dinosaur, in this case. What about the dinosaurs? We can't get around the big lizard question of the reptile reality. We know the dinosaurs were here. Even for the staunch Biblically conservative Christian; we can't get around this scientific fact. Once again, science is merely man discovering what God created and how He designed it. The big lizard question is: When were the dinosaurs here? Were they on the Earth at the same time as people? According to Fred Flintstone, they were, as he rode a Brontosaurus at work. When did the dinosaurs die? Were dinosaurs on the ark? What about dragons? Were dragons real? Were dragons a type of dinosaur? Do we still have dinosaurs with us today?

These are the tough questions we all must answer. Children to this day are fascinated with dinosaurs and other such monsters which may, or may not, be fictitious. These Cambrian creatures haunt the halls of children's bedroom walls and sandman dreams. How do we reconcile the reptilian reality with what the scriptures say? In the Genesis 1 general creation, God is said to have created "creatures" in Genesis 1:20, and "great sea creatures" in Genesis 1:21. This term "creature" can cover a great multitude of animals to include what we would call dinosaurs. Here again, we have to go back to what "yom" means in the text. Is it a twenty-four-hour day, or an era, epoch, or realm of time? Once again, were these days of creation directly consecutive, or were there gaps, or intervals, between the days or periods of creation?

The Bible uses the term "Leviathan" in four different scriptures locations. The first mention of this creature is in the oldest written book in the Bible. Job 41 gives a stunning and startling description of what anyone would describe as a dinosaur, or more fittingly, as a fire breathing dragon. "With his terrible teeth all around, his rows of scales are his pride, shut up tightly as with a seal, one so near another that no air can come between them. They stick together and cannot be parted, His sneezings flash forth light and his eyes are like the eyelids of the morning. Out of his mouth go burning lights; sparks of fire shoot out. Smoke goes out of his nostrils as from a boiling pot and burning rushes. His breath kindles coals and a flame goes out of his mouth." This is a description of a fire-breathing dragon by anyones account. Psalm 74 and 104 also make mention of the murky monster. Isaiah 27:1 gives the Bible reader this account of leviathan. "In that day, the LORD with His severe sword, great and strong, will punish Leviathan, the fleeing serpent. Leviathan that twisted serpent; and He will slay the reptile that is in the sea." Isaiah 30:6 also refers to a "fiery flying serpent."

In the 1611 King James Old Testament several verses refer to "dragons," whereas the 1982 New King James Version translates the word as "serpent." (Deuteronomy 32;33; Nehemiah 2:13; Job 30:29; Psalms 44:19, 74:13, 91:13 and 148:7; Isaiah 13:22, 27:1, 34:13, 35:7, 43:20; Jeremiah 9:11, 10:22, 14:6, 49:33, 51:34,37; Micah 1:8 and Malachi 1:3. The book of Revelation refers to the "The Dragon" in several verses mostly in chapters twelve and thirteen. Here, this is in reference to the Devil. So just for fun thought here; were these dragons/serpents the fallen angels cast out of heaven?" Don't run too far with this thought, you may become theologically weary.

What do we do with these dragons and dinosaurs? In many ancient cultures such as Great Britain, China, India, and others, had legends of these beasts which were mostly described as flying and/or fire-breathing dragons. Based on what the writer of Job tells us, we must conclude that there was some sort of creature that met this scaly description of a dragon, which we no longer have with us. Since Job gave such a splendid description of a fire-breathing dragon, is it possible these survived the flood and Job had personal knowledge of them?

Did these creatures die in the flood or perhaps in a varying timeline at some point before or thereafter? Esteemed creation scientist, Dr. Ken Ham, supports the idea that at least some dinosaurs, or dinosaur like creatures, may have been on Noah's ark. If you have not visited the Creation Museum in Petersburg, Kentucky and the nearby reproduction ark "Ark Encounter," in Williamstown, Kentucky, near Cincinnati, Ohio, I would recommend you visit both. Even though I agree and admire much of Dr Ham's research and thoughts, he and I may disagree on some items. I personally do not believe that dinosaurs, as one normally thinks of such, were on the ark. If dinosaurs were still roaming the earth at this time, I speculate that any such creatures may have died in the flood. Conventional science tells us that they all froze to death due (or got too hot and died; depending on which scientist you read) to a meteor hitting in the Yucatan Peninsula of Mexico, which caused a dusty atmosphere and blocked out the sun. This is a valid point in this type of scientific thinking. To this point of existing dinosaurs, some may say that alligators, crocodiles, turtles, komodo dragons and, other various reptiles and amphibians may be considered surviving dinosaurs.

In crypto-zoology, many are fans of the Scottish Loch Ness Monster, which is often affectionately called "Nessy' by her many followers. The nebulous Nessy is perhaps thought to be a Plesiosaur or a similar creature. Over the years, several species have been "so-called" rediscovered; mostly by westerners, who have assumed the ancient demise of these lost creatures even though locals have been aware of their existence all along. A prime example of this would be the Coelacanth fish.

Australian zoology turned then current science on its head when westerns such as Captain James Cook of England and others began to move to the island continent in the 1700's and "discovered for science" such things as black swans, the various marsupial Kangaroos, and the egg-laying hairy mammal Platypus.

The ancient Greeks were known to have found behemoth bones which may have been from dinosaurs and/or such things as wooly mammoths and the like. These bones spawned their legends and stories of giant men and monsters. It is quite likely that people have been finding dinosaur bones all over the earth over the various centuries.

However, it was not until the 1870's, that bitter rivals, scientists Othniel Marsh and Edward Cope began finding bone fossils in the American west. These were known as the "bone wars." These expeditions, and others like them, were spawned by Charles Darwin's landmark and ever controversial book, *On the Origin of Species by Means of Natural Selection*, which was first published in 1859. This work went through at least six different editions and today is simply known as *The Origin of Species*. Even though the modern version of the theory of evolution is somewhat based on Darwin's thoughts and writings on "natural selection," the modern version of the theory of evolution is somewhat expanded and different from what the Cambridge University theology student first brought forth while sailing the world's seven seas upon the HMS Beagle. As with other points of science, Darwin's thoughts and writings are beyond the scope of this book.

Before the American Civil War, there was little to no thought or discussion in the Christian world about the Creation. Almost no thought was ever given to dinosaurs, the theory of evolution, or the like, as these concepts were mostly unknown and otherwise unheard of.

PRE-DARWIN DISCOVERIES

In my ancestor's 1784 book, pages 33-36 *"The Discovery, Settlement and present State of Kentucke,"* John Filson wrote the following: *"at a salt spring, near the Ohio River very large bones were found, far surpassing the size of any species of animals now in America. The head appears to have been about three feet long --- and the thigh bones about four (feet) --- and said to weigh seventy-eight pounds the tusks are above a foot in length. The grinders about five inches square and eight inches long. These bones have equally excited the amazement of the ignorant and attracted the attention of the philosopher --- What creature is this? --- The ignorant and superstitious Tartars attribute them to a creature whom they call a Maimon --- The bones themselves bear great resemblance to those of an elephant.--- The tusk with which they are equally furnished produce true ivory --- (and this other animal is also described) (Dr. Hunter) that celebrated anatomist --- procured specimens from the Ohio examined them with that accuracy --- He discovered a considerable difference between the shape and structure of the bones --- he observed the form of the teeth that they must have belonged to a carnivorous animal whereas the habits of the elephant are foreign to such sustenance, and his jaws totally unprovided with the teeth necessary for its use: and from the whole he concluded to the satisfaction of naturalist that these bones belonged to a quadruped now unknown and whose race is probably extinct --- Happy we that is has. How formidable an enemy to the human species an animal as large as an elephant the tyrant of the forests, perhaps the devourer of man! --- To this circumstance we are probably indebted for a fact, which is perhaps singular in its kind, the extinction of the whole race of animals from the system of nature."* This location of which John Filson is referencing is likely the present site of the present Big Bone Lick State Park in northern Kentucky. The bones Filson describes are likely those of a Mammoth, or Mastodon and the "tyrant of forest" is likely to be some sort of dinosaur like a Tyrannosaurus Rex. All of this discovery, research, and speculation was several generations before Charles Darwin and those like him. Science is merely man discovering what God created and how He designed it.

Back to our original question: What about the dinosaurs? Even staunch conservative Biblical thinkers cannot deny their existence even though perhaps some still do. How do we reconcile dinosaurs with the Biblical time line? Here again, the issue of the Hebrew word for day, Yom, comes into play. Were there eons and epochs of time involved with the creation? Were there gaps in between the days of creation? Going back to Genesis 1:2, Did God create an earth with dinosaurs and then destroy it with a flood? Is this why we find an earth which was void and with darkness on the face of the deep? Is it possible that the war in Heaven happened during this same time of chaos? Did humans walk the earth alongside these giant reptiles? Dr. Ken Ham and other creation scientist provide evidence that perhaps humans and dinosaurs did walk side by side. Certain fossil evidence would support such claims. For further information on this pressing topic, read Doctor Ken Ham's book series; *Answers in Genesis,* as well as, his other books.

Regardless of what you may, or may not, think about dragons and dinosaurs, the meticulous majesty of God's creation is beyond our scope of recognition. What are the mathematical chances that we live on a planet that just so happens to be the exact and perfect distance from a proper sized and composed star, our sun? What keeps the earth in a precision orbit and tilting and spinning day by day with little to no variance? Science may, or may not, be able to explain this, but once again, science is merely man discovering what God created and how He designed it.

{Editorial note: Editor Harrison Cyrus notes that it is important to understand that the "Tree of Life" and the "Tree of Knowledge of Good and Evil are two different trees." Cyrus further comments that it almost seems as if Adam and Eve were set up for failure with regards to the Tree of Knowledge of Good and Evil. They did not make good use of their freewill. With regard to dinosaurs, Cyrus suggest that with possible "gaps" between the days, God created the dinosaurs earlier and then destroyed them before humans as humans would not be able to coexist with them. Cyrus further comments that so-called evolution science still needs a "miracle" to assert their position. Even if evolution were scientific fact; the theory still needs a prime mover.}

{Editorial Paul James Winslow asserts that the war in Heaven and the realm of the dinosaurs happened "before" the watery earth of Genesis 1:2.}

Questions and Discussion for
Chapter Three ~ Genesis: The Creation Stories
Dig-Discover-Discuss

1. How do you understand the meaning of the Hebrew word Yom יום for "day?"
   a) 24 hour period
   b) Daytime or daylight
   c) A period of time as in, "back in my day."
   d) An era, epoch, or realm of time.

2. Is it possible that Moses used the Hebrew word Yom for day in different context?

3. Did God create our world in 144 human hours, or six days as per chapter one? Or did God create the earth in one day as per chapter two?
   Is it possible that there were gaps between the days of creation?

4. Do you understand the chapter two creation story to be a different oral tradition written down by Moses; or a detailed and "different in order" continuation of chapter one?

5. Discuss the Hebrew names for God:
   God = Elohim = אלהים
   LORD God = Yahweh or Jehovah God = יהוה אלהים

6. Is God still creating an endless universe?

7. Who was the "prime-mover" or the main agent of creation? Explain the Trinity in creation.

8. Were Adam and Eve real people? What did they look like? Did they have navels? Did Adam have a chest scar from the rib extraction?

9. Did God intend for us to be vegetarians or vegans? What do the words "subdue" and "dominion" mean? Could they mean "to eat?" Did God "change His mind" after the flood with regard to us eating meat? Or did He intend us to eat meat before the flood? Explain and discuss your dietary stance.

10. How do you think the world looked when God created it? Explain

11. Where was the Garden of Eden?

12. What type of fruit was the "forbidden fruit?"
    Do we still have this fruit with us today?

13. Was the serpent in the garden the fallen angel Lucifer?

14. What did the Serpent look like *before* God cursed him to be on his belly and eat dust?

15. If Lucifer were the serpent, when did he fall out of Heaven?

16. How much time passed after Eve was created until the temptation in the garden?

17. What did the angels look like that drove Adam and Eve from the garden?

18. What happened to the Garden of Eden after the fall?

19. How do you relate the scientific theory of evolution to Biblical creation?

20. With regards to Lucifer and the fallen angels, when did the war in Heaven happen, considering "the serpent" appeared to Adam and Eve in the Garden of Eden?

21. When was the age of the dinosaurs in comparison to Genesis chapters one and two?

22. Put the following items/events in a time line order:
    a) Age of the dinosaurs
    b) Creation of Heaven and the angels
    c) Creation of the earth as in Genesis chapters one and two
    d) Garden of Eden
    e) Fall of Lucifer and the fallen angels
    f) War in Heaven

Chapter Four

Cain's Wife

East Of Eden

Since Adam and Eve were now driven east from the perfection of the Garden of Eden by the sword wielding angels, it was now time to get down in the dirt from which they came, and get on with life and work. Genesis 4 gets busy by immediately beginning with Eve having a son as a blessing from God. Adam and Eve's first son is named Cain which can mean "acquired." Scripture does not reveal how much time elapsed from the Garden expulsion to the birth of Cain, but we can biologically assume that it was at least nine months if, in fact, human pre-flood gestation periods were then nine months; if, in fact, Eve was not already pregnant before the fall. After another amount of undetermined time, Eve gives birth to her second son, Abel. It is because of these undetermined amount of time issues, that it makes Bishop Ussher's timeline somewhat untenable.

From the time that Adam and Eve left the garden until Cain's birth, there is a quick but apparent leap in time in Genesis 4:2, as Abel is named as a shepherd, and Cain as a farmer.

OFFERINGS

Here we can gather that Cain and Able, are grown men, or close to it. In Genesis 4:3 we have yet another time leap as the scripture uses the phrase "in the process of time" or "in the course of time" as some translations state it. From the text we are not sure what prompted this next action, but one must gather that the will of God implied that an offering from Cain and Abel should be made. Cain, the farmer, brought forth an offering from the fruit of the earth. Perhaps this was some sort of fruit, vegetables, and/or grain, or even some combination of all the above. The Scripture is clear to point out that Abel brought forth the "first born" of his flock. God was pleased with Abel's offering, but not so with Cain's. This brings forth the question of "why?" Was it because it was not a blood offering? This would be a good answer. Was it because it was not a "first-fruit?" This too could be a correct answer. Could it have been a poor attitude on the part of Cain? Perhaps it was a collection of all the above. Either way, God did not respect Cain's offering, and Cain was not pleased with God. The NKJV says that Cain was angry and his countenance fell. This verbiage would suggest that Cain was so angry with God, that he became unhinged, perhaps in the same manner, as a college basketball coach, or an old school baseball manager, over a disagreeable umpire call. Some may even use the term "apoplectic."

In God's grace and forgiveness, God asked Cain why he was angry, and offers him the option to "do well." With this offer, God warned Cain of the sin that awaited at his door.

MY BROTHER'S KEEPER

Genesis 4:8 suggest to us that at some point after the offering debacle, Cain persuades his brother, Able, that they should take a walk in the field. Apparently, Cain had been weaving a web of ill will towards his own blood brother after their offerings to God. Cain brings his blood-stained plan to fruition and kills his brother. This is the first murder of mankind. Sadly, millions more would occur in the many millennia to follow. We don't know how, or with what, Cain did the deed, but his brother's blood now soaked red into the soil. This now maroon mud, and crimson clay cried out to God. To be sure, our scarlet sins will find us out, and they are never beyond the ever-seeing gaze of God.

"Where is Abel, your brother?" is the first question God asked Cain. As with Cain's father, Adam, wearing his fig-o-flage in the Garden of Eden, God already knew the answer to His own question. As with Cain's father, Cain tried to be coy and deflected the question as if he, as a mere mortal, could disguise the truth with the camouflage of a lie. Then Cain replied with his most famous lie and question combination; "I do not know, Am I my brother's keeper?" Over these many centuries, we have been asking this same question in the same way; and the obvious answer has never changed. God asked again, "What have you done?" God had to first deal with the sin of deception with Adam and Eve, and the serpent. God was now going to have to deal with murder; the defacing of the image of God by another made in the image of God. Another great schism in God's fallen creation.

God was not pleased. God explained to Cain that Abel's blood was crying out to Him from the garnet ground. God gave Cain a multi-pronged punishment. The ground would be cursed more than it already was. Cain was going to be banished as a vagabond and a fugitive.

Cain replied and said his punishment was more than he could bear. He did not want to be punished and hidden from the face, or presence of God. This is where the text gets interesting. Cain replied in horror in Genesis 4:14 by stating back to God the following, "...and it will happen, that *anyone* who finds me will kill me." What? Anyone! Anyone who? We will address this more below. God promised to Cain that anyone who kills him will have vengeance unfurled on him seven-fold. Then God placed a mark on Cain. This "mark" was a sign to "others" that they absolutely were not to kill Cain.

What was this mark? The Scripture does not say. In the past, some suggested that God made Cain "black," but there is nothing in Scripture to suggest, or support this theory. Other Biblical thinkers have offered that it may have been some sort of tattoo ink, a brand, or something of this ilk. Either way, the mark was something that others would have absolutely recognized as being a warning sign from God not to kill Cain.

THE LAND OF NOD.

After the banishment and the "mark," Cain was now a young man heading east out of the land of Eden to the land of Nod, or the Land of Wandering. Sadly, Cain never seemed to repent of his sin and was content to be out of the presence of God.

The marked man Cain now finds himself a woman, "a Noddy girl" to

be his wife. I refer to the people in the land of Nod as the Noddy People. Now how can this be? God made Adam from the dust of the earth and breathed into his nostrils and he became a living man. God had Adam take a nap and took one of his ribs and made Eve. Adam and Eve sinned and were driven from the Garden of Eden and had two sons, Cain and Abel. Cain killed Abel, which should only leave us with three people on the earth; Adam, Eve, and Cain. So, where did Cain find his wife? Who was she and where did she come from? Furthermore, who were these "anyone" people who might want to kill Cain?

SISTER THEORY

The first theory was that Cain married his sister. What sister? It is common throughout the Bible, especially in the Old Testament, that daughters and wives were often not listed in the genealogies. Up to this point, Adam and Eve are not recorded in Scripture to have had a daughter. It is not until Genesis 5:4, which says, "And Adam lived one hundred and thirty years and begot a son in his own likeness, after his image and named him Seth. After he begot Seth, the days of Adam were eight hundred years and he had sons and daughters."

Genesis 4:25 says the Adam and Eve gave birth to their third son, Seth. He was to "replace" Abel. For any parent who has lost a child, there is no replacing a deceased child; no matter how many others that follow. As a point of interest, Cain's son was named Enoch, whereas Seth's son was name Enosh. Enoch can be translated as "teacher," whereas Enosh can mean "frail."

Yes, Adam and Eve did have daughters, however these unnamed and unnumbered sisters were not born until *after* Cain left the family and many years after Seth was born to Adam and Eve.

The "sister theory" would have to walk on the "unnamed in genealogies" path to have any legs on which to stand, since the sisters of Cain were not born until hundreds of years later. As a side note, Genesis 5 begins in a most interesting way, "This is the book of genealogies of Adam." Genesis 5, like Genesis 1, uses the Elohim name for God and uses the similar phrase of, "He created them male and female" as per Genesis 1.

THE NODDY PEOPLE

If the reader, does not choose the sister theory of how Cain found his wife, then where did she come from? Cain's wife is a part of this "anyone people." She was a "Noddy girl" not to be confused with a "naughty girl," or a "knotty girl" for that matter, however, this may have been true as well. She was from the land of Nod. Where did the Noddy people come from? Apparently, they were not from the lineage of Adam and Eve. How can this be? Perhaps the Noddy people have their origins in Genesis 1.

Genesis 1:27 states: "So God created man in His Own image; in the image of God He created him; male and female He created them." These people created in the image of God in Genesis 1 are not named. In a gloss-over reading, these "male and female" created people may be thought by some to be Adam and Eve exclusively. Adam and Eve were the first named created people, and were likely to be in this collective creation. Apparently, God created other people in addition to Adam and Eve. Clearly, this must be the case, as Cain was clearly aware of, and afraid of the Noddy people's presence. In the land of Nod, Cain went on to marry a Noddy girl who gave birth to his son, whom he named Enoch, who built a "city." To be sure, a mud hut, a lean-to, a tent, or a tepee in Mesopotamia does not a city make. To have a city, there must be a multitude of people. The land of Nod is where, at least some of the Noddys lived. We will get back to Cain's son, Enoch, and his city below.

THE SONS OF GOD

Another possible theory as to where Cain got his wife is from the Nephilim, the fallen ones, which fell out of heaven with the devil. The reader will want to reference the war in Heaven as described in Revelation 12. The reader will find the Devil and one third of his fallen angels, being defeated by Michael the Archangel, and being cast to the earth. In this Revelation story, the Devil, Satan, and the serpent are equated to the same creature. With the Serpent being present in the Garden of Eden, one could concude that the war in Heaven happened *before* the Garden of Eden. With this said, one third of the "stars," or fallen angels, were also cast to the earth with the devil himself. These fallen ones, the fallen angels, were also present on the earth.

Genesis 6 finally mentions the Nephilim, the fallen ones. These fallen ones were called the "sons of God." These fallen ones physically mixed with the humans and produced the giants. The Nephilim, "the sons of God," the fallen angels, mixed with the "daughters of men." This first mixing was likely with the Noddy people and the descendants of Cain. Genesis 6:4 calls these offsprings of human and heavenly extraction; "the mighty men who were of old." From this, one could conclude that the fallen ones had been around for a long time, even though they are not mentioned until Genesis 6. Were these fallen angels and the Noddy people, the ones Cain feared?

Cain's descendants, beginning with his son Enoch, were crafty artisans of various sorts. However, for all their God given talent, they became more sinful with each consecutive generation, to the point that God repented within Himself twice in Genesis 6 for even creating humans. It is during this time that we have the emergence of music and the metallurgical arts. It is likely that this talent and knowledge came through the fallen angels.

Because of the lineage of Christ in Luke 3:23-38, and related verses, all sinful humanity is thought to be "sons of Adam." If there were other people created that were not of the line of Adam, then how can we all be the sons of Adam? This is a simple deduction. Noah was a direct descendant of Adam. Noah and his family were the only ones to survive the flood by God's grace. All the Noddy people and Cain's descendants died in the flood, so, all would still be descendants of Adam and Eve. Or, did all the Noddy people and Cain's descendants die in the flood? This will be discussed more in the Noah's ark and the flood chapter.

Once again, where did Cain's wife come from? As per our above discussion:

1) She was either an unnamed sister not listed Scripture.
2) God created other people.
3) These other people could have been the mixture between the Noddy people with the Nephilim.

Where did Cain get his wife? What does the scripture say? What does the scripture not say?

{Editorial note: Editor James Paul Winslow asserts that the lineage of Cain were the "sons of the Devil" based upon their mixture with the Nephilim fallen angels.}

Questions and Discussion for
Chapter Four – Cain's Wife
Dig-Discover-Discuss

1. Where did Adam and Eve go after they were driven from the Garden of Eden?

2. How long was it before Eve conceived and gave birth to Cain?

3. How long was it before Eve conceived and gave birth to Able after the birth of Cain?

4. How long was the period of time, which is described as "in the process of time" in Genesis 4:3?

5. How old were Cain and Able before they became farmers and shepherds?

6. Why did God not accept Cain's offering from the fruit of the ground?

7. Why was Cain angry with God? Did God give Cain an avenue of redemption?

8. Why did Cain kill Able? How did Cain kill Able?

9. Are we our brother's keeper?

10. Once God punished Cain with banishment from his family; why did Cain say this punishment was more than he could bear?

11. Did Cain ever ask God for forgiveness?

12. Cain states, "anyone who finds me will kill me." Who was "anyone?"

13. What was "the Mark" that God placed on Cain to warn others not to kill him?

14. Where was the Land of Nod?

15. Cain took a wife in the Land of Nod – WHO WAS CAIN'S WIFE?
    a) Was Cain's wife his sister who is not recorded in the Bible?
    b) Did God create other people?
    c) Could this "anyone people" have been the fallen Nephilim?

    Explain your "Sister Theory" based on scripture.
    Explain your "God created other people theory,"

"The Noddy People," based on Genesis chapter 1.
Explain how one third of the angels fell to the earth – then what?

16. Why would Cain build a "city" for himself and his Noddy wife?

Chapter Five

Noah's Ark and the Flood

At the very mention of Noah and the flood, images of rainbows, a big wooden boat, doves with olive branches, and pairs of mostly African animals from the plains of the Serengeti are immediately, and instantly conjured up in one's mind. What does the scripture say? Before we get too deep into the flood, we must first examine who Noah was, and where he came from. How did all those people in Genesis live so long? We have just discussed Cain and his Noddy wife. However, Noah was not of the line of Cain. Noah was of the line of Seth, the third son of Adam and Eve.

YET HIS DAYS SHALL BE 120 YEARS

It is quite possible that Genesis 5 is yet another possible oral tradition collected, edited, and written by Moses. This is the second telling of the birth of Seth and Enosh. Also, during this early time, there appears to be two different men in the antediluvian world which were named Lamech. It is not likely that the father of Jabal and Jubal in the line of Cain, was the same man who was the father of Noah in the line of Seth. There also appears to be two men named Enoch; the son of Cain, and Enoch, the son of Jared in the line of Seth.

Adam to Seth = 130 years. Adam lived 930 years.
Seth to Enosh = 105 years. Seth lived 912 years.
Enosh to Cainan = 90 years. Enosh lived 905 years.
Cainan to Mahalel = 70 years. Cainan lived 910 years.

Mahalel to Jared = 65 years. Mahalel lived 895 years.
Jared to Enoch = 162 years. Jared lived 962 years.
Enoch to Methuselah = 65 years. Enoch lived 365 years and was taken by God.
Methuselah to Lamech = 187 years. Methuselah lived 969 years.
Lamech to Noah = 182 years. Lamech lived 777 years.
Noah to Shem, Ham & Japheth = 500 years. Noah lived 950 years.

The flood came when Noah was 600 years old.

From the inspiration of Adam, to the flood was 1656 years. Adam lived to see his Great, great, great, great, great, great, grandson Lamech born. Adam died 526 years before the flood. Noah's grandfather Methuselah likely died in, or at the Flood. Although, Noah's father Lamech died five years before the Flood. All other direct ancestors from the line of Seth were already dead. Also, remember that Enoch was "taken" by God and did not die a normal, earthly death.

The decesendants of Cain were mixed with Noddy people, which were likely mixed with the fallen ones, the Nephilim, the one third of the fallen angels to the earth, resulting in the mighty men of old as described in Genesis 6.

Cain and his Noddy wife gave birth to Enoch
Enoch had Irad,
Irad had Mehujael
Mehujael had Methushael
Methushael had Lamech
Lamech had two wives.
- Adah had Jabal
- Zillah had Jubal & Tubal-Cain
and a sister Naamah

With all of this said, it was about 1656 years from the time God inspired Adam to the time of the flood. What does the Scripture say? However, with regards to the whole creation, one must go back to the ever-elusive issue of time. Was the creation completed in one day or yom יום as in Genesis 2 or six or seven days or יום as in Genesis 1? Were there gaps between the days? Were the days 24-hour periods or were the days eons, or epoch realms of time, allowing for such things as the dinosaurs and the war in Heaven with the consequent fall of Lucifer and one third of the fallen angels to the earth. Time, as we know it, may have been a completely different situation in the antedivulian world, just as current Venusian and Martian (Venus & Mars) years are different from current Earth years. The earth's path around the sun and earth years may have been a completely different computation in the antediluvian period. Keep in mind there is an unknown gap in time from the end of Genesis 2 to Genesis 3. How long did Adam and Eve live in the perfection of the Garden of Eden with God before the temptation of the serpent? We can never know. What does the Scripture say? What does the Scripture not say?

How did those people in Genesis live so long? This may be addressed in a few different ways. Genesis 5:27 records that Methuselah lived to be 969 years old. He is the oldest person recorded in the Bible. How can this be? Is it possible that these pre-flood years were what modern people would call months? Is it possible that the antediluvian world year was shorter than a post-flood year? This is possible since the pre-flood world was completely transformed after the Flood. In classic Biblical jargon, the pre-flood world was called "Antediluvian" or thus, "before the deluge." When God created people, it was God's intent that we would live forever in a perfect creation. Methuselah's 969 years is not forever, but it is a long time. The onset of sin with Adam and Eve created a schism in God's perfect universe of creation. People would no longer live forever on this earth in their human bodies. In the antediluvian creation, human life spans had already begun to decline. This degradation of life spans became more pronounced after the flood as the earth was now going to be a much different place.

Some creation-scientists would say the atmosphere was now compromised from its original created form. It is thought that the antediluvian atmosphere was much "wetter and heavier," before the Flood than what it is now. This wetter and heavier firmament, or atmosphere, blocked out many of the harmful solar rays, which currently invade our planet. It is thought by some, that the whole antediluvian world may have been some sort of tropical paradise without the polar caps we have today. Post flood life, life spans, and life forms would be much different from the antediluvian world. Various scientists strongly suggest, from the evidence of core samples from drilling into the polar ice caps, that it is possible that the polar ice caps at various times, had vegetation and were much warmer than they are now.

"And the LORD said, my Spirit shall not strive with man forever, for he is indeed flesh; yet his days shall be one hundred and twenty years," (Genesis 6:3). "Moses tells us in a prayer recorded in Psalm 90:10, "The days of our lives are seventy years, and if by reason of strength they are eighty, Yet their boast is only labor and sorrow." Over the eons of time, human life expectancy throughout most of the world decreased up through the last few centuries. In was not uncommon for people in the middle ages of Europe to die in the forties, however some did live into what would be called old age.

According to Wikipedia, life spans currently continue to increase. As of the writing of this text in 2017, the worldwide longevity expectancy for women is 73 with men crossing the finish line at 68. Japan comes in number one with women having 87 birthday parties and their male counterparts only having 80. The United States in only ranked 26th in the world with women living to 81 and men to 77. In modern documented records, Jeane Calment lived from 1875-1997 for 122 years in France. Some in the current medical and scientific communities believe that in the future, with the correct genetics, cleaner environments, medical advancements, with better diets, and lifestyle choices, it may be once again possible to live well past the one century mark, just as God set forth. God is eternal and we are not. Only our souls will proceed into eternity, but not our earthly un-glorified bodies.

NOAH

From Adam and Eve came Seth. Where Seth got his wife is yet another Biblical conundrum since the scripture does not say. Perhaps she was a sister from the loins of Adam and Eve as recorded Genesis 5:4 of the Book of Origins. Perhaps Seth took a clue from his older brother, Cain, and wedded a Noddy girl as well. Either way, from God came Adam, from Adam came Seth, and from Seth came his son Enosh. Seth and his unnamed wife also had other sons and daughters. From Enosh came Cainan. Cainan, in turn, had Mahalalel, as well as, other sons and daughters. From Mahalalel came his son, Jared, and yet again, more sons and daughters. Jared was not to be any different from his ancestors and gave rise to his son Enoch and, once again, even more sons and daughters were born to Jared. Enoch was apparently an oddity of his generation as he is said to have walked with God. The Scripture says that God "took" Enoch, who apparently had a different passage into the afterlife than the standard human death. Enoch, in turn, passed his genes down to the ever-famous Methuselah. As with all the above, Enoch had other sons and daughters. Methuselah is best known for living the longest in the Bible at 969 years. Depending on how one does the math, perhaps Methuselah, the grandfather of Noah, died in the Flood. Sadly, in Methuselah's long life, he is only given credit for having had sons and daughters to include his son Lamech. Not to be different than all the rest, Methuselah also had other sons and daughters which apparently did not walk with God, and most likely died in the Flood. Finally, Lamech's wife gave birth to Noah and said, "This one will comfort us." Noah was the ninth generation after Adam, or the tenth generation of human beings on the earth. As was the family tradition, Lamech had other sons and daughters; brothers and sisters of Noah who sadly died in the flood.

Here the book of Genesis inserts the story of "that the sons of God," the Nephilim, who came into the daughters of men, the mighty men of old. It was at this point that God was sorry for having made man on the earth because man's heart was continually evil. The Nephilim will be discussed at length in the "Angels, Aliens, Ghosts & Giants" chapter.

Genesis 6:9 states that Noah was a just and perfect man, who walked with God. From an unnamed wife, Noah had three sons; Shem, Ham, and Japheth. Mankind continued to be corrupt, and God continued to consider destroying mankind including the animals and all the earth.

God gives Noah instruction on how to survive this great destruction. God instructs Noah to build an ark. What is an ark? An ark is a boat, a big ol' boat. But why an ark? And what was a flood?

THE ARK

Let us begin with the ark. Noah was said to have been five hundred years old when his three sons: Shem, Ham, and Japheth were born. Perhaps the three sons were triplets. Hold Noah's age of 500 years old as a mental marker. Noah's wife is not named in the Canon Scripture. Just for fun, we will call her "Joan." It is conjecture at best to suggest that the three sons, or perhaps others, to include Noah's kinfolk, or other hired hands, assisted in the construction of the ark. The negative thought is the sons may have thought their dear old dad had to be mad for building a boat for all the animals in the world, for the express purpose of escaping a worldwide deluge. The other side of the conundrum coin is the sons were helpful to their faithful father, and participated in his vision and mission from God. Genesis 11:10, informs us that Shem was one hundred years old, two years after the Flood, when he had his son, Arphaxad. This math would make Shem and his brothers, about 97 or 98 years old, while on this epic voyage.

God was specific in the description of the two main materials for the construction of the Ark. The two elements were to be gopher wood and pitch. We have no idea what type of tree Gopher wood may have been. Does this type of tree still exist? Was it all used up in the construction of the ark? Perhaps all the Gopher wood trees were otherwise destroyed in the flood. Pitch is simply any type of gooey black pine tar, or tree resin. This was used as glue and water-proofer, inside and out, over the entire structure; most important when building a boat for a flood. Because of this pitch application, the general over-all appearance of the ark would have been black. This goes contrary to most conjectured art work of the ark, which normally shows the ark being brown in color because of the hewn wood.

Besides the two-pronged materials list for the construction, God also gives Noah a specific blueprint, a schematic of instructions for the ark construction. The dimensions were to be three hundred cubits in length which is about 450 feet, fifty cubits in width, which is nearly 75 feet, and thirty cubits in depth, or close to 45 feet. For a visual size comparison; A regulation football field from goal post to goal post, is 120 yards long or, 360 feet long as compared to the 450 feet of the ark. Regulation baseball fields are about 400 feet or so at the centerfield fence from home plate. The distance between bases on a regulation baseball field is 90 feet, as compared to the 75 feet of ark width. The 45 feet of ark height is half the distance of 90 feet, between bases on a baseball diamond. Some modern cargo and naval ships have very similar dimensions. These dimensions for an ocean-going vessel are thought to be very stable and sturdy by those schooled in such specifications.

The ark was also to have a window, which was to be a cubit in size, or about eighteen inches. Also, the one door on the ark was in the side of the ark. The size of the door is not specified, but it would have needed to have been at least large enough for beasts like elephants, giraffes, and perhaps other phylum, which may have been larger than these, if there were such beast at this time. God continues to instruct Noah with the building of three decks within the ark structure which were to contain rooms, or "nests" as described in the Hebrew language. Since the ark was 45 feet deep from the bottom draft to the top rail, we can calculate or speculate that the three decks were about 15 feet each in depth. Anything beyond this blueprint of the ark is pure speculation. Genesis 7:16 tells us that God shut Noah into the ark.

In most classic and contemporary Sunday school and Bible school art, the ark had a possible V-shaped stem complete with a rounded bottom and a house boat barn on top. This may, or may, not have been so. From the simple description given in Scripture, the ark most likely resembled a big wooden box. Perhaps it did have an 18 inch "cubit ridge" or a vented window along the top as recorded in Genesis 6:16. This box shape would have sufficed, since the ark only had to float, and ride out the tempest, and tumult of the titanic flood. The ark did not have to make a traversing wake. Except for the active Hand of God, the ark had no described means of propulsion such as propellers, paddles, oars, motors, or sails. Nor did it have a rudder for steering, or a compass for navigation. It was mostly a floating box with a full cargo of eight souls, and all the various zoological wonders and oddities held within its pitched gopher wood boards and beams.

How long did it take to build the ark? Keep in mind, there were no gas-powered chainsaws to timber all those gopher wood trees, or electric powered saw mills to lumber up all the freshly fallen forest of the gopher wood foliage. Logs had to be loaded and presumed transported by human and/or animal locomotion. After the adventurous arrival to the boat building site, all the wood then had to be hewn by hand. Skillful and careful carpentry skills of measuring twice and cutting once, had to be applied as each board and beam was placed in and on the ark. How many people, besides Noah, worked in the construction, and how long did it take to build? Genesis 5:32 says that Noah was 500 years old when his three sons were born. Genesis 7:6 states that Noah was 600 years old when the floodwaters were upon the earth. With this as a broad-brush time table, we can only know from what the Scripture says that it took less than 100 years. Hired hands, or helpers, or the three sons, as builders, can only be assumed. What does the scripture say? What does the scripture not say?

THE ANIMALS

Two-by-two and side-by-side they went into the ark...and so they did. Genesis 6 plainly tells us that God commanded Noah to collect a male and female of every sort into the ark, of every creeping thing and of the birds of their kind, and so Noah did. Genesis 6 uses the Elohim אלהים name for God. This would be an "E" oral tradition that Moses collected when writing this epic story. Whereas Genesis 7, uses the YHWH יהוה name for God, which appears as LORD in our English text. This is a "J" oral tradition which was also collected by Moses for recording this story. Moses used a great deal of craft and skill as he weaves at least these two oral traditions together, leaving no stone unturned in this epic Poseidon adventure. In Genesis 7, God commands Noah, more specifically, to collect seven each of the clean animals. "You shall take with you seven each of every clean animal, a male and his female; two each of animals that are unclean, a male and his female; also, seven each of birds of the air, male and female, to keep the species alive on the face of all the earth." Were these seven pairs of clean animals, or was it some combination of males and females for a total of seven animals, such as one male and six females? This would have been a common way to collect such livestock as cattle, sheep, and goats. Cattle are referenced exclusively throughout the ark text. One could speculate that cattle were a prominent part of antediluvian life. The unclean animals are still only to be a set pair of one male and one female.

What was a clean animal? According to Hebrew and Jewish dietary laws, some animals were considered "clean," or suitable for eating, whereas some animals were not considered suitable for eating and were classified as "unclean." Oddly, these dietary laws were not discussed in the Bible until well after Noah's flood when Moses was leading the children of Israel in the Exodus out of Egypt. God reveals to Moses, in Leviticus 11 an elaborate list of clean and unclean animals, and all things pertaining thereto. However, in Genesis 9:3, God tells Noah "Every moving thing that lives shall be food for you." This is reminiscent of the Lord telling Peter to "rise Peter, kill and eat" in Acts 11. This is a dietary conundrum discussion point.

We know how big the ark was, but how many animals were on the ark? This is a perplexing question likely not to have a good answer. Many assertions, assumptions, conjectures, estimates, hypothesis, and just plain ol' good ol' guesses, have placed the numbers into the five-digit range. Perhaps thousands and thousands. The ark would have been big enough to hold a whole host of zoological wonders of little creeping things, amphibians, reptiles, birds, and mammals on the manifest. After we get past such behemoths as giraffes, elephants, rhinos, and hippos, things in the animal kingdom tend to slim down quite a bit. Horses, cows, and other large hoofed cud chewers, such as moose and buffalo, can still be on the large size. However, many standard garden variety furry woodland creatures, such as rabbits, squirrels, raccoons, opossums, fox, bobcats, woodchucks, skunks, and the such, do not take up much room. Animals of this size and sort would have been the lion's share of the load.

Children and others may also ask, "How did this floating circus, filled with the likes of such fearsome creatures of lions, tigers, and bears, keep from eating each other?" The first answer is that the majestic hand of God secured such situations. It is also certain, Noah had built cages for all the animals.

What animals were in the ark? The Scripture says all of them. We can suppose everything from aardvarks and armadillos, to yaks and zebras. The only animals listed by specific name were, cattle, a dove and a raven. At this point in the earthly time table, we may safely assume some of the original animals of creation were already extinct. On this same thought, there have been some species which had expired from existence since the time of the ark. Additionally, in this same train of thought, there have been many types and varieties of animals which have arisen since the time of the ark.

When thinking of Farmer Bob's barn yard animals of black and white Hampshire Hogs, Holstein bovines, and pin-striped Plymouth Rock Poultry, it is not likely that these particular duo-chromatic animals were on the ark. Likewise, with canines, most dogs at this point likely still resembled coyotes and dingoes. Poodles and Pomeranians were most likely not on board.

From the mouths of babes, these same children who gaze upon the Bible School and Sunday School art work of the ark, comes the inevitable question of "Were there dinosaurs on the ark?" Twenty-first century people, cannot get around the big lizard reptile wrestle. According to the most esteemed and respected authority in Christian creation thought, author, and scientist, Dr. Ken Ham, dinosaurs were on the ark. On this point, Dr. Ham and I may have to take different points of view. If dinosaurs were present at the time of the flood, it is my thoughts that they may have died in the flood if, in fact, they were not already extinct. If one wants to consider: alligators, crocodiles, snakes, serpents of various sorts, salamanders, frogs, newts, turtles, geckos, Gila monsters, Komodo dragons, and other such monitor lizards to be dinosaurs; well O.K. then, there were dinosaurs on the ark. Perhaps dinosaurs existed during this time, or perhaps they existed in a different earth age, epoch, era or realm of time. Put dinosaurs into the same context of "When was the war in Heaven, when Michael the Archangel defeated Lucifer and his third of fallen angels?" The second verse of the Bible states a watery earth was already in existence with the Creator God. As with the war in Heaven, we must ask ourselves "Is it possible that God had already created the earth once before and destroyed it?" This is neither conventional nor Orthodox Judeo-Christian thought. This is a thought provoking possible scenario unless one wants to dismiss the war in Heaven and dinosaurs.

The writer of Job described a beast in Job 41 which, by any account can be nothing other than a "fire-breathing dragon." How did the writer of Job have the working knowledge of a dragon unless he or someone he knew had seen or knew of one?

We now have different types of classifications, subspecies, kinds and varieties of animals through the human device of selective breeding, like the above mentioned Hampshire hogs and Pomeranians. In the course of time, many species of animals have become extinct since the time of the flood.

How did Noah collect such zoological oddities of Australian Kangaroos, Antarctic Penguins, and North Pole Polar Bears? This can only be attributed to the miracle moving hand of God. Genesis 6:20 says, "Two of every kind will come to you to keep alive."

There is some conjecture as to whether the flood caused the "ice age" or did the ice age cause the flood; if, there is any confluence of the two events. In Dr. Ken Ham's book, *A Pocket Guide to Noah's Ark,* page 80, it is suggested that the flood and the consequent depletion of the atmosphere led to conditions which lead to the "ice age." The term ice age is in and of itself a misnomer, as there have been a few different ice ages. Weather and climate in 1700-1850 was called the "Little Ice Age." These years vary greatly depending upon who and what one wants to read. When looking at recent art work like *Washington Crossing the Delaware,* there where chunks of ice in the Delaware River on Christmas night because then it was very cold in North America. There were many very long and cold winters and short and cool summers during the American colonial period. Ice chunks are now rarely seen in the Delaware River in December. This little ice age period was supposedly caused by a series of volcanoes in Asia, causing a shroud of pollution in the atmosphere. It is often speculated that "the ice age" occurred about 10,000 years ago. Is it possible that some animals that are now extinct, such as ice age era wooly mammoths, giant sloths, saber-toothed tigers, and the like, were either already extinct, or perhaps developed after the flood during the ice age and have since become extinct? The antediluvian world is thought to have been very different than what the world was after the flood. The same may be said for the animal kingdom. As discussed above, creation scientist and others believe that it was possible that God created His perfect world with what was called a "thick canopy," "the firmament" or a highly dense atmosphere which would have repelled much of the harmful solar rays which now bombard the earth. This thick canopy concept goes back to Genesis 1:7 when the scripture discusses the "firmament" or the waters above and below the sky. This concept would have allowed people to live "forever" as was the intention of God. Because of sin in the world, people would have to die an earthly death. 900 years is not "forever," but it is a long time. In this same thought, because of this thick atmosphere, the whole earth may have been some sort of a sub-tropical or tropical environment even at the polar caps. However, all of this is speculation at best, as the Bible does not state this. There is a common thought that it had not rained on the earth prior to the flood. There is no substantiation for this concept. The first mention of rain in Genesis was in the Garden of Eden where the text says that it had not yet rained. This was in the "dry" creation story of Genesis 2. The next mention of rain is in Genesis 7 when God tells Noah that He God is going to make it rain for forty days and forty nights. There is nothing in the interim text to support the rain, or no rain, issue one way or the other. If going with the thick canopy tropical concept of the antediluvian earth, then it is quite likely that it rained all the time to support this flora and fauna. Many will want to think that Noah built his big ol' boat in the middle of the desert, and that the earth had not seen any rain. This is going with the thought that the area in which Noah lived was a desert, much as this same area is today. One must remember, the geography and climate of the antediluvian world was a completely different place than what it is now. If it was a desert, then it was a desert filled with a gopher wood forest. Enough trees to build an ark. Forest and deserts are not synonymous.

Children may ask, were there bugs on the ark? To be sure, there were plenty of creepy crawlers on the ark with plenty of fleas, and flies, bees, wasp, and butterflies, worms, bugs, slugs, and spiders with woven webs, grasshoppers, ants, termites with mini mites to sting and bite, and all other kinds of chiggers, swarms, and hives…and unfortunately mosquitoes were substituted for unicorns.

What about the fish and the other sea creatures? A couple possibilities exist here. 1) God killed some, or all of them in the tempest of the flood as He did with the birds and land animals saving perhaps a remnant for replenishment. 2) All or some of the fish and sea creatures lived. What does the Scripture say? What does the Scripture not say?

THE FLOOD

Forty days and forty nights is how long we are told that it rained upon the earth…and it did.

In Genesis 7, God instructed Noah and his family to enter the ark. Eight souls were to embark the ark; Noah, and his unnamed wife, and Noah's three sons: Shem, Ham, Japheth, and their three unnamed wives. Additionally, all the pairs of clean and unclean animals were manifested. According to Genesis 7:1-4, Noah and all-hands-on deck, were there for seven days before it started to rain. Perhaps this was the loading period. All those animals and the supplies to feed them, didn't likely get on board the ark by themselves. It rained for forty days and forty nights. Because the waters were "above the firmament," it was able to rain for forty straight days and nights. This was the releasing of "the thick canopy," the opening of the windows of heaven. Not only did it rain for forty days and forty nights, the waters from below the earth were released as well. Genesis 7:11 describes it this way: "The fountains of the deep were broken up." This likely amounted in massive earthquakes, and perhaps volcanoes exploding with tectonic plate shifts, as well as, failing fault lines in the crust of the earth, and releasing these fountains of the deep. Between the thick canopy collapsing from above, and the upheaval from below, the whole earth was engulfed in a watery abyss.

These waters are said to have lifted the ark, and it moved about the surface of the waters. Genesis 7:19 uses two pointed words with regards to the extent of the flood. Over the centuries, many theologians, lay people, believers, and non-believers, have speculated that the flood was a localized event. However, Genesis 7:19 says that all the high hills under the whole heaven were covered. What does the Scripture say? Not only were all the mountains covered, but they were covered by fifteen cubits, or twenty-two and a half feet of water. This depth was more than sufficient to destroy all living creatures on the land as was God's intent. Were the Appalachians, Rockies, and the Andes in the Americas, the Alps in Europe, the Atlas in Africa, and the Himalayans in Asia, all covered by this deluge? What does the Scripture say? It is quite possible, however, that none of these mountain ranges even existed at the time of the flood, but rather were *caused by* the flood, with the upheaval of the land, with the volcanoes, earthquakes, and the like. When going to the high deserts of the American west, one can find sea-life fossils in the desert, and the effects of ocean water erosion. Modern science will tell us these deserts basins were at one time, an ocean floor. Was this Noah's flood?

We know where all the rain water came from, but where did it all drain off to? Due to the thick canopy now being gone in the form of rain to the earth's surface, the atmosphere was now thinner and now all this water was susceptible to evaporating beyond the now thinner atmosphere. Massive amounts of erosion, and shifting of land masses, took place during and after the Flood. When looking at a road cut through a mountain, or taking a boat ride through the Grand Canyon, one can see hundreds of geological layers. What caused these layers? How long did it take for each layer to form? Some say millions of years, whereas others say very quickly. The Mount St. Helens eruption caused major and quick geologic change. Perhaps this is another time to discuss the meanings of "yom" יוֹם the Hebrew word for "day." These great upheavals of the "fountains of the deep" likely caused the mountain ranges to rise, and great basins of the oceans and seas to occur. Genesis 8 begins with the winds of God which resulted in the waters subsiding. Interestingly, this phrase, "winds of God" רוּחַ אֱלֹהִים can mean such things as "the breath, wind, or spirit of God." Knowing this adds more richness to the text.

In the scientific world, it is thought by some, that all the land on the earth was originally mostly one mass, commonly called Pangaea. When looking at a globe, one can see where South America and Africa appear as though they have, or could have, fit together previously. The same applies for such places as New Guinea to Australia to Antarctica, Madagascar to Africa, and so forth. It is interesting to note the Mid-Atlantic Ridge, the underwater mountain range, carefully follows the contours of both the old and new worlds. It is quite possible that this break-up of Pangaea took place during the flood epic. This is what is called Plate Tectonics and Continental Drift. It is certain, the antediluvian earth was a much different place than the earth that resulted after the waters subsided.

ARK LIFE

Even though the rain lasted for only forty days and forty nights, according to Genesis 7:24, the waters prevailed for a total one hundred and fifty days. This is about five to six months afloat if you calculate that the "prevailing" waters, and the forty days of rain were consecutive. If the forty days of rain and the one hundred and fifty days of prevailing days were concurrent, then this would have been about five months. God had instructed Noah in Genesis 6:21 that he Noah had to stock pile enough food for his family, as well as, all the animals on the ark. This alone was a logistical wonder. This amount of animal fodder had to take up a considerable amount of space on the ark. The miracle Hand of God was moving here to assist Noah in all he did.

What did the eight people on the ark eat during their time on the ark? It is likely that they ate a lot of what they ate before the flood. Perhaps they ate a considerable amount of dried fruits and vegetables, and bread made from grain. Perhaps they were eating some diary products like cheese, curds and whey from the goats and cattle if they were already doing that before the flood since, cattle seemed to be a prominent before the flood. Maybe they were eating eggs from the poultry on board if they were already doing that before the flood. Perhaps they were fishing, providing they were eating fish before the flood. This depends on how one interprets "have dominion and subdue," in the last few verses of Genesis 1 with regards to food.

This was no pleasure cruise as there was always something to do. With all the multi-thousands of animals on the ark; it was always feeding time at the zoo. Various types of fodder had to be moved from the storage areas to the holding pens. Soiled bedding had to be changed and dumped overboard, or the air would have become full of foul with something other than birds.

With nature taking its course, young were likely born among some of the animals during this multi month period. There may have been more animals disembarking the ark than what were on the original boarding manifest. Due to a lack of multiple windows and doors in the ark, it was likely a most dark and dank, and downright stinky, and smelly place. If one can imagine a closed-up structure with thousands of animals and eight people for multiple months; this could have gotten a bit pungent over the course of time.

POST FLOOD - MOUNT ARARAT

At the end of this 150-day Neptunian tour, the ark and its crew rested upon the Mountains of Ararat, in what today is called eastern Turkey. Based upon the Biblical phrase, "in the Mountains of Ararat," this does not specify a certain peak in the Ararat Range. This makes locating the exact landfall a difficult task. This has been confounded and complicated over the centuries and decades, by various governments in the Turkey region, who have not been too partial to western Christians exploring and probing their Muslim mountains.

Now this is where the time gets tricky. How long were Noah, his family, and the animals on the ark before they got on dry land? Here is the Biblical time line.

Genesis 7:1-4
Noah loads the ark for **7 days** before the rains fall and the fountains were broken up.

Genesis 7:11
Noah enters Ark on the **17th day of 2nd month in 600th year of his life.**

Genesis 7:11
40 days and 40 nights of rain.

Genesis 7:24 & 8:3-4
150 days the waters prevailed before ark resting on Mount Ararat. This 150 days figures out to **13 days in the 2nd month**, followed by **four 30 days months** and **17 days in the 7th month**.

Genesis 8:4-5
Estimated **74 days** of the ark resting on Mount Ararat.
The ark rested from the **17th day of the 7th month to the 1st day of the tenth month before the tops of the mountains were seen.**

Genesis 8:5
The tops of mountains were seen.

Genesis 8:6
After **40 days** Noah opened the window

Genesis 8:7-12
Raven and Dove **14-day** release sequence

Genesis 8:13
1st day of 1st month of 601st year, of Noah's life, Noah removes covering and sees ground is dry.

Genesis 8:14
27th day of 2nd month, (of 601st year) of Noah's life, the earth was dry and Noah left the ark.

Total of about 370 days or (about 377 days if counting the 7 days of loading in Genesis 7:1-10) on board the ark from time embarked to debarked. If using an ancient lunar calendar, there are 29.5 days in an actual lunar month. There are about 354.3 days in an actual lunar year as such things are counted. Keep in mind, antediluvian time calculations with regards to moon cycles and earth rotation may have been different from current rotations and time calculations.

When comparing Genesis 7:6 to Genesis 8:14, this puts all on board right at about one year. Dr. Ham's calculations in his book, *A Pocket Guide to the Global Flood* on pages 94 and 95 put the time at 371 days. Dr. Ham and I are very close in agreement. Keep in mind that Noah may have been using some sort of ancient lunar calendar and when Moses wrote this account of the flood, he likely was trying to harmonize at least two or more different oral traditions and the math involved.

600th year of Noah

2nd month 17th day	3rd month	4th month	5th month	6th month	7th month 17th day
7 days of loading prior to 17th day. 40 days and 40 nights of rain/ Fountains of the deep broken up.	150 days the waters prevailed and receded on the earth.				Ark rested on Mount Ararat.

601st year of Noah

8th month 1st day	9th month	10th month	11th month 1st day	12th month	1st month	2nd month 27th day
Mountains were seen	40 days later Raven & Dove are leased.		waters dried up.			Noah, family and all animals out of the ark.

The raven never returned after first release.

After three releases and 14 days, the dove does not return to the ark.

Here is my mathematical calculation:
...after the 17 days in the 2nd month of Noah's 600th year ...
13 days in the remainder of the 2nd month of Noah's 600th year.
30 days a month multiplied by the 11 months following = 330 days.
27 days in the 2nd month of the 601st year of Noah's life.
Thus: 13 + 330 + 27 = 370 days on the ark plus the 7 days of loading in Genesis 7:1-10.

The first inhabitants to leave of the ark were birds. First, Noah released a raven, which is described as flying to and fro. Next, Noah releases a dove. After coming back empty handed, the dove returns to the ark. After a week, Noah releases the dove for a second time, this time with different results. This second time, the dove returns with an olive leaf in her grasp. This symbol of a dove with an olive branch has become an international symbol for peace. Likewise, ravens and crows are often associated with darkness and evil. A third time, Noah released the dove, and this time she did not return to the ark.

Genesis 8:13 uses the strange phrase of Noah removing the covering of the ark and looked and saw that the ground was dry. What was this covering? Perhaps it was something as simple as a piece of wood, leather, or cloth, which covered the window. It is at this point, God instructs Noah release all the animals, and for him and his family to leave the ark.

Additionally, God commanded Noah's Family to be fruitful and multiply and fill the earth. Noah buildt an altar and took one of all the clean animals, and made a sacrifice to God. God smelled the aroma of Noah's burnt offering sacrifice, and promised within Himself that even though mankind was evil, that He would not destroy the earth with water. Genesis 8:22 says, "While the earth remains, seedtime and harvest, cold and heat, Winter and Summer, And day and night Shall not cease."

God also informed Noah and his family that they are to eat of any of the animals; however, they are not to eat of the blood, because it is their life. Because of this, the fear of Man will be within all animals. God also warned against human murder because man is made in the image of God.

Then God set a rainbow in the cloud. This was to be God's promise to mankind that He would never again destroy the earth by flood. Sadly, this symbol of the rainbow of a promise of peace to mankind and the world from God, has been hi-jacked by the homosexual movement as one of their symbols. What a great confusion this is. Because of the sinful nature of people, the flood was implemented to wash away sin to include homosexuality.

<u>WOMEN</u>

The question is often debated, thus, one of the driving forces behind this book, "If all of the people in the world are "sons of Adam" through the sons of Noah, then how are there so many different colors, races and ethnic groups throughout the world? This is a big question. Here is a viable answer.

The Scripture states Adam and Eve had Seth after Cain killed Able. The Scripture also says that Noah was a direct descendant of Seth. This is the connection between the first family in the Garden of Eden to Noah and his three sons, who disembarked the ark after the flood.

What about Cain and all the Noddy people? Quite simply, they all died in the flood… or did they? We have established that Noah was of the linage of Seth. This is what the scripture says. What about "Joan," Noah's wife? What was her linage? Was she like Noah, also of the house and linage of Seth, or was she, "Joan" of the fallen family tree of Cain? This we cannot know because the scripture does not say. What we do know, is that somehow the "giant genes" of the Nephilim, the fallen angels, somehow survived the antediluvian world, and rode out the storm of the flood, to the dry side of the ark on Mount Ararat. The giants made themselves known again to the twelve spies, that went into the Promised Land under the direction of Moses during the Exodus period, as well as, via the Philistine giant Goliath, who was slain with a smooth stone slung by the young shepherd boy, David, who would be king.

Noah and "Joan" had three sons: Shem, Ham, and Japheth, who also had one wife, making eight souls that were on the ark. As with "Joan," what was the pedigree of these three wives? Were they of a pure line from either Seth or Cain, or some mixture in between? With the separation of families and gene pools after the many generations after the ark, different colors, races, and ethnic groups could have occurred naturally. If this explanation does not suite you, then perhaps it was the moving Hand of God who once again created more people of various colors, and placed them in various locations throughout the world.

It was not beyond the creative hand of God to breath into the dirt, and once again inspire and create a more diverse population. What does the Scripture say? However, the scripture says in Genesis 9:19 that the whole earth was populated from these three sons.

The genealogy of Japheth begins in Genesis 10. Japheth is considered the progenitor of the European, or so-called Caucasian, or white races of Europe, Iran, and India. The family tree of Ham begins in Genesis 10:6. His household was spread into Africa, and parts of southwest Asia and is thought to be the father of the so-called Negro or black races. The lineage of Shem is also traced in the end of Genesis 10, as well as, in Genesis 11, after the Tower of Babel saga. Shem is the father of the Jewish and Arab races, or the Semites. However, in recent times, the term Semetic most usually only pertains to Jewish people. This will be expounded upon in the genealogies in The Tower of Babel chapter.

GRAPES

This next part of the story is one of the most neglected and, perhaps, feared sections of all the Scripture. Noah goes from being a ship captain and zoo keeper, to a farmer and vinedresser. With Genesis 9:28 telling us that Noah lived for another three-hundred and fifty years, we are not certain how long it was after Noah and his kin exited the ark until the fateful following events. What we can know is that all the family was still seemingly living as a somewhat contiguous community. Apparently Ham and his unnamed wife, had had at least one of their four named sons.

Ham's sons listed in Genesis 10:7 were Cush, Seba, Havilah, and lastly Canaan. With Canaan being listed last, it is likely that Canaan was the youngest. We could conclude that all four of Ham's sons were already born to him and his wife. As per similar situations, we may dangerously assume, daughters were also born to this post diluvian union.

We can only speculate Noah and his kinship clan, were still living in the general region where they reached landfall on the slopes of Ararat. The Scripture does not expound upon this geographical point as it is not overly germane to the story. Wherever it was, apparently it was most suitable for a vineyard.

In Genesis 9:20-21, the text quickly asserts that Noah became a farmer, planted a vineyard, got drunk and became naked. Was the art of winemaking a known skill to Noah and other people in the antediluvian world? Was this fermenting feat of the fruit of the vine something that Noah came upon by accident? When looking at what Jesus said in Matthew 24:38, "For in the days before the flood, they were eating and drinking, marrying and giving in marriage until the day that Noah entered the ark." Based on this verse, straight from the mouth of Christ, if one understands the word "drinking" as "drinking wine," then one could conclude that wine making was known before the flood. However, did Noah, himself, have this skill? What we can know is that this was the first of about two hundred and sixty times wine is mentioned in the Bible. Additionally, grapes are mentioned nearly fifty times throughout the Holy Scripture. For those given to such notions "grape juice" or unfermented wine, is specifically *not* mention anywhere in the Bible. Modern refrigerators, were not put into wide use until the 1930's in the United States. The American Temperance Society was founded in 1821 to rebel against the ill effects of alcoholism. In response to this, Dr. Thomas Bramwell Welch invented "unfermented sacramental wine" for the purpose of communion wine for his church in Vineland, New Jersey in 1869. With this said, when the Bible says "wine," then that is exactly what the Scripture means. This would also include Jesus turning the water into wine in His first miracle in John 2 at the wedding in Cana. In the John 2 account, the Greek words οινου and οινον are used from the base form of the word οινος which simply translates as "wine." Here, the text states the following, "Everyman at the beginning sets out the good wine, and when the guest have well drunk, then the inferior. You have kept the good wine until now!" This verse is certainly not talking about grape juice. Once people are drunk on the high dollar Ernest & Julio Gallo good tasting wine, then set out the cheap Mad Dog 20/20. Likewise, in I Timothy 5:23, the New King James Version says, "No longer drink only water, but use a little wine for your stomach's sake and your frequent infirmities." Here, the word for wine in Greek is spelled οινω. What about grape juice!? In Acts 2:13, the Bible uses the phrase "new wine." Is this grape juice? In the Acts account, the disciples are accused of drinking new wine or being drunk, for speaking in various known foreign tongues or languages. One does not get drunk on grape juice. The word for new wine or sweet wine is γλευκος or gleukos, which is where we get our English word glucose or sugar. When the Bible says "wine" in scripture, then that is exactly what it was; wine. What does the Scripture say? Wine was a big part of the culture throughout the Bible. With this, the Scripture warns of the abuse of wine in such places as I Corinthians 6:10 and Ephesians 5:18.

SIN & CURSING

Sadly, and strangely, Ham saw his father drunk and naked. This was not likely the first time Ham saw his father undressed. However, it was likely the first time Ham saw Noah drunk. Living arrangements of early primitive and provincial people were more exposed and intimate. Many modern people often have a separate bedroom and sometimes a private bathroom. During these early times, most families likely lived in a commonly shared room of a small hut, or shack type dwelling, or perhaps a tent, or lean-to type structure. Privacy then, as we know it today, was at a premium.

Why was this event different? Was it the drunkenness that made the situation different, or was it the nakedness, or something else? Why did Ham report to his brothers, Shem and Japheth, that he saw their father drunk and naked? However, this issue goes deeper.

After Ham reports his unfortunate sighting, his two brothers took some sort of garment or blanket, and walked backwards inside the domicile with the covering between them, and covered their drunk and naked father. They were careful in their actions not to see the nakedness of their father. There is no mention as to the whereabouts of "Joan," the absentee wife of Noah, during this obtrusive event. Genesis 9:24 and following speaks to what happened.

"So Noah awoke from his wine and knew what his younger son had done to him."

"Then he said, 'Cursed be Canaan; a servant of servants he shall be to his brethren.'"

"And he said, 'Blessed be the LORD, the God of Shem and may Canaan be his servant. May God enlarge Japheth and may he dwell in the tents of Shem; and may Canaan be his servant.'"

The keystone words to this cursed event are: "what his younger son had done to him," with emphasis on 'done to him.' The big question is, what does "done to him," mean? Some scholars say Ham merely embarrassed, defamed, or dishonored their father by announcing to his siblings that he had seen the state of his father's drunkenness and nakedness. Was Noah's curse caused by his embarrassment? Why did Noah have such an apoplectic reaction?

Historically, some scholars believe the textual phrase, "done to him," is in the reasonable realm of possibility that Ham somehow sexually violated his father and caused the strong pronouncement of perpetual servitude against Ham's son, Canaan.

Why was Canaan, the son of Ham and not Ham himself cursed? Here again, this falls squarely into the broad barrel of our accumulated Biblical conundrums. This may have been a prophetic announcement of Noah. This cursing of Canaan by Noah, is similar to God cursing Adam, Eve, and the serpent in the garden. Did Noah's curse cause the underclassment of Ham's descendants, or did Noah foresee it as a vision? It was God's intent for all of humanity to live in harmony with each other and with Him. Human actions and sin have caused the inequity with genders and races.

The broader scope of the Noah saga is that humans were sinful and God wanted to redeem His creation. In spite of the sin of people, God still loves us. Just as the first animals were sacrificed to cover the sin and nakedness of Adam and Eve, the world had to be saved and cleansed of its sin. God gave the world a gigantic bath via the flood. God still redeems us through the one man in Jesus Christ. God saved the world then in one man being Noah. The New Testament gives three mentions of Noah. The first being in Hebrews 11 where the writer of Hebrews gives a thumbnail sketch of the Old Testament. The second reference of Noah is in I Peter 3 where Peter gives a parallel of Christian baptism to the eight souls being saved through water. In II Peter 2, Peter once again mentions Noah being saved from the destruction while others perished, which is coupled with the fallen angels not being spared due to their sin.

Jesus Himself gives credence to the flood and mentions it in Matthew 24 and in Luke 17:27. Jesus compares the eating, drinking and marrying before the flood of sinful people and they were caught unaware; just as sinful people will be caught unaware when He returns to reclaim those who belong to Him. Did the flood really happen? Dig, discover and discuss. What does the scripture say? What does the Scripture not say?

{Editorial note. Harrison Cyrus mentions that it is difficult to "timeline" the traditional Ice Age speculated to be 10,000 years ago; with the Flood. If the Flood and the Ice Age are paired, then this pushes the date of the Flood back farther than most Creation Scientist believe it to be or the Ice Age was more recent than 10,000 years.}

Author note: If current Global Warming is caused by humans, then what caused the Ice Age? Likewise, what reversed it?

Questions and Discussion for
Chapter Five – Noah's Ark and the Flood
Dig – Discover – Discuss

1. Is the Noah and the ark flood story true?

2. What do the words "Antediluvian" and "Pangaea" mean?

3. Based on what Genesis says, had it rained on the earth before the flood?

4. What was the form of the earth in the Antediluvian period? a) Was it still in the possible Pangaea form? b) Was all the ground cursed because of Adam? c) Was all the earth tropical? d) Were there deserts and were there ice caps at the poles? e) Did the earth before the flood look just like it does now?

5. How did the people in Genesis live so long? Were these years as we now understand years?

6. Explain the following scripture in Genesis 6:6: "And the LORD was sorry that He had made man."
Why did God use a flood to destroy the earth?

7. Explain the Genesis 6:9: "Noah was a just man, perfect in his generations, Noah walked with God."

8. God gives Noah the blueprint instructions for the ark.
   How big was the ark, and how many decks did it have? How many doors and windows did the ark have?
   What is gopher wood? What is a cubit? What is pitch?
   What was the general appearance of the ark?

9. How long did it take to build the ark and who built it? Where was the ark built? Was it near water?

10. How many and what types of animals were on the ark? Did the animals on the ark look like the animals we have today? What is the difference between a clean and unclean animal? According to scripture, were all the animals in pairs?

11. Were Dinosaurs on the ark? Consider Dr. Ken Ham's views. Explain. Did God destroy the sea creatures? Explain.

12. How did Noah gather all the animals from all over the world?

13. What are "Fountains of the great deep"?

14. How deep was the flood and how much of the earth was covered? Did the flood cover all of the mountains we have today, or did the flood cause these mountains?

15. What did the animals eat? How did Noah keep the predators from eating the other animals?

16. Did some of the animals give birth on the ark?

17. Where did Noah and his family live on the ark and what did they eat? Explain.

18. Explain how Noah and his family fed and cleaned up after all the animals?

19. How long was Noah, his family, and the animals on the ark before getting out?

20. Explain the issue of the raven and the dove.

21. Where did the ark land? Which modern day country is the likely location?

22. What did Noah sacrifice for a burnt offering after getting off the ark?

23. What did God say people could now eat? What was the restriction?

24. Explain: "Fruitful and multiply."

25. What promise did God make to Noah and humanity with regards to earthly destruction and what was the symbol of this promise?

26. Noah planted a vineyard, made wine, drank it and got drunk and naked. Discuss what may have happened to Noah at the hand of his son Ham.

27. Why did Noah curse Canaan, the son of Ham instead of Ham himself? What was the punishment? How has this curse affected us today if any?

28. Were Noah's wife and the three wives of Noah's sons of the lineage of Adam? Were the 3 wives of three different colors or ethinc groups? Did the Nephilim genes come through the flood through these three wives? Explain how we all are still descendants of Adam through Noah?

29. Did the flood cause the ice age? Or did the ice age cause the flood? Is there any collelation between the two events? Discuss.

Chapter Six

The Tower of Babel

The Geneanologies Of Shem, Ham & Japheth

1 n the beginning of Genesis 9, God instructed Noah's family to be fruitful and multiply and fill the earth and indeed they did. After all the doves, olive branches, rainbows, grapes, and wine; the sons of Noah and their wives began to once again fill the earth with people. A further comparison of genealogies is paralleled in the Genealogies section in the first part of the "List Chapter." Here is what lead up to the Tower of Babel narrative.

Genesis 10 gives us the following lines of descent: Oddly, Japheth, the youngest, is listed here first. **Japheth** has the following sons: **Gomer,** Magog, Madai, **Javan**, Tubal, Meshech, and Tiras.

From **Gomer** came the following:
Ashkenez, Riphath, and Togarmah.

From **Javan** came the following:
Elishah, Tarshish, Kittim, and Dodanim.

"From these the coastline peoples of the Gentiles were separated into their lands, everyone according to his language, according to their families, into their nations." Genesis 10:5

The sons of **Ham** were:
Cush, Mizraim, Put and **Canaan.**
The sons of **Cush** were:
Seba, Havilah, Sabtah, **Raamah**, Sabtechah, and **Nimrod**.

The sons of **Raamah** were:
Sheba and Dedan.

The sons of **Canaan** were:
Sidon, Heth, the Jebusite, the Amonite, the Girgashite, the Hivite, the Arkite, the Sinite, the Arvadite the Zemarite, and the Hamathite.

Special mention is here given to Nimrod. Cities which arose from Nimrod, the mighty hunter were:
Babel, Erech, Accad, and Calneh, all in **the land of Shinar**.
In the land of Assyria, Nimrod built the following cities:
Nineveh, Rehoboth Ir, Calah, and Resen.

Mizraim the second son of Ham had the following sons:
Ludim, Anamin, Lehabim, Nathtuhim, Pathrusim, from whom arose the Philistines, and Casluhim, from whom arose the Caphtorim.

"Afterward the families of the Canaanites were dispersed. And the boarder of the Canaanites was from Sidon as you go toward Gerar, as far as Gaza; then as you go to Sodom, Gomorrah, Admah and Zeboiim, as far as Lasha. These were the sons of Ham according to their families, according to their languages, in their lands and in their nations."

Sons were also born to **Shem**:
Elam, Asshur, **Arphaxad,** Lud, and **Aram.**

Aram also had sons:
Uz, Hul, Gether, and Mash.

Arphaxad also had a son:
Selah.
Selah begot **Eber**.

Eber had two sons:
Peleg and **Joktah**.

Joktah had a baker's dozen of sons to include:
Almodad, Sheleph, Hazarmaveth, Jerah, Hadoram, Uzal, Diklah, Obal, Abimael, Sheba, Ophir, Havilah, and Jobad.

"And their dwelling place was from Mesha as you go toward Sephar, the mountain of the east. These were the sons of Shem according to their families, according to their languages, in their lands, according to their nations." Genesis 10:31

The middle section of Genesis 11, "the Tower of Babel chapter," gives us an alternative genealogy. It follows a different branch with the sons of **Eber**. Eber had the two sons, **Peleg** and **Joktah**. The first genealogy follows the line of Joktah. This second line is the lineage in which most Bible readers will be interested; the line of Peleg.

From **Shem** came the following line:
Arphaxad to Selah to Eber to Peleg to Reu to Serug to Nahor to Terah.

Terah was the father of **Abram (Abraham)** and his two brothers, Nahor and Haron. This is the chosen line of the Patriarchs, the Hebrews, the Children of Israel, the Jews. A fuller presentation of this Terah family tree is laid out in the Genealogies section of the List Chapter.

From the above scripture, one can conclude that the Tower of Babel story was, at some point, concurrent to the above genealogies. Genesis 10:5, 20, and 31 state that each family group from Shem, Ham, and Japheth each had separate and diverse languages according to families, lands and nations. Apparently, these family-language-nation groups split-up *after* Genesis 11:9 after "the LORD God scattered them abroad over the face of all the earth."

Genesis 11 begins with the phrase "Now the whole earth had one language and one speech." Genesis 11 uses the YHWH יהוה LORD name for God, making these verses most likely a "J" oral tradition. However, Genesis 11:7 uses the familiar "Us" pronoun for God in the phrase, "come, let Us go down and there confuse their language." This is very samiliar to the phrase in Genesis 1, "Let Us make man in Our image," which was an "E" oral tradition. This phraseology also brings to mind the Genesis 18 story of God saying, "I will go down now and see" as God and his two angels were visiting Abraham and Sarah. Here again, this "Us" concept reaffirms the Trinity of God, in the form of God the Father, Jesus the Son and the Holy Spirit. Genesis 11:7 uses the "E" oral tradition and parallels Genesis 11:5-6.

THE TOWER

The Tower of Babel story is an oddity within an oddity of all the stories in the first eleven chapters of Genesis. The Tower story itself, like Genesis 1, does not mention any particular person by name except for God. However, Genesis 11 is bookended with the name filled genealogies. It takes place on the Plain of Shinar. This was part of the domain of King Nimrod, the Mighty Hunter son of Cush, the grandson of Ham. Supposedly, this area was in the lower end of Mesopotamia, or near the modern confluence of the Tigris and Euphrates rivers, which, in turn, empty into the Persian Gulf, and ultimately into the Indian Ocean. Strangely, this *may have been* near the original location of the Garden of Eden, in the antediluvian world – just a thought. If this were the case, it would have been nearly eight hundred miles away from the possible location where the ark made landfall in the mountains of Ararat, and perhaps some 292 years later after the flood. As mentioned before, life spans began to decrease dramatically after the flood. In Genesis 6:3, God informed Noah, before the flood that the future life span of humanity would be limited to 120 years.

From the inspiration of Adam to the Flood, it was about 1,656 years according to the genealogies in the earlier chapter of Genesis. Based on the genealogy in Genesis 11:10-32, it was 292 years from the ark landing in the mountains of Ararat to the birth of Abram. From this, we can sum up that Abram was born about 1,948 years after the inspiration of Adam.

"This is the genealogy of Shem; Shem was one hundred years old and begot Arphaxad two years after the flood." With this as a baseline, the reader can calculate the following:

Shem to Arphaxed = 2 years Shem lived 500 years
Arphaxad to Salah = 35 years Arphaxad lived 403 years

Salah to Eber = 30 years Salah lived 403 years
Eber to Peleg = 34 years Eber lived 430 years
Peleg to Reu = 30 years Peleg lived 209 years
Reu to Serug = 32 years Reu lived 207 years
Serug to Nahor = 30 years Serug lived 200 years
Nahor to Terah = 29 years Nahor lived 119 years
Tereh to Abram = 70 years Terah lived 205 years

And as with some other Genesis genealogies, "they had 'other' sons and daughters."

As with the construction of Noah's ark, the materials list for the tower would also be simple: "baked bricks and asphalt." Nothing more, nothing less. These mud bricks were most likely baked by the sun, or baked in high temperature ovens or kilns. Modern day Afghan hut builders still use sun baked mud bricks to build most of their structures. This asphalt substance would have been an oil based gooey tar like substance. The "Then they" people in Genesis 11:3 may be dangerously assumed to be the dynasty descendants of Nimrod which conjured up this idea of a tower which would reach into the heavens. It is not only possible, but also likely that slave labor was employed to build this behemoth bridge to heaven. It is not likely that most people freely engaged in this tower building activity of their own volition as most common, salt of the earth folk, were likely trying to scratch out a living from the soil on which they lived. Tower building was not likely high on their family survival agenda.

"Let us make a name for ourselves lest we be scattered abroad." The following pressing questions begs to be asked. Why were "they" concerned about "making a name for themselves?" Why were they concerned about being "scattered abroad?" Ultimately, why did they want to build a tower into the heavens? Were they trying to reach God or heaven? Were they trying to get God to acknowledge that they were there upon the face of the earth? In the end, we cannot reach God by the works of our own hands. We cannot climb up to God by any ladder, steps, staircase, tower, or by any means, to include our own strength, or deeds. We can only reach God in Heaven with faith in Jesus through the leading of the Holy Spirit with the saving grace of God reaching down to us – it is the gift of eternal salvation.

"But the LORD came down to see." God saw that the people were of one mind and purpose and of one language. God further comments: "now nothing that they propose to do will be withheld from them." How does this compare to the current state of humanity, and the technology that we now have within our hands which is well beyond baked mud bricks and asphalt? Most western teen-agers and adults hold more computing power within their hand-held personal devices than what took rooms full of computers to launch and sustain the early NASA/Apollo programs. These same space programs of American Astronauts and Soviet Cosmonauts may be considered by some as a twentieth century style Tower of Babel with mankind "reaching into the heavens."

Communication is the key – don't lock yourself out. Without certain purpose, and good communication, nothing productive happens. God confused their language and scattered them over the face of the earth and they ceased building the tower. Therefore, the name of the place is Babel. Later this area would become the region of Babylon. So, their fear of being scattered abroad indeed came to fruition. Likewise, their fear of not having a name also came to be, as "they" are not mentioned by name in the text.

What did the tower look like? Traditionally, it is thought to be a "ziggurat" in construction. This ziggurat structure style is a stair-step or spiral design which was broad at the base and became thinner as each terrace neared its pinnacle. In some respects, these Babylonian towers which were built in some number, were similar to the pyramids which would eventually be built in nearby Egypt, and in the Americas as well.

It is difficult to speculate which of the line of Shem, Ham, or Japheth may have been present, during this Tower of Babel event. What is clear, is that people of the earth were once again dispersed from the Tigris-Euphrates river valley into all the world as described in Genesis 10.

SCATTERING

How did people get into the far reaches of the earth from the Plain of Shinar? When looking at a flat map, or better yet, a spherical globe, one can see that this Plain of Shinar was indeed the original "middle earth." This was the perfect place from which to disperse the planet's population. This area is currently called "the Middle East." This is where three of the worlds' seven continents all come together.

A contiguous confluence of continents. Western Asia, eastern Europe, and northern Africa are all connected to Mesopotamia. This was the perfect launching point for all humanity to disperse into all the world.

For all the hunter-gatherer, nomadic, and early agricultural people, their mode of transportation was usually one of three common varieties. Remember, there were no planes, trains, or automobiles; likewise, there were no helicopters, scooters, motorcycles, all-terrain four-wheelers, tricycles, bicycles, unicycles, roller blades, roller skates, skate boards, or pogo sticks. There were however, boats of various sorts to include: barges, catamarans, canoes, clippers, galleys, gondolas, kayaks, keelboats, johnboats, longboats, flatboats, ferryboats, houseboats, sailboats, skiffs, schooners, junks, dinghies, dugouts, rafts, and out-rigors, and eventually yachts, and ships for those willing to brave the high seas, lakes, bays, gulfs, and rivers, creeks, tributaries, streams, swamps, shores, and shoals. Those traveling in the snow, they may have had sleighs, sleds, and perhaps snowshoes, and eventually skis. For the post Tower of Babel people, riding in a cart pulled by an animal, or team of animals, was one possibility of terrain travel. If this did not suit you, then actually riding astride a beast of burden was the norm. This would have mostly consisted of donkeys, mules, oxen, or perhaps horses, or camels. Those not fortunate enough to have hooves, they had best been well heeled. The standard default of good ol' fashioned foot walking would have been en vogue. Bare-footed, boots, sandals, shoes, or otherwise shod, would have been the fashion of the day.

A great day of traveling may have been twenty miles. Ten miles a day was most likely the reasonable goal as challenges and hurdles were sure to be afoot. New to the post flood world were: tumultuous oceans, desolate deserts, snow-covered mountains, impenetrable jungles, raging rivers, ravines, rocks, rills, hills, crashing waterfalls, high plains, and plateaus with treacherous cliffs, and other such natural boundaries. Most all these places were also sure to include: thorns, thistles, tangles of briars, sharp rocks, sticks, and prickly pines, with stinging spines, cactus nettles, and other such sore foot stones along the way. These human travel hurdles would be the defying deterrents and funnels to determine where, when, and how human travel may have occurred. Many families or tribes would have been most content to stay fairly stationary, if the ability to gain food, fodder, and forage via fishing, hunting, herding, and/or planting and harvesting was stable. Other clans and kinfolk would have been more mobile, and prone to have the traveling bone to seek what was beyond the next peak or valley. In time, individuals and families would slowly expand westward and northward onto the plains of Europe, while others would have spread westward and southerly down the valley of the great Nile and into the hinterlands of Africa. Many others would have traversed northward and eastward into the great endless expanse of Asia, and from here, eventually into the Americas from Alaska down to Argentina. Some would have traversed to the far-flung reaches of Australia. One can only speculate how many millennia these miles of migration took. As discussed before, different languages, and diverse and distinct ethic groups would have developed from years of separation and isolation.

As a point of interest, *The American Heritage Dictionary of the English Language,* which I have used since I was in elementary school, has a language family tree in the back cover. The chart displays the Indo-European family tree of languages for the better part of Europe and Asia. This concept of all these languages spawning from a single source was developed from Sir William Jones in 1786 in Calcutta, India. Oddly, Hebrew and the other Semetic languages do not appear in this chart of languages, however, Greek does. This Indo-European Family Tree theory would be complementary to the Tower of Babel event.

{Editorial note: Harrison Cyrus suggests that the tower of Babel story may have been of Egyption roots since Moses was brought up in the house of the Pharoah and the pyramid builders of Eygpt. Cyrus asserts that the Pyramid builders were more likely of the line Shem and not Ham.}

Questions and Discussion for
Chapter Six – The Tower of Babel
Dig – Discover – Discuss

1. Is the Tower of Babel story true?

2. How long was it from the Ark to the attempted building of the Tower of Babel?

3. Why are no individuals listed by name?

4. Where is the plain of Shinar?

5. Why were the people building the tower?

6. Which two items were used in the building of the tower? Reference Genesis 11:3. Discuss the possible engineering technics that were involved in the construction of the Tower

7. Who likely built the tower?
   Discuss the possible widespread use of slave labor.

8. What two issues were the people fearful of?

9. In Genesis 11: 7, what does, "Come Let Us go down" mean? Who is "Us?"

10. What two actions did the Lord take against the people to cease the building of the tower?

11. If all of the people of the earth came from the three sons of Noah, then how did the earth become filled with various races, colors and ethnics groups? Explain.

12. Discuss how long it may have taken for people to migrate to the far reaches of the Americas and Australia. Discuss the development of language considering the Proto-Indo-European family of languages.

13. Did God create more people to fill the earth?

Chapter Seven

I will go down now and see

In The Flesh

"In the beginning was the Word and the Word was with God and the Word was God. He was in the beginning with God. All things were made through Him and without Him nothing was made ... And the Word became flesh and dwelt among us ..." – John 1:1-3, 14a

As discussed before hand, Jesus the Christ, and the Holy Spirit, were a part of the eternal trinity with God the Father, from before the beginning of time and creation. Some deist thinkers, like Thomas Jefferson and others who were prevalent during the birth of the United States, saw God as a distant creator who set everything into motion and then stepped away. Is this true, or was the Creator more hands-on with His Creation? Christians will vote for the God who was involved with His creation. Not only was He involved with His creation, but He also loved us and dwelt among us.

All orthodox Christians believe that Jesus was born to the Virgin Mary after divine conception of the Holy Spirit and dwelt among us. But did God, or perhaps, Jesus, "visit" us before Jesus' physical birth? Was there ever a pre-nativity physical presence of God, or perhaps Jesus in the Old Testament? The Old Testament reader will find many of these epic events in scripture where God, or perhaps Jesus was in physical form appearing to people.

A pre-nativity physical flesh and blood appearance of God in the Old Testament is called a Theophany. A similar technical term is called a Christophany. The Christophany term expressly implies that the pre-nativity physical form of God was specifically Jesus Christ.

From the very beginning we find God physically walking in communion beside His creation of humanity. Genesis 3:8 records Adam and Eve hearing the walking of God in the Garden. Here God spoke directly in an audible voice to the first family along with the fallen angel serpent. This may be considered a thinly veiled reference of God in the flesh walking among us, but let us continue to journey down this path.

CLEFT OF THE ROCK

We find throughout much of the Old Testament that God either appears and/or speaks to His people. How did God appear to them? Was He visible or invisible? Was He only heard and not seen? On Mount Sinai, God appeared to Moses in the burning bush in Exodus 3. Throughout Exodus, God appears and meets with Moses many times. In Exodus 33:11, God speaks with Moses "face-to-face." But did Moses actually see the face of God? Further on in Exodus 33:20-23 the scripture says the following: "But He said, you cannot see My face; for no man shall see Me and live. And the LORD said, Here is a place by Me, and you shall stand on the rock. So it shall be, while My glory passes by, that I will put you in the cleft of the rock, and will cover you with My hand while I pass by. Then I will take away My hand and you shall see My back; but My face shall not be seen." Previously in Exodus 33, God said that He would not come into the midst of the people, lest He consume them.

Thus far, these appearances of God to man seem to be spiritual in nature or super-natural; instead of actually face-to-face in the flesh. Let us continue this quest for God in the flesh.

God starts speaking to Abraham, formerly known as Abram the Chaldean from the land of Ur, in Genesis 12. (I personally have been in the Land of Ur. The "Ur" name for this geographical location is an adept description of this dusty and desolate place). As before, these early discussions seem to only to have been "in the spirit." In Genesis 17 and 18, we find two different oral traditions of God appearing to Abram and Sarai, who was now renamed Sarah. These are the two "laughing" chapters in which God reveals to the elderly couple that they would give birth to Isaac. Previously, to the son of promise, Isaac, being born to Abraham and Sarah; Hagar, the female Egyptian slave, gave birth to Ishmael, through the seed of Abraham. Even though he was first born to Abraham, Ishmael was not to be this son of promise. This has been a source of discontent for time and eternity for the Arab nations. Ishmael was called a "wild man" in Genesis 16:11-12 and that every man's hand would be against him. No truer thing has ever been said.

JAKE AND ELWOOD WITH GOD

Theophany and Christophany – here is where the rubber meets the road in our journey to find God in the flesh in the Old Testament. In Genesis 18, we find Abraham sitting under the terebinth trees in Mamre. Abraham is said to have lifted up his eyes and saw three men. What? Men! Well, O.K. this is fine, there were other people in the area. Abraham recognizes that one of them is actually the LORD God! How or why Abraham recognized God in the flesh is certainly a conundrum, but some how he did. Abraham addressed him as "Lord." The evidense that these three unique fellows were in the flesh is that Abraham instructed Sarah to make some cakes, more likely what we today would call biscuits, or rolls, while he went with a young male servant to slaughter a calf. With a meal of veal, milk, butter, and biscuits, God and His two "men" dined in the desert.

Spirits, ghost, mirages, and other such supernatural beings as, angels, avatars, and aberrations do not eat biscuits. This was God in the flesh announcing to Abraham and Sarah that they would have a baby at the appointed time. Sarah could laugh, and Sarah could hide, but no tent canvas was going to cloak her from becoming pregnant, and giving birth to Isaac, regardless of her advanced age, as everything is possible with God, if only we believe. This eating episode is reminiscent of Jesus eating after the resurrection in Luke 24 and John 21.

After God and the two men ate their meal, God determined to tell Abraham what His plans were, while the two men proceed on to Sodom to carry out their mission from God. This is where the great bargaining saga between God and Abraham played out over the souls of Sodom.

If one of these three men who wandered into the terebinth trees of Mamre was God Himself in the flesh, then who were these other two fine fellows? Further reading in Genesis 19 overtly tells us that the two companions with God were actually angels, who assisted Abraham's nephew, Lot, in Sodom. They were so human in form that the homosexual men of Sodom wanted to have sex with them. Often, the question is asked, "What does a real angel look like?" In this case, they looked like human men. Other Biblical appearances of some angels and other heavenly beings can be quite different.

As discussed earlier, God told Moses that he could not look on the face of God and live. Apparently, the more human and subdued form presented to Abraham and Sarah was not the "full glory" of God which appeared to Moses on Mount Sinai. God can appear in any form. Apparently, the Mamre version was more palatable for human eyes than was the full glory form of Mount Sinai.

Genesis 19 tells us that when Lot saw the two men, the two angels, Lot bowed his head to the ground. They looked like men, but there must have been something special or spectacular about their appearance. Once, in Lot's house, he offered to wash their feet and they ate again; this time unleavened bread to go along with an un-described feast, which showed the appearance of their perceived humanity. As a special note here; the word "angel" simply means "messenger."

As the evening progressed, the homosexual men of Sodom tried to knock the door down on Lot's house so to have sex with the two angels. The two angels pulled Lot inside of his own house for his safety. To Lot's credit, he was going to protect his angelic visitors at all cost. To Lot's dishonor, he offered his two teenage daughters to the homosexual men just to get them to go away. A further reading will reveal that Lot's two daughters were actually "naughty" and not "Noddy" as was Cain's wife.

The two angels blinded the homosexual men of Sodom and were the agents of destruction for the city of Sodom, as they accomplished their mission from God, while God rained fire and brimstone on Sodom and Gomorrah. The reader cannot be certain of the background of Lot's wife, but she became a salt of the earth kind of gal, a real pillar in the community, because she did not listen to the instruction of the two angelic men. We do not have any further record of the two angels after they led Lot and his two naughty daughters out of the smoked scorched city. Since these two angels were on a mission from God, perhaps these two angels were named Jake and Elwood. The only angels named in the Canon are Michael the archangel, and Gabriel the messenger, which spoke to the Virgin Mary.

WRESTLE-MANIA EXTRAVGANZA

Just like his grandfather Abraham, Jacob had a super-natural encounter with God in Genesis 32. Jacob had just left his Uncle Laban's household. After years of toil, he married his two cousins, Leah and Rachel. Also, in this bride bargain, he also acquired their two hand-maids Bilhah and Zilpah. From all four of these brides, Jacob now had eleven sons. It was time for him to get away and have some time by himself and try to get a good night's rest, but a good night's rest he would not receive.

As Jacob was on the far side of the Jabbok stream in solitude looking for a good night's sleep, instead of finding sleep, he found a Man, a wrestling Man. This was to be the ultimate big-time wrestling, an all-night, ultimate wrestle-mania extravaganza. After many dark hour rounds, the wrestling Man was not able to prevail over Jacob. However, the wrestling Man was able to dislocate Jacob's hip. Not only was Jacob's hip nearly broke, but the dawn of the day was about to break on the eastern horizon. After their allnight grappling session, the wrestling Man requested of Jacob that He be paroled. "Let Me go for the day breaks." Jacob replies to the ultimate wrestler and says to Him before his morning parole, "I will not let You go unless you bless me." Now under the thin veil of the darkness of the night, the ultimate wrestler asked Jacob, "What is your name?" Jacob answers back and says, "My name is the Deceitful Supplanter, but I go by Jacob for short." Then the wrestling Man says to Jacob, "Your name shall no longer be The Deceitful Supplanter, but rather Israel, the One Who Struggles with God."

Before leaving his father, Isaac's tent, Jacob had wrestled away the birthright, and inheritance of his twin brother, Esau. His hairy red brother traded his birthright for a bowl of red bean soup.

As a turn-about of fair play, Jacob asked the Wrestler, "Please tell me what Your name is." Masked by darkness and a cape of mystery; the Wrestler answered back to Jacob in a counter move, "Why do you ask Me My name?" The wrestler blessed the newly named and maimed Israel as the sun broke across the eastern horizon. The now crippled Israel called this place, Penuel, פניאל "The Face of God," as Israel now knew that he had seen God "face to face" פנים אל־פנים and that he had been on the canvas matt in the squared circle, and had wrestled with God in the flesh.

THE ULTIMATE WARRIOR

Moses had many supernatural close encounters with God throughout the book of Exodus. However, now it was going to be a passing of the torch of the mantel of leadership for the children of Israel. After their many years of marching in the wilderness, in their quest to reach the long sought after Promised Land, there was going to be a change of command.

Joshua, the son of Nun, was now going to stand in the sandals of Moses, as Joshua was going to marshal the Israelites onto the west bank across the stormy banks of the Jordan River, into the Promised Land. Newly in command, Joshua planed his campaign against the walls of Jericho. As Joshua surveyed and reconed his objective, he saw a Warrior. But this was no mere warrior, this was the ultimate warrior, arrayed in full battle rattle, with a sword drawn in His hand. In military fashion, Joshua password challenged the ultimate warrior to identify Himself and asked Him, "Are You for us or against us." The ultimate warrior replied and said, "No, but as the Commander of the LORD's army." Notice here, that the ultimate warrior did not state whose side that He was on; but rather, that He was the Commander of the LORD's Army. In our freewill, we must choose to be on God's side.

Joshua immediately fell on his face and began worshipping the ultimate warrior as Joshua recognized Him as God. Like Abraham on the plains of Mamre, we are not certain how or why Joshua recognizes God as God in the flesh. Joshua asked the Ultimate Warrior what his orders were, as the Israelites were about to march around the walls of Jericho until they came-a-tumbling down. The ultimate warrior commanded Joshua to remove his sandals as he was on holy ground. This is amazingly similar to what God commanded Moses to do when he saw the burning bush on Mount Sinai. We know this could not have been a mere messenger of God, an angel, because in Revelation 22:8-9, when John fell down to worship the angel, the angel told John not to worship him, the angel, as he was his fellow servant.

Joshua now had his marching orders from God in the flesh, the Commander of the LORD's army. In the end of Joshua 5, Joshua was on a mission from God. For a week, Joshua led his Israelite army with ram's horns and shouts before the Ark of the Covenant, and the walls of Jericho came-a-tumbling-down.

THE FIERY FUNANCE

One of my favorite gospel songs is, *Daniel Prayed*. One of the lines is that Daniel prayed: morning, noon, and night. Not only did Daniel pray, he also wrote the book of Daniel. Daniel 3 contains one of the most astounding Christophanies in the Old Testament with the fiery furnace story. In Daniel 3, King Nebuchadnezzer, king of Babylon, declared that if you did not worship the prescribed gold image, then you shall be cast immediately into the midst of a burning fiery furnace.

As it turned out, Shadrach, Meshach, and Abed-Nego did not worship the gold image at the time when they heard the sound of the horn, flute, harp, lyre, and psaltery in symphony. Furthermore, this bold trio told King Nebuchadnezzer that their God, would be able to deliver them from the flames of the burning fiery furnace and from the king's hand as well. This flame retardant trio went on to tell the King of Babylon, "But if not, let it be known to you, O King, that we do not serve your gods, nor will we worship the gold image which you have set up."

At this point, King Nebuchadnezzer had had enough of the three young men from Israel. He had his mighty men of valor bind them up and cast them into the fiery furnace. They were bound head to toe in their coats, trousers, and turbans. The King's wrath was so hot against the tied trio, that the king had the fiery furnace heated up even more so, that it was "exceedingly hot." The extreme heat killed his mighty men of valor as they cast Shadrach, Meshach, and Abed-Nego into the inferno. After they were cast into the flaming fiery furnace, being bound head to toe, they fell down into the midst of the furnace.

This should have been the end of the three young men as they were barbequed in Babylon. Although, the king was astonished, and asked his counselors how many men were cast into the fire; was it not three? His counselors answered back and confirmed that the number was indeed three. Then King Nebuchadnezzer exclaimed, "Look, I see four men loose and walking in the midst of the fire and they are not hurt and the form of the fourth looks like the Son of God." The king asked them to come out of the fire. When they did, there was not even the smell of smoke on their now unbound and unburned bodies.

After this event, King Nebuchadnezzer promoted the three young men. The king blessed the God of Shadrach, Meshach, Abed-Nego, and "His Angel." Oddly, this is the only mention of the "Son of God," the fourth being, in the Babylonian blaze. We can clearly see that this was God, Jesus, or perhaps an angel who saved them in this miracle from the furnace.

Whether we call them Theophany or Christophany, we can see in scripture that God the Father or Jesus the Son, made Himself known to people in the flesh prior to the nativity. Even though God told Moses that no man can see My face and live, somehow, God appeared to many people in a human form, which was not His Full Glory, and they lived. Jesus, the Word, became flesh and dwelt among us. Can God, or an angel, still appear to us today? The unknown writer of the book of Hebrews tells us in Hebrews 13:2, "Do not forget to entertain strangers, for by so doing, some have unwittingly entertained angels." Do you believe in angels? Do you believe that Jesus is the son of God?

Sadly, such major world religions as Islam and Judaism will not acknowledge that God could ever be in physical form, thus their main reason for rejecting Jesus Christ born of the Virgin Mary. However, this type of thinking is quite obviously contrary to the word of God as recorded in the Old Testament Scriptures. Do you believe that Jesus was concurrently 100% man while also being 100% God? Do you believe that God and/or Jesus appeared to people in the Old Testament before the Nativity? Dig, discover, and discuss. What does the scripture say? What does the scripture not say?

Editorial note: {With regards to how Abraham and Joshua were able to recognize God in His human form, Harrison Cyrus suggests that God put it into their hearts.}

Questions and Discussion for Chapter Seven – I will go down now and see
Dig – Discover – Discuss

1. Was Jesus Christ present at creation or was Jesus created by God? Who was the "prime mover" of creation?

2. Explain what a Theophany is and how is it different from a Christophany, as described in this chapter?

3. Has God, in physical "human form," appeared on the earth before the nativity? What is the scriptural evidence such as walking, talking, eating, and so forth?

4. Is Jesus 100% God and 100% Man at the same time? Explain and discuss.

5. How did the individuals in the Biblical storries know if they had seen a Theophany/Christophany of God, or an angel? How would we as modern westerners react in the presence of a supernatural being?

6. Did God physically wrestle with Jacob, and did Joshua see God dressed as a warrior? Were these stories just symbolic metaphors?

7. With God's visit to Abraham and Sarah, did God and the two angels really talk and eat food? Were God and the two angels in actual human form?

8. Did God destroy Sodom and Gormorrah because of homosexuality? Discuss the ramifications of homosexuality in our modern context.

9. Do you believe that the fiery furnace story really happened? Who, or what, do you believe King Nebuchadnezzar saw as the fourth form in the furnace? Discuss what this story means.

Chapter Eight

Angels, Aliens, Ghosts & Giants

Angels

The first mention of an angel is in Genesis 3:24, if one does not count Adam and Eve's encounter with the "serpent," as the chief fallen angel, Lucifer, in the opening of Genesis 3. The Cherubim were the sword wielding angels, who were placed by God, to guard the Tree of Knowledge of Good and Evil, in the Garden of Eden from Adam and Eve after they were cast out. Was there more than one sword wielding angel? As per an earlier discussion; any time a Hebrew noun has an "im" ים ending, it becomes plural, just as putting an "s" on an English noun makes it plural. With this said, this was a troop of Cherub type angels armed with their flaming swords.

Just what is an angel? What do they look like? How big are they? Do they really have harps, and wings, and fly? How many angels are there? What is a fallen angel? Are there male and female angels? Do angels marry each other? What is an archangel? Do we all have guardian angels? Is there an Angel of Death? Do we become angels when we die? In short, the word "angel." in both Hebrew and Greek, simply means "messenger:" "aggelos" αγγελος in Greek and "malak" מלאך in Hebrew. In the KJV, the term "angel" or "angels" appear nearly three hundred times.

Two of the most common classifications of angels mentioned in scripture are the above Cherubim and their heavenly counterparts, the Seraphim. Classic European art often depicts the Cherubim as the cute cuddly fat baby cupid type angels, complete with undersized wings and perhaps a loin cloth or nothing at all, as they lounge around on clouds, playing harps and shooting their darts of love. The actual role of the cherub was usually that of a guard or guardian as in the Garden of Eden. In Scripture, they are usually represented with the appearance of an animal or a mixed humanoid/animal. Cherubim are mentioned nearly one hundred times in the Old Testament, as well as, once in the New Testament in Hebrews 9. These angels are highlighted extensively in Exodus 25 and 37, I Kings 6, and Ezekiel 1 and 10, as well as, other locations. Ezekiel 10:8 clearly states that the cherubim had the form of a man's hand under their wings. All appear to have wings.

The seraphim technically only appear in Isaiah 6. They appear to have three pair of wings and they do fly. The second set of wings covers their face and the third set covers their feet. It is possible that they may appear as six-winged fiery serpents. These Isaiah seraphim are similar to the four creatures of the throne room of Heaven found in Revelation 4, in that they were guardians in the LORD's throne room, saying "Holy, holy, holy," and had three pair of wings. Compare these heavenly creatures of the Revelation Throne Room to those of the Ezekiel "wheel" cherubim. The Throne Room Creatures are described as a Lion, a Calf, a Man, and an Eagle with six wings and full of eyes. The Cherubim of Ezekiel 1 and 10 are full of eyes, and faces which look like a man, a lion an ox, and an eagle.

Collectively, between the cherubs and seraphs, they all seem to have wings, perhaps six, and they like to say "Holy, holy, holy," while being on guard in the Throne Room of the LORD while having the face of a man, a lion, an eagle, and an ox or a calf. None of them seem to be cute cuddly fat cupid babies.

What is an archangel and how many are there? According to Canon Scripture, only one archangel is named; Michael. In an odd verse in the book of Jude, Michael is identified as "the archangel," as he disputes with the devil over the body of Moses. The Greek uses the same phrase, using the definite article "the," as opposed to "an archangel." "Michael and his angels" is the phrase used as he leads the war in Heaven against the Devil and his fallen angels in Revelation 12. Daniel 10 also makes a reference to Michael where he is referred to as, "one of the chief princes."

The only other named angel in Canon scripture is Gabriel, the messenger who appeared to the Virgin Mary in the Gospel of Luke 1:26. Gabriel, announced that the Virgin Mary, was highly favored and would conceive through the Holy Spirit and give birth to a son and call His name Jesus. Strangely enough, the Catholic New American Bible also entitles Michael as "the archangel," insinuating that there is only one archangel. However, in an extra-Biblical account, Gabriel and Uriel in the book of I Enoch, are named as archangels, as is Raphael is mentioned in the Apocrypha book of Tobit. Here, these four angels are considered equal "archangels."

As mentioned in an earlier discussion, God through the form of the Holy Spirit, is everywhere. But what about guardian angels? Don't we all have one, and are they not with us everywhere we go? This is an interesting question. Many adults often tell children that everyone has a guardian angel. What does the scripture say? In Matthew 18:10 Jesus tells us, "Take heed that you do not despise one of these little ones, for I say to you that in Heaven their angels always see the face of My Father who is in Heaven." This may be one of the few verses that deal with the concept of guardian angels. Ordinarily, one verse in scripture is not enough upon which to build a theology or the foundation for faith. However, when the source is Jesus, there is no higher authority on which to build. In modern popular music, guardian angels are often mentioned. One example is the song, *Workin' Them Angels,* off the 2007 album entitled *Snakes and Arrows,* performed by the Canadian rock trio RUSH. Their drummer and lyricist is Neil Peart. Mr. Peart has been an open atheist his entire adult life. Yet many of his lyrics for decades have had many veiled acknowledgement, of God, Heaven, Hell, angels, demons, and other various elements of spiritual sorts. In this song, the character sees himself as someone perpetually living on the edge of life, like a motorcycle rider on a dangerous and twisting road, testing both life and fate in the absence of faith, thus, working his guardian angel overtime. Once again, are there guardian angels?

Is there an angel of death? In gothic culture, this is often referred to as the Grim Reaper, a gray clad cloaked skeleton type minion with an old timey reaping sickle. In Exodus, God moved through Egypt and killed the first born of the Egyptians. In Revelation 14:17-20, we have the image of an angel with a sickle thrusting it into the earth "...the blood came out of the winepress up to the horses' bridle for about 184 miles." God uses a great army of angels to bring death upon the earth in a variety of ways in the book of Revelation. More specifically, we see the four horsemen of the Apocalypse. We can assume that the mounted riders are some sort of angels or otherwise heavenly host. The first of these fierce riders is the white horse with a crown and a bow for conquering. The second of this fearsome foursome is the red horse of war swinging his sword. The third of these cavilers of destruction is the black horse of famine, holding a pair of scales to divi out portions of poverty and starvation. The final of the four palominos of plunder is the pale horse, who is also known as the pale rider, … Death … and Hades followed with him. Here is a Biblical image of a so-called angel of death. (Revelation 6:1-7)

In most Christmas and other holiday art in both ancient and contemporary thought; Angels are often portrayed and thought to be beautiful, mostly female or at least effeminate in appearance. Are angels male, or female, or neither? This feminine appearance may be attributed to men in the middle ages as being brutal and barbaric, whereas women during this time were more gracious and genteel. The latter qualities seeming to be more God-like, thus, the feminine appearance of angels in middle ages and holiday art. Going by the names discussed above, they would appear to be male at least in supernatural appearance. The two "men" who dined with Abraham and Sarah in the desert were described as "men." The homosexual men of Sodom were most determined to have sexual relations with them due to their stunning appearance. As discussed earlier, the heavenly beings were described as having the appearance of a "man." This "man" title could be interpreted as "human," but what does the scripture say?

Jesus discussed the concept of marriage in Heaven with the Jewish Sadducees in Mark 12:25, "For when they rise from the dead, they neither marry nor are given in marriage, but are like the angels in Heaven." From what Jesus tells us, heavenly beings apparently are asexual, being neither male or female in their supernatural state. This verse here also alludes to when Christians die and go to Heaven, that they do not become angels; but rather are a different class of heavenly beings which are "like," or similar, to angels.

It is important to note that angels are not free agents. Angels do not have freewill as do humans. Angels are only the messengers of the Creator God Almighty and never act on their own volition. The one time an angelic action of choice did happen, was with the war in heaven where

Michael the archangel drove Lucifer and his third of fallen angels from the realm of Heaven. This evil angelic action is the tap root of the *problem of evil*. The writer of Hebrews quotes Psalms 8, and tells us that God created people a little lower than the angels, or humans are a different class of beings in both Heaven and on Earth. Paul, in I Corinthians 6:3, tells us "Do you not know that we shall judge angels?" This verse is certainly a "theological conundrum." Why would we, as humans, who are flawed from birth, judge angels who do not act on their volition? Whereas, the angels will not judge humans according to II Peter 2:11. From this we can conclude that in Heaven, in their supernatural form, there is neither male or female angels in the conventional sense. Also, contrary to conventional thought, when we die, we do not become angels, but rather a different class of heavenly beings. If one wants to consider all classes of heavenly beings as "angels," then this would be the only case in which we, as humans, become angels.

How many angels are there, is a question many people have asked over these many eons of time? In Matthew 26:53 Jesus tells his Maundy Thursday evening Garden of Gethsemane captors that He could call upon twelve legions of angels. In the first century Roman Army, a legion could have anywhere from three to six thousand members or sometimes more. Based on this heavenly military math of Jesus, there could have been at least 72,000 angels who were on alert at any given time. Daniel 7 gives us an account of, "…a thousand thousands ministered to Him; Ten thousand times ten thousands stood before him." If the horsemen of Revelation 9 are, in fact, angels, then there are at least 200,000,000. How many angels are there? Apparently, many.

So how big is an angel? If we are looking at the visitors of Abraham, they are "man-sized." The beloved disciple John gives us an interesting measurement in Revelation 21. "Then he measured its wall; one hundred and forty-four cubits, according to the measure of a man, that is, of an angel." When measuring Heaven, John attempted to give us a cubit measurement. A traditional Biblical cubit is the length of a man's finger-tip to his elbow. This could be quite subjective as this would be different with all people. This is usually thought to be about eighteen inches. However, John was quick to point out, that this was an "angel cubit" and not a mere man measurement. John was trying to relay that the supernatural dimensions of Heaven are like time and eternity, and cannot be measured by the contrived measurements of mankind.

"Did it hurt?" has been a most often used pick-up line used by guys and gals alike. The most common response might have been, "Did what hurt?" Then the player would coyly respond by saying, "Did it hurt when you fell out of Heaven?" Here the player was implying that the approached person was so beautiful, that they must have been an angel straight out of Heaven. However, the fallen angels were cast out of Heaven by God and defeated by the archangel Michael, because of their sin of following the Chief Fallen Angel, Lucifer. As per the previously discussed war in Heaven, one third of the angels fell from Heaven. Apparently in part, they fell to Earth and Hell as well.

II Peter 2:4 tells us the following: "For God did not spare the angels who sinned, but cast them down to hell and delivered them into chains of darkness to be reserved for judgment. Jude 6 tells us "And the angels who did not keep their proper domain, but left their own abode, He has reserved in everlasting chains under darkness for the judgment of the great day."

Finally, do angels sit around on clouds and play harps? Well according to the book of Revelation, they do. In chapter fourteen of the Apocalypse, the writer John, records the one hundred and forty-four thousand sealed souls from the twelve tribes of Israel singing in the presence of "The Lamb," Jesus, and apparently playing harps. These heavenly beings were twelve thousand from each of the tribes of Israel. Since they are the heavenly souls of people, they are not angels in the truest meaning of the words. In Revelation 15, those who had overcome the 666 beast, were standing on the crystal sea having harps and singing the song of Moses and the song of the Lamb. The above examples were humans in heaven, so once again, they were not true angels. But do not lose heart about true angels not having harps. In the throne room of Heaven, in Revelation 5:8, the four living creatures and the twenty-four elders each have a harp, as well as, a golden bowl full of the prayers of the saints. There it is in black in white, true angels in Heaven having harps.

There are some church denominations which exclusively have "a cappella" music, which merely means "in chapel style," and do not believe in having musical instruments in the church because they say there is no basis in the New Testament for having musical instruments in the church. Although musical instruments, like the harp or lyre, are common features of praise in the Old Testament, most particularly with King David and the Psalms. Also, the book of Revelatioin list heavenly host having both harps and trumpets. So, should there be musical instruments in the Church?

THE ANGELS OF THE APOCALYPSE

The book of Revelation is full of angels from the get go with the first one listed in the first verse. There are several different groupings of angels and heavenly beings listed in the Apocalypse. This first grouping is the individual angels who are aligned with the seven churches of the Apocalypse. These "church angels" are equated to stars and the churches as lamp stands.

Rev. 1:1 = His Angel.
Rev. 2:1 = the angel of the church of Ephesus.
Rev. 2:8 = the angel of the church in Smyrna.
Rev. 2:12 = the angel of the church in Pergamos.
Rev. 2:18 = the angel of the church in Thyatira.
Rev. 3:1 = the angel of the church in Sardis.
Rev. 3:7 = the angel of the church in Philadelphia.
Rev. 3:14 = the angel of the church of Laodiceans.
Rev. 3:5 = angels who are confessed to with regards to the Book of Life.

Revelation 4 presents a second major cast of heavenly beings. These are the four living creatures and the twenty-four elders of Heaven's throne room. As discussed above, these four creatures are very much like the seraphim which are full of eyes and which continually say, "Holy, holy, holy," with the first one looking like a lion, and the others like a calf, a man, and finally an eagle. The Twenty-four elders are quite possibly symbolic of the twelve sons of Jacob and the twelve disciples of Jesus. These twenty-four elders are not given a physical description and are dangerously assumed to look like human people. In actions, they are falling before the throne of God, and casting down their crowns while praising God. The four living creatures and the twenty-four elders each have a harp and a golden bowl full of the prayers of the saints. Additionally, they are singing a new song.

Rev. 5:2 = the strong angel with a loud voice.

Rev. 5:11 = ten thousand times ten thousand and thousands of thousands loud voice angels.

Rev. 7:1 = four angels holding the four winds of the earth. Same angels as those in Rev. 9:14?

Rev. 7:2 = Another angel from the east with the seal of God commanding the four wind angels.

Rev. 7:11 = All the angels stood around the throne. (same as Rev. 5:11 angels?)

The next major set of angels are the seven angels with the seven trumpets which are coupled with the seven plagues. With each trumpet blast, another plague is brought upon the earth. The fourth trumpet blasting angel is aligned with another "angel" who announces the three woes. This additional angel is sometimes identified as an eagle.

Rev. 8:2 & 6 = seven angels with seven trumpets.

Rev. 8:3 & 5= another angel with golden censer and incense and the prayers of the saints.

Rev. 8:7 = The First Trumpet – plague on third of vegetation.

Rev. 8:8 = The Second Trumpet – plague on third of the sea.

Rev. 8:10 = The Third Trumpet – plague of the Wormwood Star on third of fresh water.

Rev. 8:12 = The Fourth Trumpet – plague on third of the sun, moon, and stars being darkened.

Rev. 8:13 = Angel or eagle announcing the three coming woes of the next three trumpets.

Rev. 9:1 = Fifth angel sounding of first woe: fallen star/Satan.

Rev. 9:11 = Angel of the bottomless pit whose name is Abaddon in Hebrew and Apollyon in Greek.

Rev. 9:13-15 = Sixth angel sounding of second woe: Release the four winds angels (same as 7:1?)

Listed with this sixth angel is the revisiting of the four winds angels which were introduced in chapter seven. Along with them are the two hundred million horsemen. The question here is: are these two hundred million horsemen human cavalrymen or mounted angels?

Rev. 10:1-Rev. 11:1 = a mighty angel clothed with a cloud, with a rainbow on his head with a face like the sun & his feet like pillars of fire.

Rev. 10:3 = The voice of the seven thunders.
Rev. 11:15 = Seventh angel sounding of third woe:
the announcement of Christ kingdoms on Earth.
Rev. 12:7 = Michael the archangel and his angels fight the Dragon (the Devil) and his third of fallen angels (the fallen stars of Rev. 12:4.)
Chapter fourteen presents "The three angels of proclamation."
Rev. 14:6 = The first angel of proclamation is a flying angel who preaches the gospel to every nation and tribe and tongue of people.
Rev. 14:8 = The second angel of proclamation announces the falling of Babylon.
Rev. 14:9 = The third angel of proclamation warns in a loud voice the eternal penalty for receiving the mark of the Beast.
Rev. 14:10 = The holy angels who witness the torment of the damned.
Rev. 14:15 = Another angel with a loud voice
instructing Christ to thrust in His sickle.
Rev. 14:17 & 19 = Another angel with a sharp sickle.
Rev. 14:18 = Another angel with the power over fire.
These next seven angels represent the last seven plagues of God with their golden bowls of wrath.
Rev. 15:1-8 = Seven angels with the seven last plagues
and seven golden bowls of the wrath of God.
Rev. 16:1= The seven angels are instructed to
pour out the wrath of God on the Earth.
Rev. 16:2 = First golden bowl: Loathsome sores on
those who took the mark of the Beast.
Rev. 16:3 = Second golden bowl: The sea turned to blood killing all within.
Rev. 16:4 = Third golden bowl: The rivers are turned to blood.
Rev. 16:7 = "Another Angel" proclaims the righteousness of God.
Rev. 16:8 = The fourth golden bowl: The scorching of men by the sun.
Rev. 16:10 = The fifth golden bowl: darkness and pain.
Rev. 16:12 = The sixth golden wowl: Euphrates river dried up.
Rev. 16:17-18 = The seventh golden bowl: earthquakes and destruction.
Rev. 17:1-7 = One of the seven angels shows John future judgment.
Rev. 18:1 = Another angel with great authority announces that Babylon is fallen.

Rev. 18:21 = A mighty angel with a millstone and threw it into the sea.

Rev. 19:17 = An angel standing in the sun, invites the birds to eat the fallen warriors of the earth.

Rev. 20:1 = The angel with the key to the bottomless pit with a great chain in his hand.

Rev. 21:9-17 = One of the golden bowls angels shows John the bride of Christ and measures Heaven.

Rev.21:12 = An angel at each of the twelve gates of Heaven.

Rev. 22:6-9 = John is told not to worship the angel as angels are our fellow servants of God.

Rev. 22:16 = Jesus tells John that He has sent His angel to testify of these things.

It is difficult to calculate how many angels and heavenly beings are in Heaven, and how many were mentioned in the Book of Revelation, but certainly, there were many.

GIANTS

Genesis 6:4 is perhaps one of the most bizarre verses in the Bible on several levels. It begins with the mention of "the Nephilim" הנפלים as they are called in the Hebrew. This Hebrew Nephilim word has also been interpreted as simply the "fallen ones" but many times as "giants."

Where did these giant fallen ones come from? This most unique verse says, "when the sons of God came into the daughters of men and they bore children to them." WHAT!? Who were these "sons of God?" Were these the same as the fallen angels from the war in Heaven? May we dare ask, were they some sort of aliens? Whoever or whatever they were, they appear to have been some sort of supernatural being not of this natural world. Even more odd is that they were supernatural beings that were somehow sexually compatible with human women and able to reproduce human born children. If this were not strange enough, the wording of this verse states that these giants were called the mighty men of old and men of renown. We are *only* in the sixth chapter of Genesis. It is likely that Genesis 6, should be read concurrently with the previous chapters of Genesis.

As we will discuss below, these Nephilim giants roamed the earth for many more centuries beyond the flood of Noah up to the time of King

David. Where did these mighty men of old come from and who were they? What does the scripture say? We know that there was the war in Heaven and a third of the angels fell. Were these "war in Heaven fallen angels" the same or part of these "sons of God" listed in Genesis 6? Perhaps!? It would appear that some fallen ones fell to earth. Whereas, some fell straight to Hell. Perhaps, in some natural or supernatural form, some were able to move between both realms just as the "un-fallen" messengers of God, the good angels, who were able to make lateral moves between the physical and spiritual dimensions.

In Numbers 13, Joshua and Caleb were the only two spies of the twelve, who went into the Promised Land, and wanted to take it. The other ten spies were afraid because of the giant people who were already there. These were the descendants of Anak. The ten unwilling spies described themselves as grasshoppers in the sight of these giants, who were referred to as "men of great stature". We know from scripture that there were giants who roamed the earth from the dawn of time, up through the time of King David.

In Deuteronomy 2, God tells Moses not to contend with the nation of Moab. In Deuteronomy 2, the Moabite people called the Emin people giants who were as tall as the Anakim. These same Anak giants are mentioned in Deturomony 9, "a people great and tall." In Joshua 15, where Caleb drives out the three sons of Anak: Sheshai, Ahiman, and Talmai. The Bashan king, King Og, is also called a remnant of the giants as mentioned in Joshua 12. In the end of Deuteronomy 3, King Og's bed is said to be over thirteen feet long; nine cubits in Hebrew measure.

The young son of Jesse, David, later to be the second King of Israel, fought and killed a Philistine giant named Goliath, who was estimated to be about nine feet and nine inches tall. More than a good two feet taller than the former NBA basketball player Shaquille O'Neil. Just as Shaq was a big broad man, so was Goliath, based upon the weight and measurements of his weapons and body armor mentioned in I Samuel 17. Goliath's coat of mail, the small interlocking rings of bronze, was five thousand shekels or perhaps one hundred and twenty-five pounds, whereas his iron spearhead was a respective five thousand shekels, or perhaps sixteen pounds. The Philistine giant Goliath was also known to have had at least one brother, Lahmi the Gittite, and three sons, Ishbi-Benob, Saph, and a third son, who had six fingers on each hand and six toes on each foot. David and his warriors are recorded to have killed these other giants in II Samuel 21. After David and his warriors killed these Philistine giants, there is no further mention of giants in scripture.

Today we have "giants" among us. We call them NBA and NFL athletes. Many college and pro basketball players are near, at, or well over seven feet tall. The same can be said of many of the three- hundred-pound behemoth college and pro football lineman who are usually well over six feet tall. To be sure, this is still a far cry from the Philistine giant Goliath who topped out at nine feet and nine inches tall as Hebrew cubits are calculated. In the 1800's, in the American west, some suspect bones were dug up under the assumption that these bones may be human giant bones. However, some of these bones were later confirmed to be bones of ancient animals such as Mastodons. They could be Bigfoot bones, for those given to such possibilities.

Is it possible that there really are real modern giants who still walk among us? Not only is it possible, it is true. In the last two hundred years, we have documented facts of modern giants. Ella Ewing was born in 1872 in Missouri. She was documented to have been 8'4" tall before dying in 1913. As with others with this physical situation during this time, she was employed by the traveling circus of the time in what were unfortunately called "freak shows." Johan Aason was officially measured at 8'9" but was rumored by some to have been as tall as 9'2" which would have made him the tallest documented modern giant before he was buried in Montana. Robert Wadlow was from Alton, Illinois. He was born in 1918 and died at the early age of 22. He topped out at the lofty height of 8'11" and holds the record for the tallest modern giant. This is just to name a few. This is still almost a foot shorter than the rather robust warrior giant Goliath who was slain by a small smooth stone slung by the shepherd boy David, who would be King of Israel.

Most modern giants began life with what would be called "normal" growth rates. Usually in late childhood, they began to have enormous growth spurts. They normally had a long list of health problems and usually died young.

There are numerous records and reports throughout the world, of various time periods and places which recall giants. Some people have reported to have bones from graves. In the last century and a half, some have even had photos of either the actual living giant, or their bones, or other artifacts.

Are these modern giants the result of recessive genes reserved over the centuries and left over from the fallen Nephilim? Or are these contemporary giants the result of misguided genetics, or modern diet, and/or environment or otherwise? Dig-discover-discuss.

GHOSTS, SPIRITS and other ABERRATIONS

The 1611 King James Version uses the phrase "Holy Ghost" for the third part of the Trinity, which most Christians today refer to as the Holy Spirit. Most Christians and other people of faith, we believe in spiritual beings, such as God, angels, and other heavenly beings, as well as, the Devil, demons, and other lesser malevolent minions, and malefactors. Orthodox Christianity believes we have an eternal spirit and/or soul, which will either abide in Heaven with God, for those who belong to Jesus Christ, or in an eternal torment in Hell with the Devil and his fallen angels.

In the German language, the word for our English word Ghost is "Geist." In the Hebrew, the words ghost, geist, spirit, soul, and even breath, and wind are called "ru'ach" רוח which are basically the same words. God inspired or breathed the breath of life or wind into Adam, and made him a living soul in Genesis 2. What does the scripture have to say about ghosts? Older King James Versions use the phrase, "gave up the ghost," to refer to, "breathing his last breath." In these instances, the spirit or soul of the person was referred to as ghost.

In I Samuel 28, King Saul, the first king of Israel, sought a woman who had a "familiar spirit" as she was referred to in various older translations. A woman who was a medium in newer translations. In popular thought, she is commonly called the "Witch of Endor." King Saul knew he was about to die in battle. God did not answer Saul in either dreams, prophets, or by the Urim, or the casting of lots, or dice. King Saul was in the guise of a commoner, as he sought out the Witch of Endor, the woman with the familiar spirit. Oddly enough, King Saul had already exiled or otherwise dispatched all the wizards, witches, warlocks, and such soothsayers from the land. The lady medium of Endor thought this was a trap. She asked the disguised King Saul for assurance that she would not be outed for conducting an outlawed séance for him. King Saul obliged her safety and asked the witch to summon up the prophet Samuel. Once she had called up Samuel from the spirit world, she was aghast at the ghost, and asked King Saul not to punish her. King Saul asked her, "What do you see?" the Endor witch replies and says, "a spirit ascending out of the earth …an old man coming up covered in a mantle." Saul knew that it was Samuel, and bowed his face to the earth. Samuel strangely asked Saul, "Why are you disturbing me by bringing me up?" Saul wants to know from Samuel what his fate will be in combat the following day. The spirit Samuel informs Saul that the Philistines will overtake him, as well as, his sons, and that on the morrow, Saul would be joining him in the spirit world.

With all of this said, are there ghosts walking among us? Can our spirits be summoned from the grave and eternity? How does this scripture affect how we understand ghost, spirits, death, Heaven, Hell and the afterlife? What does the scripture say? During the crucifixion of Jesus and the two criminals with Him, Jesus tells the one thief on the cross, that he would be with Him in Paradise that same day. The Apostle Paul tells us in I Corinthians 15:52 that the dead in Christ would be raised from the grave at the last trumpet blast. A similar verse is given to us in I Thessalonians 4:16-17. Does this mean that Christians "Rest In Peace," (aka R.I.P) in a quiet and timeless grave until the trump of the LORD? If we look at I Thessalonians 4:14, we will see "God will bring with Him those who sleep in Jesus." This phrase would infer that Christians are already with God in Heaven. Either way, it works out the same, since eternity is timeless. If we were to die and then go to the grave without time, then rise to the Lord at the sound of the trumpet, this would be the same as going to Heaven directly. Ultimately, we will be united in eternity with Christ in Heaven.

In Matthew 14:22-33, while the disciples were in their fishing boat on the Sea of Galilee, the disciples saw a figure walking on the water coming towards them during a storm and thought it to be a ghost. After they had said, "It is a ghost!" Jesus said to them, "Be of good cheer, it is I, do not be afraid." It is for certain, that Jesus will come to us during the storms of our life. Immediately upon Jesus identifying Himself, Peter asked Jesus to join Him. For a short while, Peter was the only other person to have ever walked on water, until his faith failed and he sank. Once again, Jesus is always there to save us when we sink in doubt and sin when our faith fails. One can only imagine that the bold, and seemingly fearless, fisherman Peter wanted to walk on the water with Jesus as a matter of faith. However, Peter was still human. Perhaps, in his eager ego, he glanced back with pride at his fishing partners, James and John as well as his own fisherman brother, Andrew and said, "Hey Y'all! Hey Andy! Look at me!" And he sank. Jesus did rename Simon, as Peter, "Rock." And rocks sink.

Even though Jesus could walk on the water, Jesus did actually go under the water once. His own cousin, John the Baptist, baptized Jesus in the Jordan River. The Spirit of God descended in the form of a dove and lands on Jesus. Who knew that Jesus "needed' to be baptized? He did not, but Jesus did so as an example for us. The words spirit or spirits appear hundreds of times throughout all the scripture.

The question remains; do ghosts, ghouls, and other such disembodied spirits still haunt old houses, hospitals, battlefields, accident scenes, and grave yards? This ghost topic is especially brought to our minds during the fall festival of Halloween. (Halloween and other holidays will be discussed further in detail in the appendix). Is it possible for spirits to transverse the dimensions of Heaven and Hell to Earth? Is the occult real? Are the powers of darkness real in our three-dimensional world? Just as with the good guardian angels, are personal demons about seeking whom they may devour? Are there really such people as mediums, witches and other such séance seers and sooth sayers? Are they able to summon spirits and souls as the Witch of Endor did with King Saul? Certainly, there are spirits and a spirit world. If not, our faith in Jesus Christ is null and void. Do spirits exist? What does the scripture say? What does the scripture not say? <u>A strong note of caution should be placed here</u>. Attempting to summon spirits & souls, and seeking after the dead with séance's, seers, soothsayers, witches, wizards, warlocks, and various dime store palm readers, is a dangerous and slippery slope into the activities of the occult, and should be avoided by all believers, at all times, at all cost.

ALIENS

Above, we mentioned the word "alien." This is a fun word for those who enjoy the various pseudo-sciences, UFO's, crypto-zoology and the like. What is an alien? An alien is defined as any sort of being not of this world. There is a very fine line between the definition of an alien and that of a supernatural angel or other heavenly being also defined as not being of this physical world. Are aliens the same as the Nephilim of Genesis? God created the whole entire endless eternal universe. What is the mathematical possibility that we earthlings are the only planet that has intelligent life, out of the endless universe that God created? Openly, most people would not admit to acknowledging that there may be intelligent life beyond our own planet, saving God and the angels in Heaven of course. However, many folks may privately allow, that there *may be* others in the universe. This is played out in the common popularity of such movies and TV shows as *STAR WARS* and *STAR TREK*. Some people, Christian, or otherwise, like to enjoy the notion that we may not be alone.

There are more than a few people who claim to have seen either an alien, an angel, or even a ghost. Could most people be able to discern one from another, based on the description of angels in scripture? For some Christian thinkers, it goes against their Christian Orthodoxy to acknowledge there may even be the possibility of extraterrestrial life. However, there is nothing in scripture to suggest one argument over another, as to whether aliens, as we think of them, exist in the great vast black abyss of the eternal sky. What we can know for certain is that if "they" exist, they were certainly created by God.

Erich von Daniken in his 1968 book, *Chariots of the GODS,"* openly espouses that there are aliens and they have visited humans on planet earth. One of the topics he covers is what is commonly called the "Nazca Lines," which are located in the Andes Mountains of western Peru. There are as many theories as to why these lines exist in the remote mountains of South America as there are mountains.

These lines are etched about four to six inches deep into the dark iron oxide pebbles which cover the lighter colored sub-surface. Who made these lines? Many scientist and others believe these lines were made by the local Nazca people. They may have been put there for religious reason, perhaps as prayers to their gods to bring rain to this most arid of lands. The lines have been there for thousands of years, because very little rain falls there, and oddly, the wind seldom blows there, thus making this location most like the surface of the moon. Some lines are extremely straight lines, which may proceed for miles with little or no variation in degree. Other lines are animals, spirals or other things in nature. When the lines are in the shape of an animal, the drawing is made of one continuous non-crossing line, much in the similar manner, as there is only one grove on each side of a vinyl album. If you were born after 1980, vinyl albums are those big black round flat things with music on them, similar to a CD, only bigger and blacker.

Some of these animal etchings are the size as of a several football fields. Many of these drawings can only be seen for what they really are from the air. One of the mountains is completely leveled off flat. It resembles a landing strip, or an airport for aircraft. How and who did this, and why?

One must also consider such oddities as the gigantic engraved stone heads at Easter Island, the precision cut "H-Blocks" at Pumapunku, Bolivia, and the Paracas, Peru skulls. Who made these statues at Easter Island? How did they make them? Why did they make an army of mostly identical giant, elongated stone heads on such a remote island in such an isolated location? Who, how, and when were the precision cut "H-blocks" made at Pumapunka, Boliva? These stones were apparently quarried about six miles away, at the Lake Titicaca area. Most of these hewn stones weigh many metric tons and are cut with such a precision that modern engineering would find it a challenge to duplicate the stone cutting and the engineering required to move them six miles. The local Inca tribes take no credit for the existence of the H-blocks and other local oddities. What about the Paracas, Peru skulls which were discovered in 2014. These are very odd elongated skulls which seem to have questionable DNA findings. Many groups of people throughout the world, mostly in Africa, typically practice manipulating their own skulls to make them long and/or large. However, these Paracas skulls seem to be different. Were we visited from above? We know that we have been visited by angels. Have we been visited by aliens? Are angels, aliens, and ghosts the same? Could these "alien phenomenon" be related to "The Nephilim" of Genesis? Once again, if we, as modern people, were in the presence of an angel, an alien, a ghost, or other, could we discern the difference? This is a conundrum.

In Ezekiel 1, Ezekiel attempts to describe what he saw. What was it? "A whirlwind coming out of the north; a great cloud with raging fire." "The color of amber in the midst of fire." Ezekiel described the four living creatures who came from within the whirlwind. They were the familiar creature refrain of a man, a lion, an ox, and finally an eagle. These creatures each had four faces and four wings. Their legs were straight and the color of burnt bronze with feet like calves. The creatures ran back and forth like a flash of lightening. Wheels in the middle of wheels with rims full of eyes, and went in all four directions.

"When they went, I heard the noise of their wings, like the noise of many waters like the voice of the Almighty, a tumult like the noise of an army and when they stood still, they let down their wings." Could this be the description of modern helicopters or other modern machines of war? Could this have been an alien space ship or something else? Ezekiel, after much description, finally describes this "Whirlwind" like the appearance of a rainbow in a cloud on a rainy day. This was the appearance of the likeness of the glory of the LORD.

Compare the vision of Ezekiel to the vision of John's Apocalypse recorded in Revelation 9. These creatures, or mechanical beast, are best described by John as locust or scorpions. "The shape of the locust like horses prepared for battle. On their heads were crowns of something like gold and their faces were like the faces of men. They had hair like a woman's hair and their teeth were like lion's teeth. And they had breastplates of iron, and the sound of their wings was like the sound of chariots with many horses running into battle. They had tails like scorpions and there were stings in their tails." Is this a description of a modern military attack helicopter? Or is it something else? What does the scripture say? Modern attack helicopters like, Army Apaches and Marine Corps Cobras, could be compared in appearance to locust or scorpions. The sound of helicopter wings could be compared to that of horses running into battle. The rounded split windshields of these war birds could be described as a "face." These helicopter tails with side mounted machine guns and rockets could be described as "stings" by a biblical era writer.

In Genesis 5:24, Enoch was "taken up" by God. A most similar story is recorded in II Kings 2 where Elijah is taken up in a "whirlwind" into heaven which is described as a "Chariot of Fire" with "Horses of Fire."

The question begs to be asked, Were these some sort of spaceships, or just merely wind and fire and horses? The Old Testament writers even with clear vision of the events, would not have had the volcabulary to describe an interstellar space craft, if in fact, these were the vehicles of transport.

Considering the vocabulary and knowledge of post civil war Americans in the late 1800's, how would they describe a smart phone or a laptop? Are angels in their various forms the same as aliens? Do aliens even exist at all? Are these the Nephilim? Dig, discover, and discuss.

{Editorial note: Editor Kellie Cyrus states that Christians in Heaven become "like" angels. So the question remains: Do we become actual angels or just something "like" angels?}

{Editorial note: Editor Pam McIntosh compounds the author's thought that Christians should not experiment with the occult of any sort or level.}

Questions and Discussion for
Chapter Eight – Angels, Aliens, Ghost and Giants
Dig – Discover – Discuss

1. What are angels αγγελος and what is their primary purpose?

2. Do angels have freewill? Are they free agents?
   Explain the war in Heaven and the fall of Lucifer and one third of the angels?

3. What do angels look like? Are angels created with wings? or do they have to earn them as "Clarence" did in the Christmas movie, "It's a Wonderful Life?"

4. Do angels sit on clouds and play harps?
   How many angels are there?
   How big are angels?
   Are there male and female angels?
   Do angels get married?

5. According to Scripture, which two angels have names?

6. According to Scripture, how many archangels are there?

7. In traditional and current art, why do angels usually look like women?

8. Have angels come to earth in the form of human people? According to Hebrews 13:2, do angels still come to earth? Do you believe angels can still "cross-over" from either Heaven or Hell to interact with humans as per Hebrews 13:2?

9. According to Matthew 18:10, do guardian angels exist?

10. Do you believe there is an angel of death? Why?

11. Are there such things as Ghosts? What is the difference between an angel and a ghost? If you as a twenty-first century Christian were to have an encounter with a ghost, a disembodied spirit, angel, alien, avatar, or aberration; could you discern which type of entity it was? Explain.

12. Considering an endless universe and an all-powerful Creator God, is it possible that aliens exist?
Is there anything in the Bible to suggest either way that aliens "do" or "don't" exist?
Angels are often defined as being "supernatural-not of this physical world."
Aliens are often defined as being "extra-terrestrial-not of this physical world."
What is the technical difference between an angel and an alien? Discuss.

13. Do you believe the Genesis 6 Nephilim are the same as the war in Heaven fallen angels described in Revelation 12? Explain.

14. Do you believe that the Genesis 6 Nephilim had sexual relations with human women and produced human giants?

15. Do you believe the young David, son of Jesse, actually killed the nine-feet, nine-inch, Philistine giant with a sling and smooth stone?
Do you have alternative thoughts on this story?

16. When Christians die, do they go straight to Heaven or Rest-In-Peace in their graves until the Second Coming?

17. Do Christians become angels when the go to Heaven or become another class of heavenly beings?

18. Can spirits or ghosts be summoned from the grave in a séance by a witch, or other enchantor?

Chapter Nine

Jonah

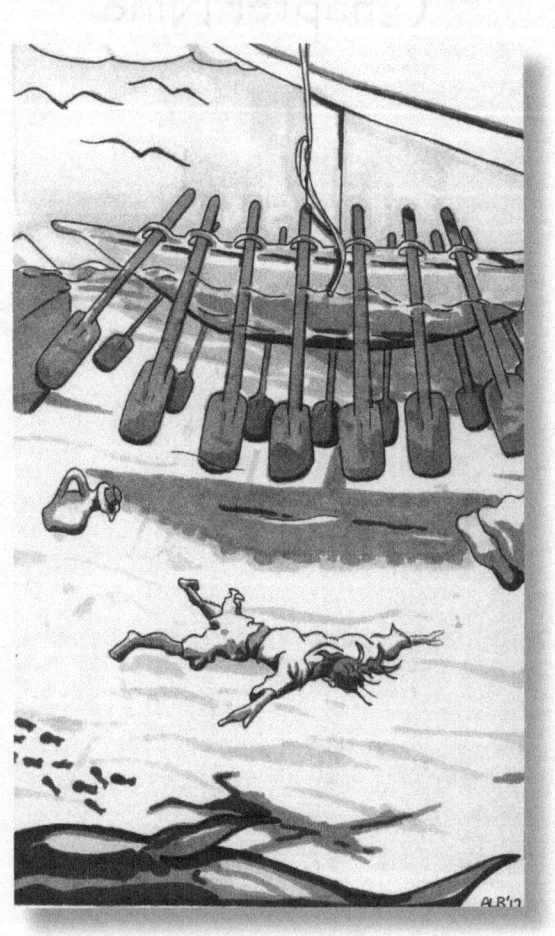

"Now the word of the LORD came to Jonah the son of Amittai, saying, Arise, go to Nineveh, that great city, and cry out against it; for their wickedness has come up before me," is how the book of Jonah begins. The book of Jonah falls correctly into the grouping of minor prophets which are gauged by their small book size. Jonah only has four short chapters. In spite of the book being written in the third person, the reluctant prophet is thought to be the likely author of this work bearing his name.

As with Noah's Ark and other Bible School and Sunday School artwork, there is a great amount of discussion and/or confusion such as "Jonah and the Whale," or is it "Jonah and the Great Fish?" What does the scrirture say? Jonah 1:17 says the following: "Now the LORD had prepared a great fish to swallow Jonah. And Jonah was in the belly of the fish three days and three nights." These three days and three nights will be referenced later.

Some quasi scientific Biblical thinkers would say, "Oh, but it had to be a whale, because there is no fish big enough to swallow a man alive. Jonah would have had to have air to breath and if he was in the belly of a whale, then he would have air to breath." OK, where to start? If it was a whale, then we will say, and dangerously assume, that it could have been a Sperm Whale, which would have a mouth suited for swallowing something as big as a grown man. However, if this were the case, we will wag this fish tale this way. After Jonah was swallowed, he would have ended up in the "belly" as the scripture says, and not likely in the lungs. If Jonah was in the belly and not the lungs, he still would not have been able to gain access to oxygen to breath even if he were in an air breathing sperm whale. The digestive system would have eaten Jonah alive. One could continue with this fish story and say that the whale had the hiccups for three days and nights, thus allowing for air to be in the belly of the whale for Jonah to breath. Now this would be the greatest fish story ever told.

As with the whole concept of God and our faith in Him, we, as mere created creatures, cannot limit God, the creator of the whole universe with our own whims of what we think the Bible *should* say to suit our own spiritual views. Whereas we should adjust our spiritual views to what the scripture says. The Hebrew text simply uses the word "fish," דג which, oddly enough, is pronounced as "dog" in English. What is glossed over here is that God "prepared a great fish." Here the operative word is "prepared." This was not an ordinary previously existing fish or sperm whale. It was a special creation with a special purpose. A fish with a mission from God. God is allowed to do this. This is the miraculous, creative hand of God doing His will for His own purposes. As we have just discussed, no fish or sea mammal in the ocean is capable of swallowing a man alive and sustaining him for three days and nights. This had to be a specially prepared fish, just as the scripture says. Unfortunately, most people get "caught" hook, line, and sinker, with the concept of the great fish. However ... Attention Please! The great fish is *not* to be the point of the story.

God had called Jonah to be a prophet; a missionary to go to the city of Nineveh. However, Jonah, with pride and perhaps anger in his heart, thought he knew better than God. Jonah did not want to go to the city of Nineveh because he thought they were not worthy to hear the word of God because they were "wicked." Somehow, Jonah failed to realize that this same "wickedness," was the very reason for him to go there in the first place.

Instead of Jonah going straight forward and toward Nineveh as he was commanded by God, Jonah went his own way in the opposite direction towards Tarshish, and away from the presence of the LORD. Tarshish is thought by some to be in the western Mediterranean Sea. This may be the modern seaport town of Tartessus, Spain. There are various towns, churches, and certain places all through the Mediterranean Sea region which claim to be Tarshish, or other locations which were visited by Biblical figures. Nineveh, on the other hand, was on the banks of the Tigris River in the Babylon/Assyria region. Jonah was at the coast at Joppa, and set sail with the sailors. The New International Version calls the seamen on the ship "sailors," whereas the King James, New King James and The New American Bible calls them, "Mariners." Jonah paid his fare and went down into belly of the ship. It wasn't long before God sent a tempest on the sea and the tiny ship was tossed to the point that it was about to be broken up in this titanic struggle on the way to Tarshish. The seaman became afraid and were crying out to their sea faring gods: perhaps Poseidon and/or King Neptune. They began to throw their cargo into the deep and dark abyss with hopes of lightening their load. Meanwhile, in the belly of the ship, Jonah was asleep, and oblivious to the dangerous deep. The captain of the ship awakend Jonah from his deep sleep and asked him, "What do you mean sleeper? Arise, call on your God; perhaps your God will consider us, so that we may not perish." Perhaps both Poseidon and Neptune were on shore leave as neither responded to the SOS distress call of those in peril on the sea. But the Eternal Father of Jonah was strong to save. After the casting of lots, it was determined by the perishing privateers that Jonah should be cast-a-way, and eventually down the plank and overboard he went. But, before he was cast off the stem, or stern, starboard, or port, the sailors inquired of him why he had caused them this tumultuous trouble? What was his occupation? Where was he from? He told them that he was a Hebrew, and that he feared the LORD God above, who created the land and sea. At this point the men of the sea knew that Jonah was fleeing from the presence of the LORD and they were very afraid. The mariners asked Jonah what they must do to calm the raging seas. Jonah instructs them to throw him overboard, but they refused to do this, and rowed and oared the vessel with even more vigor, but the sea raged even more against their efforts. At this point, the sailors started praying to Jonah's God, and asked that they not perish due to Jonah. Finally, they tossed Jonah to the waves, and the sea stilled for them. They offered a sacrifice to the God of Jonah, and took vows to the same. It is at this time that Jonah was swallowed by the great prepared fish of God's hand of special creation. Compare this story to the story of Jesus sleeping in the boat during the storm on the Sea of Galilee in Mark 4.

While in the belly of the beast, Jonah prayed and compared his plight to being in Sheol, or in the pit of the underworld, at the bottom of a mountain. Floods and waves, with weeds wrapped around him. Finally, Jonah's prayers end with thanksgiving to God. Finally, after three days and nights, the great prepared fish vomited Jonah up onto dry land.

Jonah, being three days and nights in the belly of the beast for his sins, has often been paralleled to Jesus being in the tomb or perhaps, Hell, to bury all our sins before being resurrected on Easter Sunday.

Jonah 3 begins with, "Now the word of the LORD came to Jonah the second time saying, Arise, go to Nineveh, that great city and preach to it the message that I tell you. Jonah arose and went to Nineveh."

What we don't know is, where was Jonah vomited up onto dry land? We can either speculate that it was some deserted, un-charted island, or perhaps a known isle or the mainland. If on an island like Cyprus, then Jonah was going to have to take yet another ship to the mainland, with nothing to pay his passage. This must have been a most interesting conversation with the second ship captain. Would Jonah be able to convince another captain to allow Jonah to be manifested on his ship after hearing about his luck. Was the captain willing to take this risk after listening to the bad luck, ill-fate, or lack of faith, Jonah was having at the time? Perhaps he was simply vomited back up on the eastern shore of the Mediterranean Sea.

After Jonah's second attempt to venture to Nineveh, he finally arrived at his Tigris River town destination. Jonah describes the city of Nineveh as a three days journey in extant. With this being the description, Nineveh could have been about sixty miles across the entire city. The thought is that he might have walked twenty miles in one day which would have been considered a full day's journey at this time and place. Some calculate ancient Nineveh was similar in size to the greater Los Angeles area. After the first day's tread and trek, he cries out against the city and said that it will be overthrown in forty days. Here is yet another example of "forty" being used as a time marker of God's work in the Scriptures. It is likely Jonah took great joy in shouting down the city of Nineveh, considering all of the trouble he had had in getting there. Although, he brought this trouble upon his own head. The root cause of most of the trouble we have as individuals is often caused by our own hands.

This was perhaps the shortest and yet most effective sermon ever preached. Jonah spoke less than a dozen words and the people of the city responded. The people of Nineveh first believed in God, then proclaimed a feast and put on sackcloth as a sign of repentance. The king of the great city even took off his royal robe and put on sackcloth and covered himself with ashes. The king of Nineveh further went on to make a decree saying: No man or beast was to eat or drink anything. Additionally, every man and beast should be covered with sackcloth, cry out to God, and turn from their evil ways. In the king's decree, he only hoped that God would turn his wrath from the city so that they all would not die.

God saw that the king and people of Nineveh were sincere in their repentance and relented from the disaster He said He would bring upon them. That is what God does, we repent, and God forgives us. Even though we don't deserve forgiveness, God forgives. This forgiveness displeased Jonah, and he was exceedingly angry –What? This is reminiscent of the story Jesus gives us of the prodigal son returning home from his life of sin and riotous living and his father forgiving his wayward son. The older brother of the prodigal son, was most unhappy with this forgiveness of sin. None of us are worthy of forgiveness, but all Christians must be thankful when anyone comes to the saving grace of God.

Jonah prays to God and informs God that he somehow knew that this act of repentance of the people of Nineveh and forgiveness from God would happen, much to the personal dismay of Jonah and his jaded heart. This is exactly what Jonah knew. He knew God would forgive them. Jonah wanted condemnation to fall heavily upon the city of Nineveh. This is why Jonah explains to God why he attempted to flee to Tarshish. Jonah, much like Cain, was apoplectic. Jonah asked God to take his life. One could clearly conclude that Jonah really did not like the people of Nineveh. God asked the distraught Jonah if it was right for Jonah to be angry.

In Jonah's anger and self pity, which may be compared to a selfish five-year-old not getting their way, Jonah went east of the city, built a shelter, and sat there to pout. It was Jonah's hope that God might still smite the city.

God made provision for Jonah, even though Jonah certainly did not deserve it. God made a "prepared plant" to rise up and cover Jonah from his misery. Jonah was very grateful for the prepared plant. However, in the morning, God also prepared a worm to eat the plant and destroy it. Additionally, God caused a great east wind, and had the sun beat down on the head of Jonah to the point that he wished he was dead.

"Then God said to Jonah, "Is is right for you to be angry about the plant?" And he said, "It is right for me to be angry, even to death!" God once again responds and states, that you Jonah had pity on the plant for which you had no labor in the growing, but should I God not have pity on the great city of Nineveh which had more than one hundred and twenty thousand people who cannot tell their right hand from their left who have much live stock.? And then? ... And then...? Apparently, the very end of the text has quite possibly been lost to the ages, as the text ends here in the most odd and abrupt fashion speaking about livestock. What do you think?

Taken as a whole, this is a very odd story. The point of the story is not the great fish or the whale, but rather the moving and redemptive hand of God. God uses a reluctant prophet to do His will. In spite of the reluctance of Jonah, God's will still prevailed. Jonah, in his own sin and self-righteousness, is still used to do the will of God. It is most likely that Jonah loved God with a deep passion. He also hated the people of Nineveh with an equal zeal because of their sin against God. Are Christians today like Jonah? Do we hate others who do not love our God? Are we reluctant to go to those who hate us and our God? Are we our brother's keeper? It is the will of God that we all come to Him. God wills to save us all. "That if you confess with your mouth the LORD Jesus and believe in your heart that God has raised Him from the dead, you will be saved...for whoever calls upon the name of the LORD shall be saved. (Romans 10: 9 & 13). Go looking for Jesus before He comes looking for you. Jesus Himself mentions the Jonah saga in his preaching to Scribes and Pharisees in Matthew 12.

Questions and Discussion for
Chapter Nine – Jonah
Dig – Discover – Discuss

1. Do you believe Jonah was a man after God's own heart with passion and zeal?

2. Throughout the story, Jonah is angry. Where is his anger directed and why?

3. Compare and discuss Jonah to the "older brother" in the "prodigal son" story as told by Jesus in Luke 15.

4. Where are the cities of Tarshish and Ninevah?

5. Compare Jonah sleeping in the ship to Jesus sleeping on the boat in Mark 4. Contrast Jonah and Jesus' individual reactions to the storms. How did the two different ship crews react to the storms?

6. Discuss Jonah's mind set during the storm and the bargaining during the storm.

7. In Jonah 1:14-16, did the "life & death" faith of the sea mariners stick after they cast Jonah overboard?

8. Do you believe that the Jonah and the whale or the great fish is true? Do you believe the sea creature was naturally occurring?
   Was this creature a special creation of God for such a time as this? Discuss the meaning of the Hebrew word דג pronounced in English as "dog."

9. Compare Jonah's three days in the belly to Jesus' three days in the tomb –discuss.

10. Discuss the meaning of the verse, "Nineveh was an exceedingly great city, a three-days journey in extent."

11. Explain and discuss Jonah's spirit, disposition, and attitude when he gave his "Yet forty days and Nineveh shall be overthrown" sermon.

12. Discuss the immediate and corporate repentance of Nineveh.

13. Discuss Jonah's anger with God after God's forgiveness of Nineveh. Discuss modern western Christian's attitudes towards Muslim Terrorist. How are these attitudes similar to how Jonah felt towards the people of Nineveh?
    Are Christians often reluctant missionaries to people who are diametrically opposed to their Christian faith?

14. Discuss the special creation by God of the shade plant and the worm.

15. Did Jonah fulfill the will of the Lord?
    Did Jonah get his heart right with God?

16. The book of Jonah ends in a most odd way discussing livestock. Is it possible we are missing the end of the book of Jonah?

Chapter Ten

Mary

In the Bible, when thinking of the name "Mary," most will immediately turn their minds to the figure of the Virgin Mary, the wife of Joseph and the physical mother of Jesus Christ. This Mary is one of the most central figures in both the New Testament and all Christianity. However, she is not the only woman in the New Testament bearing the name of Mary. Others with this Mary moniker who may come to mind are Mary Magdalene, Mary of Bethany, as well as, others. Sometimes there is confusion over which Mary did what. We will attempt to help sort out the various Marys of the New Testament with who they were and what they did.

THE VIRGIN MARY

We will begin with the mother of Jesus, who was of the family line of King David. We first find this Mary in the two different birth narratives in the gospels of Matthew and Luke. The Luke 1:26 account introduces us to the young Mary who is visited by the Angel Gabriel. As with anyone experiencing a super-natural angelic appearance, this had to be an overwhelming event to the young woman. There were no cell phones, computers with Skype, cars, or any of the other various modern wonders and devices that currently invade and pervade our modern lives. All this technology now seems like some sort of a common everyday magic, or miracle, which is mindlessly taken for granted as being routine. To be visited by an angel of the LORD face to face, had to be an indescribable and terrifying event for anyone, especially to a first century teenage Nazarene girl.

The Angel Gabriel is only one of two angels to be named in the Canon Scripture, with Michael, the Archangel, being the other. The angel Gabriel announced to the young Mary that she was going to have a baby, even though she was an engaged virgin who had not known a man, or not yet had physical sexual relations. Not only was she going to have a baby, but this baby was going to be conceived by the over-shadowing of the Holy Spirit. This baby, was going to be the divine Son of God and the savior of the world. This baby was going to be simultaneously 100% human and 100% God. This is certainly a conundrum for many non-believers, and a source of controversy and debate for those not of the faith. However, this is at the core of Christianity. Without this miracle of the moving hand of God at its foundation, with Mary being a virgin, who gave birth to the divine God-child, the whole of Christianity is null and void.

What had begun as a normal day in Nazareth for the young Mary, this angelic announcement changed her life perspective forever. Mary accepted her mission from God and said, "Let it be to me according to your word." Mary is also informed by the angel Gabriel that her relative Elizabeth was also six months pregnant, even though she was of an advanced age, which is reminiscent of the late age pregnancy of Sarah, the wife of Abraham. Not only was Elizabeth pregnant in her old age, but she was going to give birth to a baby boy who was going to grow up to be the last Old Testament style prophet; the forerunner of Jesus Christ. He would be known as John the Baptist; not to be confused with John the Disciple, the brother of James and the son of Zebedee. This John the baptizer wore camel hair and leather belts and ate wild honey and locust, and said of himself that he was not worthy to even carry the sandals of Jesus while being the voice of one crying out in the wilderness saying, "Prepare the way of the LORD!" This John would go on to baptize Jesus in the Jordan River, spurring the earthly ministry of Jesus. At the baptism of Jesus, the Holy Spirit descended upon Jesus from Heaven in the form of a dove.

After this announcement from the Angel Gabriel, Mary visited her nearkinswoman Elizabeth and her husband Zacharias in the hill country of Judah for about three months. While Mary was with Elizabeth and Zacharias, she shared with them the news of her own divine pregnancy. It is not clear in the scripture, if Mary stayed with her relatives in the hill country of Judah, until Elizabeth gave birth to John.

We can only speculate that Mary was a teen-ager, who was living an ordinary life in Nazareth until her angelic visit. We have no realistic way to determine her age with any certainty. We can only know that she was old enough to be engaged, according to the common cultural and social norms of Jewish marriage customs and traditions of the time. Mary is listed as being a virgin who is "betrothed," or engaged, to a man named Joseph, in the city of Nazareth, who was also of the family line of King David.

Nazareth was a small town in the Galilee region of the northern area of Israel about half way between the Sea of Galilee and the Mediterranean Sea in the Jezreel Valley. Outside of being the childhood hometown of Jesus, there seemed to be little significance to the town of Nazareth. Eventually, one of Jesus' disciples, Philip, exclaimed in the Gospel of John, "Can anything good come out of Nazareth?" One person in the town of Nazareth, who would be central to world history, was a simple man named Joseph.

Joseph was known by his trade as a carpenter. As just mentioned, Joseph, like his betrothed wife to be, was also of the line of King David. However, Joseph was not a king, but rather a simple carpenter. This simple but, yet important trade, was central to the common economy in Nazareth as most things during this time would have been made from either wood, stone, bone, bricks, leather, wool, cotton, flax, or some other type of natural items. Joseph is identified as a carpenter in Matthew 13 and again in the Gospel of Mark 6. Jesus is also identified as a carpenter, as it was common in those days in Israel for sons to follow their fathers in their trade. Matthew states the following: "Is this not the carpenter's son?" Whereas, the Gospel of Mark identifies Jesus as being a carpenter Himself. Joseph was also visited by an unnamed angel and told not be afraid to take the now pregnant Mary as his wife, as what was conceived in her was of the Holy Spirit. This was revealed to Joseph in a dream.

Joseph was well within his betrothed rights, to have Mary stoned to death for assumed adultery, or, at the very least, divorce her, or to have her "put away." In the divine dream, God puts upon Joseph to take this betrothed and pregnant woman to be his wife as recorded in the first chapter of Matthew's gospel. To be sure, this out of wedlock pregnancy had to be quite the small-town scandal in Nazareth. This social scandal may have persisted throughout the lives of Joseph, Mary, and Jesus. This scandal may have been compounded by the fact that Mary proclaimed that Jesus was of Divine conception.

In Roman Catholic circles, Mary is most esteemed; blessed among all women, and considered to be clean of any original sin, or thus immaculate, and venerated above all others to the point of being almost worshipped by some. She is considered nearly divine, the Queen of Heaven, with prayers being offered to her by some. She is most always referred to as "The Virgin Mary." In contrast to the Old Church, the Holy Scripture tells us that Mary and Joseph went on to have other sons and daughters. Mary is supposed to have remained in a perpetual state of virginity throughout her whole life in Catholic doctrine, thoughts, and beliefs. The Gospels of Matthew and Mark give us lists of Jesus having other siblings. Mary and Joseph were the parents of these children. Conservative and traditional Roman Catholic thought is most staunch on the perpetual virginity of Mary and will hypothesize that these other children were from a previous marriage of Joseph. However, there is nothing in Scripture to substantiate this concept. Matthew 13:55-56 and Mark 6:3 state that Jesus had four brothers: James, Joses, Simon, and Judas as well as an unknown number of unnamed sisters. Mark 3 also speaks of Jesus' brothers and Mary. The Apostle Paul in his letter to the Galatians, refers to James, the Lord's brother. However, it is paramount to point out that Mary was a physical virgin at the point of Jesus' conception and birth which was of the Holy Spirit, the third part of the Holy Trinity. Matthew 1:25 states that Joseph "did not know her till she had brought forth her firstborn son, and he called His name Jesus." It is equally paramount to point out that Joseph, the carpenter of Nazareth, was *not* the physical father of Jesus. Although, the lineages of Joseph and Mary are both listed as being of the line of King David. Joseph was "supposed" to be the father of Jesus, as pointed out in the Luke 3 genealogy. Joseph served in the role as the ever-important earthly father to raise Jesus as his own son and to have passed on the carpentry trade to Him.

We know that Jesus was born to Mary and Joseph in Bethlehem, and they apparently stayed there until he was about two years old when the magi appeared at the house with their gifts of gold, frankincense, and myrrh.

After conferring with the visiting magi, King Herod of Jerusalem threatens to kill the baby boys in Bethlehem, who were two years of age and younger. After this slaughter by King Herod, Joseph took his fledgling family on their flight away from Bethlehem to Egypt and they stayed in North Africa until of all of those wanting the life of the young Jesus had died. After the pilgrimage in North Africa to Egypt, Jesus lived in Nazareth with His family where He learned the carpentry trade from His earthly father Joseph.

Luke 2 relays the following story to us when Jesus was twelve-year-old. Joseph and the family were returning from Jerusalem when Jesus was separated from the family and was eventually found in the Temple with the teachers. Jesus said He was being about His father's business. When they arrived in Nazareth, Jesus was said to be subject to them and that Jesus increased in wisdom and stature and was in favor with God and man. Unfortunately, this is the only account that we have of Jesus' early life. We can only speculate that Jesus lived near His family and perhaps with, or near, His mother Mary in Nazareth as a carpenter until His baptism by His nearkinsman, John the Baptist. This return trip from Jerusalem to Nazareth is also the last account we have of Joseph. We can only suppose that Joseph died in Jesus' adolescent life, or twenties, before Jesus began His ministry at about thirty years of age since the disciple, John was given charge of Mary at the cross in John 19:27.

Mary, the mother of Jesus, is once again seen at the marriage at Cana of Galilee in John 2. During the wedding celebration, apparently, the party goers ran out of the "good wine." Here, Mary informed her Son, "They have no wine." In a most striking and stern reply, Jesus tells His own mother, "Woman, what does your concern have to do with Me? My hour has not yet come." Oddly, Mary instructed the servants to do whatever Jesus says to do. In spite of Jesus' trite reply to his mother, Jesus instructed the party servants to fill the six stone water pots with water to the brim; and so they did. Immediately, Jesus instructed the party servants to draw some of this "water" out of the twenty to thirty-gallon pots and take it to the master of the feast. The servants took the then water as they were told. The master of the feast tasted the water (which was now wine). The feast master called the bridegroom and cross examined him. "Every man at the beginning sets out the good wine, and when the guest have well drunk, then sets out the inferior (wine). You have kept the good wine until now!" It was quite obvious that Jesus was the supreme wine maker. This was not

Welch's grape juice. We will not see the Virgin Mary again until the last week of Jesus' life, where Mary is listed among the women of the cross in the Gospel of John. Jesus addressed John the Disciple and his mother Mary directly from the cross before He died, "Behold your son," and "Behold your mother."

OTHER MARYS

Other, lesser known Marys are also referred to in the New Testament. Perhaps the most obscure of these other Marys is "Mary of Rome." This Mary is mentioned by Paul in his letter to the Romans in a list of other saints in Rome striving and serving for the cause of Christ. (Romans 16:6)

Another equally obscure Mary, is the mother of John Mark. John Mark is the missionary assistant of the Apostle Paul and the author of the Gospel of Mark. This Mary is mentioned in the Acts of the Apostles in Acts 12:12, which was penned by Doctor Luke, who also authored the Gospel of Luke.

Mary the wife of Clopas only appears in the list of women of the cross in the John account. It is possible that she may be the same as the Mary, mother of James and Joses. Likewise, Clopas may or may not be the same person as Cleopas, one of the Emmaus road walkers with Jesus.

In the Gospel of Matthew, Mary the mother of James (the Less) and Joses as she is also referred to, as "the other Mary." It is possible that this Mary is the mother of Jesus. The Matthew account, as with the Mark and Luke accounts do not list Mary the Mother of Jesus, in their accounts of the women of the cross. Only the Gospel of John lists Mary the mother of Jesus being at the crucifixion. Jesus did have two brothers named James and Joses along with Simon and Judas. Although, this is only a valid point of conjecture.

MARY MAGADALENE

Mary of Magdala, or the moniker of Mary Magdalene, as she is better known, was from the town and/or region of Magdala. This town was on the western coast of the Sea of Galilee, where the four fishermen disciples cast their nets for fish, before Jesus turned them into fishermen of men.

She was one of the more prominent female followers of Jesus. Mary is first mentioned in a list of women, of whom evil spirits were cast out of by Jesus. In Luke 8:2-3, Mary is recorded to have had seven demons cast out of her. We cannot be certain as to "who' or "what" these evil spirits were, as the scripture does not stipulate. Any guessing would be mere speculation at best. Other women on this list were Chuza, the steward of Herod, and Susanna.

This Mary is the same Mary who was spoken to by two angels at the tomb of the resurrection. Jesus, in the Gospel of John, spoke to Mary Magdalene and told her not to touch Him as, He had not yet ascended to His Father. Jesus instructed Mary Magdalene to go tell the disciples that He was ascending to His Father. For centuries, in false secular pseudo church teachings, stories, and movies, Mary Magdalene has often been much maligned for having a poor reputation as a prostitute. But was she? What does the Scripture say? The Scripture does not even begin to elude to her being a prostitute. Perhaps, one of the casted out demons may be construed as "the demon of prostitution." This is at best a theological stretch. If this Mary was not a prostitute, then who was? We will explore this further down the text.

In French Merovingian tradition, Mary Magdalene is said to have married Jesus and had children with Him. This is one of the greatest apostasies against Jesus and the Christian faith. If this apostasy were to be true; then the foundation of Christianity would be crumbled to dust. We become a part of Christ through our faith in His blood sacrifice in death and His resurrection. We do not gain access to Christ through a genetic blood line. Once again, what does the scripture say? What does the scripture not say?

MARY OF BETHANY

Last, but certainly not least, on the list of women named Mary, is Mary of Bethany. The small town of Bethany was just a short walk of about two miles southeast of Jerusalem near the south end of the Mount of Olives. This Mary is often associated with her sister, Martha and their brother, Lazarus, who was raised from the dead by Jesus. It is important to point out, that this Mary is always seen at the feet of Jesus, but why? Luke

10:39 says the following: "...Mary who also sat at Jesus' feet and heard His word." This is the story of Martha serving Jesus, while Mary was more interested in listening to Jesus. In the story of Jesus resurrecting Mary and Martha's brother from the dead, we once again find this Mary at the feet of Jesus in John 11:32. "Then, when Mary came where Jesus was, and saw Him, she fell down at His feet, saying to Him, Lord, if you had been here, my brother would not have died." Why was this Mary of Bethany always at the feet of Jesus? Let us explore the text a little further.

In John 8, we find the story of the woman caught in adultery. This took place at the Mount of Olives and the Temple, very near Bethany, where Lazarus, and his two sisters, Mary, and Martha lived. Here, the Scribes and Pharisees brought a woman to Jesus who had just been caught in adultery. Sadly, there is no mention or record of the man of who was with her, in this duet of sin. The Scribes and Pharisees boldly informed Jesus that this woman was caught in the very act of adultery. These same scholars further informed Jesus that the Law of Moses commanded them that she should be stoned to death. Stoning was the practice of a group of individuals who were armed with self righteous rocks and stones, for the purpose of, pelting to death a targeted individual, whom they deemed worthy of death due to their sins. Such was the case on that early morning at the Mount of Olives near the Temple.

After the Scribes and Pharisees had leveled their charges against the woman caught in adultery, they were ready to unleash their salvo of stones upon the woman. But first, they asked Jesus what He thought, by testing Him with the hopes of catching Him in a legal web. Jesus, in His calm and cool demeanor, simply stooped down to the dust, as if He had not heard them and began to scribe something in the dirt with his finger, much in the same fashion as a baseball pitcher does on the backside of the mound before he begins to hurl his game. What did Jesus write in the dust with the tip of his finger? We can only speculate. Just as coolly and calmly as Jesus stooped to the ground, he arose from the dust and straightway said to the Scribes and Pharisees. "Hee that is without sinne among you, let him first cast a stone at her," as the 1611 King James Version says. The air was now stilled with stunned silence. Jesus once again bowed Himself to the earth, and once again traced something unto the surface of the ground with the same calmness of a child in a sandbox. Beginning with the oldest to the youngest, they all dispersed from their rock-slinging-circle, leaving Jesus with the woman who was standing in their midst.

We can only imagine the horror and fear which may have been pounding through the arteries of the woman caught in adultery. For the second time, Jesus rose from the ground and said to the woman, "Woman, where are those accusers of yours? Has no one condemned you?" She likely responded in a trembling and yet humble and gracious tone, "No one Lord." Then Jesus said, "Neither do I condemn you; go and sin no more." WOW!!! Jesus was in no way ignoring the fact that the woman sinned, as all sin must be forgiven. Rather, the point was two-pronged, as fellow sinners are not to condemn other fellow sinners, as we are not worthy to do so. The second point was, "Go and sin no more." We are to turn from our sinful ways and follow Jesus. This is the real Jesus who came not to condemn the world, but rather to save us from our sins. Hold on to this thought of a woman at the Mount of Olives, who was caught in adultery, whom Jesus saved from being stoned.

All four Gospels give an account of Jesus going to a house in the town of Bethany, where Jesus had a mysterious woman anoint His body with an expensive substance. Who was the woman and why did she do this at the feet of Jesus? This parallel story is recorded in Matthew 26, Mark 14, Luke 7 and finally in John 12. Here are the following common themes:

THE HOUSE IN BETHANY

The Gospel of Matthew, written by Matthew the disciple, addresses the house in Bethany this way:

"And when Jesus was in Bethany, at the house of Simon the leper…"

The Gospel of Mark describes the house in Bethany in this manner:

"And being in Bethany at the house of Simon the leper, as He sat at the table…"

Doctor Luke in the third Gospel mentions the house in Bethany in the following:

"Then one of the Pharisees asked Him to eat with him. And He went to the Pharisees' house and sat down to eat."

In verse 40, Jesus addresses the Pharisee by name as Simon.

In the Fourth Gospel, John the disciple records the house in Bethany this way:
"Then, six days before the Passover, Jesus came to Bethany, where Lazarus was who had been dead,
whom He had raised from the dead. There they made Him a supper; and Martha served."

In verse 4, the disciple Judas Iscariot is listed as Simon's son. From these verses, we may piece together that the father of Judas Iscariot was named Simon and that this Simon was a Pharisee, as well as, a leper. Leprosy was the dreaded skin disease which was somewhat common during this time in Israel. Pharisees were one of the leading Jewish religious classes in Israel during the time of the New Testament.

THE WOMAN AND THE FLASK

The Gospel of Matthew records the woman with the flask in this manner:
"...a woman came to Him having an alabaster flask of very costly fragrant oil"

The Gospel of Mark records the woman with the flask in this manner: "a woman came having an alabaster flask of very costly oil of spikenard"

The Gospel of Luke records the woman with the flask in this manner:
"And behold a woman in the city who was a sinner, when she knew that Jesus sat at the table in the Pharisee's house, brought an alabaster flask of fragrant oil."

The Gospel of John records the woman with the flask in this manner:
"Then Mary took a pound of very costly oil of spikenard, anointed the feet of Jesus, and wiped His feet with her hair. And the house was filled with the fragrance of the oil.

From the above set of parallel verses, we can conclude that a Woman

(Mary? Which Mary?) had an alabaster box full of very expensive fragrant spikenard oil

THE ANNOINTING

The disciple Matthew in his Gospel describes the anointing of Jesus in this way:
"…and she poured it on His head as He sat at the table."

John Mark in his Gospel describes the anointing of Jesus in this way:
"Then she broke the flask and poured it on His head.

Doctor Luke, the companion of Paul, in his Gospel describes the anointing of Jesus in this way:
"…and stood at His feet behind Him weeping; and she began to wash His feet with her tears
and wiped them with the hair of her head; and she kissed His feet and anointed them with the fragrant oil."

The Disciple John in his Gospel describes the anointing of Jesus in this way:
"Then Mary took a pound of very costly oil of spikenard, anointed the feet of Jesus, and wiped His feet with her hair. And the house was filled with the fragrance of the oil."

From the anointing we can gather that the Woman anointed both Jesus' head and feet and wiped them with her hair after she washed Jesus' feet with her tears.

THE INDIGNANT ONES

Matthew relays to us the following about the indignant ones:
"But when His disciples saw it, they were indignant, saying, Why this waste? For this fragrant oil might have been sold for much and given to the poor."

Mark relays to us the following about the indignant ones:

"But there were some who were indignant among themselves, and said, Why was this fragrant oil wasted?

For it might have been sold for more than three hundred denari and given to the poor. And they criticized her sharply."

Luke relays to us the following about the indignant ones:

"Now when the Pharisee who had invited Him saw this, he spoke to himself saying, This man, if He were a prophet, would know who and what manner of woman this is who is touching Him, for she is a sinner."

John relays to us the following about the indignant ones:

"But one of His disciples, Judas Iscariot, Simon's son, who would betray Him, said, Why was this fragrant oil not sold for three hundred denari and given to the poor? This he said, not that he cared for the poor, but because he was a thief, and had the money box; and he used to take what was put in it."

Lots of different points can be gathered together from this set of verses: The host of the house, Simon, the Leper Pharisee, was not pleased with the "sinner woman" being in his house. Simon was also recorded as being the father of Judas Iscariot. Judas Iscariot, one of the disciples, along with some of the other disciples, were not pleased with the woman and what they perceived as an expensive waste of the fragrant oil which may have been sold for three hundred denari and given to the poor.

THE MEMORIAL

Matthew shares with us in his Gospel the following about the memorial regarding the woman:

"But when Jesus was aware of it, He said to them, Why do you trouble the woman? For she has done a good work for Me. For you have the poor with you always, but Me you do not have always. For in pouring this fragrant oil on My body, she did it for My burial. Assuredly, I say to you, wherever this gospel is preached in the whole world, what this woman has done will be told as a memorial to her."

Mark shares with us in his Gospel the following about the memorial regarding the woman:

"But Jesus said, Let her alone. Why do you trouble her? She has done a good work for Me. For you have the poor with you always, and whenever you wish you may do them good, but Me you do not have always. She has done what she could. She has come beforehand to anoint My body for burial. Assuredly, I say to you, wherever, this gospel is preached in the whole world, what this woman has done will also be told as a memorial to her."

Luke shares with us in his Gospel the following about the memorial regarding the woman:

"Then He turned to the woman and said to Simon, Do you see this woman? I entered your house; you gave Me no water for My feet, but she has washed My feet with her tears and wiped them with the hair of her head. You gave Me no kiss, but this woman has not ceased to kiss My feet since the time I came in. You did not anoint My head with oil, but this woman has anointed My feet with fragrant oil. Therefore I say to you, her sins, which are many, are forgiven, for she loved much. But to whom little is forgiven, the same loves little. Then He said to her, Your sins are forgiven. And those who sat at the table with Him began to say to themselves, Who is this who even forgives sins? Then He said to the woman, Your faith has saved you. Go in peace."

John shares with us in his Gospel the following about the memorial regarding the woman:

"But Jesus said, Let her alone, she has kept this for the day of My burial. For the poor you have with you always, but Me you do not have always."

Jesus rebuts, Simon His host, as well as Simon's son, Judas Iscariot, the disciple, as well as, the other disciples at the dinner. Jesus tells them that this was not a waste of fragrant oil. Because you will always have the poor with you and you always have the opportunity to do good to them. Jesus goes on to defend the woman and says that her actions were a preparation for His own burial. This woman, which was, in fact, a sinful woman, has her sins forgiven and what she has done should be always remembered throughout the world as a memorial to her.

BETHANY CONCLUSIONS

In the broader scope, from what the scripture says: we can conclude all the following from the anointing at Bethany.

1) The dinner took place in Bethany.
2) The dinner was in the house of the Pharisee, Simon the Leper, the father of Judas Iscariot.
3) Judas Iscariot and the other disciples were in attendance.
4) Recently raised from the dead, Lazarus and his two sisters Mary and Martha were in attendance.
5) A sinful woman brought an alabaster box full of one pound of fragrant oil costing 300 denari.
6) The sinful woman anointed both Jesus' head and feet.
7) The sinful woman additionally washed Jesus' feet with her tears and wiped them with her hair.
8) Judas, as well as, the other disciples were "indignant" about their perceived waste of the oil.
9) Simon the Pharisee was inwardly critical of the sinful woman anointing Jesus.
10) Jesus instructs the dinner party that they can always tend to the poor.
11) Jesus forgives the sinful woman of all her sins and memorializes her anointing.

With all of this said, was Mary Magdalene the Mary prostitute of the New Testament?

For millennia, she has been maligned as being a prostitute. She has been marked with this moniker for no reason. There is absolutely nothing in scripture to even mildly suggest her being a scarlet women of the evening. Some may want to speculate that one of the seven demons which were cast out of her was the "demon of prostitution," however, this is a Bible page thin speculation at best. If this was the case, then what were the other demons, and where is the Biblical foundation for such a premise? There is none. Mary Magdalene as a prostitute is a false premise. Furthermore, the heretical myth of Mary Magdalene and Jesus being married and bearing children, which became the fore-runners of some of the royal households of Europe, is nothing more than a fabled falsehood. This is a false secular narrative to discredit Jesus Christ and the whole of Christianity.

This is *not* a Biblical conundrum. The Gospel of John *clearly* states who the "Mary Prostitute" is. John's Gospel in both 12:3 and 11:2 states that Mary of Bethany was the woman who anointed Jesus' head and feet and washed His feet with her tears and wiped them with her hair. Simon the Pharisee lived in the same town of Bethany, as did Lazarus and his two sisters Martha and their sister Mary. Due to the close proximity of them all living in the same small town of Bethany, Simon the Pharisee is easily able to identify this Mary as a "sinner woman." Can we, as Bible readers, equate: "sinner woman" to "prostitute?"

Each time we see Mary of Bethany with Jesus, she is at Jesus' feet. Why is this? Is it possibly because Mary of Bethany was so thankful to Jesus for Jesus possibly saving her life? This is the Biblical textual conjecture: Was the woman caught in adultery at the Mount of Olives the same as Mary of Bethany? It is a distinct possibility. The geography works as Bethany and the Mount of Olives are contiguous to each other just east of Jerusalem. Jesus certainly saved the life of this woman caught in adultery from a gruesome death by stoning at the hands of Pharisees and others. It is near certain that this saved woman would forever be thankful for having her life saved by Jesus.

Based on what the scripture says, we can safely conclude that Mary of Bethany was some sort of a "sinner woman," perhaps a prostitute. However, can we assert that this was the same woman who was about to be stoned for adultery at the very nearby Mount of Olives? This is a possible speculation. These are dig and discover discussion points. Do you believe that Mary Magdalene is the prostitute of the New Testament or do you believe it was someone else? Was it Mary of Bethany? In the end, Jesus can forgive all of us for all our sins, regardless of the stain of sin. In the end, we must go and sin no more.

{Editorial note: Harrison Cyrus questions why was Simon the leper disdainful towards the "sinner woman." Why did Jesus show more compassion for the sinner woman than Simon the leper?"}

{Editorial note: Editor David Foster ascerts that the figure of Mary Magdalene was seen as a female equal to the twelve male disciples by Jesus. Foster further suggest that the overall teachings of Jesus supports the notion of equality between the sexes. The early church "fathers" of 2000 years ago and since would have simply found it unacceptable to have a woman as a spiritual equal. This type of thinking was also contrary to the writings of the Apostle Paul in his letter to the Galatians in 3:28. "There is neither Jew nor Greek, there is neither slave nor free, there is neither male nor female; for you are all one in Jesus Christ." Foster points out that all of the compilers of the Canon were male, as well as, all of the early church clergy were men. These gender inequities have reached down to us today. Foster also argues that the full message of Jesus was lost due to our own prejudices which is why we have fallen short of God's glory.}

Questions and Discussion for
Chapter Ten – Mary
Dig – Discover – Discuss

1. How many women in the New Testament were named Mary? List them here.

2. Do you believe that Mary the mother of Jesus was a virgin at the conception and birth of Jesus? Discuss.
   Do you believe, based on Matthew 13:55 and Mark 6:3, that Mary, the mother of Jesus, had more children by Joseph?
   Or, do you believe, based on Scripture that she remained a perpetual virgin? Explain.

3. Based on Luke 8:2, do you believe that Mary Magdalene was a prostitute? Why?
   Do you believe that one of the demons that Jesus casted out of Mary Magdalene could have been the demon of prostitution?
   If Mary Magdalene was not a prostitute, then which Mary, if any, was? Explain.

4. Do you believe that Mary of Bethany was the woman at the anointing of Jesus feet at Bethany? Explain and discuss.

5. In John 8, is it possible that Mary of Bethany was the woman at the Mount of Olives, near the Temple, who was caught in adultery, whom Jesus saved from being stoned to death? Explain.

6. Why did Simon the leper show distain for the sinner woman? Are there times in our lives in which we as Christians show disdain for those we perceive as unsaved? Why?

7. Why did Jesus show more favor for the sinner woman than for Simon the leper? Why did Jesus distinguish a difference in the hospitality of Simon the leper by hosting the dinner, and the anointing and foot washing by the sinner woman?

Chapter Eleven

Merry Christmas

"In the beginning was the Word, and the Word was with God, and the Word was God. He was in the beginning with God. All things were made through Him and without Him nothing was made that was made. In Him was life, and the life was the light of men. And the light shines in the darkness, and the darkness did not comprehend it … And the Word became flesh and dwelt among us, and we beheld His glory, the glory as of the only begotten of the Father, full of grace and truth."

This above scripture is recorded in the beginning of John's Gospel. These few verses are a compact composite of several foundational Christian beliefs and orthodox theology. Not only does this small amount of scripture record the creation with Christ as the prime mover of creation and the Trinity of God the Father, the Son, and the Holy Spirit; but also, the physical birth of Jesus, the Christ, the Christmas event. We know that the Christmas event of Jesus' physical birth in Bethlehem was not Jesus' first appearance to planet Earth. We know that Jesus was recorded several times in the Old Testament in the forms of Theophanies or more specifically, in Christophanies as, *God in the flesh*.

We have seen Christmas movies, church plays, Christmas cards, and various Christmas art portraying the shepherds with their angelic choirs in concert with the "three" wise men from orient are, with their camels and Christmas star. How accurate is this composite of shepherds and wise men congregating around the Bethlehem manger of the Messiah? Sadly, in short, it is not.

Before we get too far ahead of ourselves, we must begin with the prophecies of the coming of the Messiah, the Christ, the Anointed One.

THE PROPHECIES

Taken as a whole, the Old Testament scripture points toward the birth and ministry of Jesus Christ. A few scriptures stand out amoung the many. The magi point out to King Herod, the following: "But you Bethlehem, in the land of Judah, Are not the least among the rulers of Judah; For out of you shall come a Ruler Who will shepherd My people Israel," which is a New Testament paraphrase pulled from the Old Testament minor prophet Micah 5:2. It is quiet possible that these three kings of the orient, were familiar with this text because of the Babylonian capitivity.

Another familiar Old Testament text pointing towards Jesus' birth is found in the major prophet text of Isaiah 7 "Behold, the virgin shall conceive and bear a Son, and shall call His name Immanuel."

THE GENEALOGIES OF JESUS

The Gospel of Matthew directly begins with a genealogy of Jesus originating with Abraham. This genealogy ends in this particular way: "And Jacob begot Joseph, the husband of Mary, of whom was born Jesus who is called Christ." Complementary to the Matthew genealogy, the Gospel of Luke, starting in Luke 3:23, gives us a reverse order genealogy which reads in this manner: "Now Jesus Himself began His ministry at about thirty years of age being (as was supposed) the son of Joseph, the son of Heli." Besides being a reverse order, this genealogy goes all the way back to Adam, "…the son of Seth, the son of Adam, the son of God."

What is perplexing about these two genealogies, is that they both appear to come through Joseph. We know that Joseph is only the "supposed" father of Jesus, the earthly father of Jesus, since Jesus was conceived through the Holy Spirit, not having a physical/biological earthly father. This makes Jesus 100% Divine and concurrently, 100% human being, as he was birthed by the Virgin Mary in Bethlehem.

Can we ask the question, which line is of Mary? Which line is of Joseph, if any? Traditionally, wives, mothers, sisters, and women, taken as a whole, were generally not included in Jewish genealogies. The Matthew genealogy begins with Abraham and runs through King David and King Solomon. This is referred to by some as the majestic or royal genealogy of Jesus. Whereas, the Luke genealogy begins with Jesus and runs in reverse order. From Jesus, this line goes all the way back to Adam. This is sometimes called the physical genealogy of Christ. In this Luke genealogy, Nathan instead of King Solomon, follows his father, King David.

A point to consider: Was Joseph the son of Jacob as per Matthew, or was Joseph the son or Heli as per Luke? Was Mary the daughter of Heli with Joseph being the son-in-law of Heli? Some scholars will assert that the later is the case with Mary being the daughter of Heli with Joseph having the honor of being the son-in-law of Heli. This is a Biblical conundrum of the first order. This is another dig and discover discussion point.

It would appear in doing this genealogy puzzle that the Luke genealogy is most likely the genealogy of Mary and the Matthew genealogy is of Joseph, the non-biological, earthly father of Jesus. A fuller description of genealogies is discussed under the Genealogies section in the List chapter. An interesting biological question therefore is, did Jesus only carry genes from Mary, or did Jesus only carry divine genetics? We can never know the answer to this scientific and theological conundrum. However, the better question is: Do you belong to the family of God through the blood of Jesus which was sacrificed for you? Are you an adopted son or daughter of God?

VISIONS AND DREAMS

The Christmas story is in three different New Testament locations. The most brief account is the above mentioned description in the first chapter of John's gospel. This is proceeded by the classic Luke account with the shepherds and angels. "Lights Please." No one has ever read this account with more sincerity, conviction, and purpose than the blanket dragging child of Linus Van Pelt, the younger brother of Lucy Van Pelt, and neighbor of Charlie Brown, in the children's Christmas cartoon classic by Charles Schultz in 1965. Finally, the Matthew account is concerned with the magi and the mystical Christmas star. Strangely, the original gospel, penned by Mark, does not have a Bethlehem birth narrative of Jesus. Mark rather shoots straight and "immediately" into the adult ministry of Jesus. Jesus was baptized by his near relative, John the Baptist. John baptized Jesus in the Jordan River while the Holy Spirit descended upon Jesus like a dove.

The Gospel of Luke gives us the narrative of the angel Gabriel visiting Mary in Nazareth in chapter one. As discussed in the Mary chapter of this book, Gabriel announced to Mary of the pending divine intervention of the Holy Spirit which resulted in the virgin conception and birth of Jesus. Prior to Mary's dream, Mary had a near relative, Elizabeth, who was married to Zacharias. Zacharias had a vision in the Temple while he performed his duties of the priesthood. In this vision, the angel Gabriel informed Zacharias that his late age barren wife would bare a son and that he would be named John. This John would be known as John the Baptist. He would be a prophet in the spirit of Elijah. Zacharias doubted the announcement of Gabriel, so Gabriel stated that Zacharias would be mute until the birth of John.

Matthew 1 reveals to us another vision. An unnamed angel appeared to Joseph in a dream. In this dream, the angel said to Joseph, "Joseph, son of David, do not be afraid to take to you Mary your wife, for that which is conceived in her is of the Holy Spirit." After the birth of Jesus, the family is divinely warned again in a dream to take their flight to Egypt in Matthew 2. After the death of Herod, the angel of the LORD appeared to Joseph and informed him that it was once again safe to return Israel. An even bigger angel event is yet to be discussed. Additionally, the wise men were also divinely warned in a dream that they should not return to Herod.

THE LUKE ACCOUNT

"And it came to pass in those days that a decree went out from Caesar Augustus that all the world should be registered," or taxed, as it says in the KJV, is how the Luke Christmas nativity narrative begins. Judea, as this Roman province was known at the time of Jesus' birth, was on the extreme eastern frontier of the Roman Empire. Judea was south of the province of Syria, along the western edge of the Arabian Desert and the extreme eastern coast of the Mediterranean Sea. Most of northern Africa which was along the northern edge of the great endless expanse of the Sahara Desert from Egypt, to Libya, to the kingdoms of the Vandals and Cyrene, to

Carthage and Mauretania, the land of the Moors, in northwest Africa, was all under control of the Caesars south of the Mediterranean Sea. All the various provinces of Asia Minor, also known as Turkey, as well as Greece, Macedonia, Dacia, and the lands of the Visigoths, all of Gaul, later to be known as France, the entire boot of Italia, as well as the Iberian Peninsula of Hispania with the various groups of Spaniards and Portuguese, were also paying alms to the Empire on the Seven Hills of Rome. To the north, most of lower Germania, Belgica, and the other surrounding low countries were under the thumb of Rome. Across the English Chanel, the northern end of Britannia later to become Scotland, was left mostly unconquered due to the ferocious Celts. The Romans purposely built Hadrian's wall in about 120 AD, to keep out the kilted warriors. However, the lower part of Britannia fell beneath the oversight of the Eagle of Rome. So all of the world was to be registered for a census and taxed under Caesar Augustus, to include the lowly town of Nazareth in Galilee.

Since Joseph, the carpenter of Nazareth, was of the house and lineage of King David, he was obliged to go to his ancestral home town of Bethlehem, to be registered for census and taxes. In much of traditional Christmas art, and theater, we see the traveling duo traversing south out of Nazareth to Bethlehem, with the obviously pregnant Mary, attired in light blue, astride a gray donkey, escorted by the brown clad Joseph, leading the beast of burden with a short leather tether with perhaps a shining star above them. We don't know if any of these colorful details are accurate according to scripture and history. However, all these unknown artistic details are likely scenarios somewhat close to the truth. It is likely it took the Nazarene couple at least a few days to traverse the roughly seventy miles south through the rugged hill country of Judea, either by foot, or by beast, or cart. Despite classic and modern art, and theater, they were likely in a caravan, with fellow travelers for safety. Not only were they not traveling via train, plane, or automobile, they were likely not on a smooth paved road. This trail of travel for them was most likely a crude mud, dirt, and/or rocky gravel road. However, it is possible that the occupying Romans had upgraded it a bit for their own convience. Common hazards of travel during this time would have been the despised robbing highwaymen, taking advantage of weary and unwary travelers. The weather would have always been a constant concern, since travlers were perpetually exposed to the elements while traveling. There was the possible threat of wild animals such as lions, bears, and so-forth, or packs of wild, or strange roving dogs. Signage may not have been the best, so getting lost was always a possible peril. Memory from previous travels would have been your best sign post.

We can only imagine the brave disposition Mary had to have, to endure this treacherous trek, being so advanced into her pregnancy. What was going through the mind of Joseph? He had in tow, this young woman of whom he is only engaged to, about to give birth to a divine son. What was it going to mean to be a father? What were going to be the challenges of trying to raise a divine son? In the mean time, he was about to face an unknown registration by the local Jews and occupying Romans. It is likely that the roads going in the general direction of Bethlehem and greater Jerusalem, had to be filled with anxious and weary travelers, not really knowing what to expect from the Roman officials once they reached their registration destination.

As per the scripture, due to the concentrated crowds, "…there was no room for them in the inn." Mary and Joseph are presumed to be in some sort of stable, cave, or barn since this is where mangers, or feed troughs, for animals are located. It is here in the humble surroundings that the Virgin Mary gives birth to Jesus the Christ. In short, Jesus was born in a barn. Here we have half of our traditional setting of the birth of Jesus. Joseph, Mary, and the baby Jesus, are surrounded by perhaps some cattle, some sheep, goats, and maybe a gray donkey, as per the traditional art and theater. We can not say with any certainty what animals were present, if any, but this is at least a likely livestock cast of critters. Mary is said to have wrapped Jesus in swaddling cloths and laid Him in the manger or the feed trough. Swaddling clothes are usually thought to be mere simple strips of cloth wrapped around a baby for warmth just after birth. How humble was this? How horrifying this must have been for Mary to have given birth in the smelly and unsanitary conditions of a barn. We have no record of there being any kind of doctor, nurse, or even a mid-wife, being present at the birth of Jesus. We don't know how much experience Joseph had in child birthing. We can only speculate "none" would be a good hypothesis, as most single men were not engaged in such activities then, or now. Regardless, this is how Jesus the Christ, the Savior of the world came into this world.

SHEPHERDS AND SHEEP

"Now there were shepherds in the same country living out in the fields, keeping watch over their flocks by night." This is where a great speculation begins. What time of year was Jesus born? Christians and nonbelievers alike celebrate the birth of Jesus on the twenty-fifth of December. Is this when it happened? The specific year, time of year, or date, is unknown. Many speculate that it was during warm weather, since the shepherds were out in the fields by night. Most livestock are in the fields regardless, of time of the year. Where else would a flock of sheep be? (see author note).

Being a shepherd was the "McJob" at the time. Something most didn't want to do, but many did. This occupation would have been relegated to the young, or otherwise socially, and/or economically disenfranchised. Being out in the weather twenty-four seven has its own built in obstacles. Here, one bears the brunt of scorching sun, blowing wind, pelting rain, sleet, or even snow. If it was not your watch at night, then you slept on the ground, in the dirt, dust, mud, and mire. Most shepherds did not bring a padded posture-pedic, complete with box springs, with them to the field. An extra woolen wrap would be the best one could hope for in the field. Sleeping on the ground for endless nights on end, can be challenging, even for the most hardy of souls. A good shepherd would always have his rod and his staff. This hook and crook would be for redirecting and retrieving lost and troubled sheep from treacherous situations, as well as, for fending off predators and perpetrators both two and four-footed. The safe charge of the sheep would have been the singular focus for the shepherds tending them, in the stead of those who owned them.

From almost the very beginning, the Scripture is full of shepherds. Starting with the slain by his brother Cain, Able was a shepherd, then the first patriarch, Abraham, and his sons, Isaac and Ishmael, and his grandsons, Jacob and Esau, were all men of the field. A great dispute arose between Abraham and his nephew, Lot, over grazing rights. Jacob and his father-in-law, Uncle Laban, also had disputes over ownership of sheep. On the mountains and moors of Midian, Moses was a shepherd with his father-in-law, Jethro, before shepherding the children of Israel out of their bondage in Egypt. From shepherd's crook, to sling-shot, to scepter, King David did more than his share of sheep herding. Apparently, God has a special place in His heart for shepherds. It was quite appropriate that shepherds were present at the birth of Jesus.

Sheep are money. The primary economic purpose of sheep would be wool. Wool is mostly used for clothing. Unlike leather, wool is renewable and obtainable, without having to kill the sheep. However, 'sheep-skins' were used for parchment, and their intestines would be used for strings for musical instruments. Sheep would also be used to a lesser amount for their meat known as mutton. More so with goats, a female 'nanny goat,' produces a rich quality of milk. A steadfast shepherd would do all he could, to care for and protect the sheep which were in his watch-care. For those not familiar with sheep and similar livestock – in short, they stink. Sheep are not at the top end of the learning curve in the animal kingdom. In short, "Sheep are stupid." Domestic sheep are mostly a helpless sort in the animal kingdom. They don't posses much in the way of self defense. Even though goats have horns, as do male ram sheep; sheep do not have any sort of shells or armor. Nor do they posses any sort of talons, claws, fangs, or sharp teeth. Neither do they have keen eyesight. As with most all grass-eaters, they do have great peripheral vision, however, this is off-set by poor depth perception. Although, their eyes rotate in their sockets to keep their vision level to the ground when their heads are down to sheer the grass. Sheep do not run too fast or too far, but can run around aimlessly for a short distance when threatened. All through the Bible, sheep and shepherds are referred to. Christ Himself is referred to as the "Lamb of God" in the books of John and Revelation. In contrast, John 10, Jesus refers to Himself as "The Good Shepherd." We as people are also referred to as lost, or helpless sheep. Sheep are one thing, but a whole host of singing angels is a whole other matter.

IN EXCELSIS DEO

"And there were in the same countrey shepheards abiding in ye field, keeping watch ouer their flocke by night. And loe, the Angel of the Lord came vpon them, and the glory of the Lord shone round about them, and they were sore afraid," as is stated in the old King James. As with Mary and others in scripture, being visited by heavenly beings, one can only imagine the awe and fear the simple shepherds must have felt in their hearts. One moment they are watching their flock by night, just like any other night. Then suddenly, an angel appears to them. As with the other angels; what did it look like? How big was it? Only these shepherds can know the answers to these questions. Even with all their amazement, they listened to the heavenly messenger of God from the realms of glory.

"Then the angel said to them, Do not be afraid, for behold, I bring you good tidings of great joy which will be to all people. For there is born to you this day in the city of David a Savior who is Christ the Lord. And this will be the sign to you: You will find a Babe wrapped in swaddling cloths, lying in a manger."

Not only were the shepherds trying to absorb the mere appearance of the heavenly host, they also were trying to digest this message from the angel. They were trying to process the concept of celestial good tidings from Heaven, as well as, the birth of a baby who is to be the Messiah, of whom all of Israel had been looking and waiting for, for centuries. While just seconds earlier, they were hoping the wind would stop blowing, hoping it would not rain, that a predator, or a thief would not show up, and that the morning sun would soon shine on their face. But more than the morning sun was about to brighten their brows. "And suddenly there was with the angel a multitude of heavenly host praising God and saying: Glory to God in the highest, And on earth peace, goodwill toward men."

How many heavenly host were in this number? Did the night sky split open with a bright and shining light? Once again, what did they look like? Was this multitude different in appearance from the first angel? How big were they? What did they sound like? Did they have harps, or trumpets, or other musical instruments? Only these shepherds can only know these musical angelic details.

"So it was, when the angels had gone away from them into heaven, that the shepherds said to one another, Let us now go into Bethlehem and see this thing that has come to pass, which the Lord has made known to us." This had to be the apex of all that had ever happened, or would ever happen, in their simple shepherd lives? Even though we only have this short discourse which was exchanged between the shepherds, we can be sure, this angelic appearance was something they discussed much and often for the remainder of their lives. However, the question must be asked. Of all the people in the greater Jerusalem and Bethlehem region; why did

God chose to reveal this message through His angels to this lowly lot of common shepherds? Was it because, the priestly class at the Temple would not have accepted a baby born in a barn to an unmarried couple from Nazareth, to be the long awaited Messiah? Was it because the political ruling class would feel threatened by a possible usurper to their scepter? We cannot be certain of God's eternal plans, but we can know from Scripture, that both above situations were, in fact, the case. As discussed above, why not invite shepherds? God seems to have a special place in His heart for shepherds since He has been using them to do His work from almost the very beginning. We don't know how many shepherds were addressed by the angels. We also don't know if they all came into town with the flock in tow; or if some of the shepherds stayed in the field with the sheep?

"And they came with haste and found Mary and Joseph and the Babe lying in the manger. Now when they had seen Him, they made widely known the saying which was told them concerning this Child. And all those who heard it marveled at those things which were told them by the shepherds. But Mary kept all these things and pondered them in her heart. Then the shepherds returned glorifying and praising God for all the things that they had heard and seen as it was told them." We are not certain as to how the shepherds found the family of the Nativity. We can speculate that either the angel told them specifically where this particular manger was; or simply, the shepherds were familiar with all of the possible stable sites which were in Bethlehem since they were livestock effecienados. Did the Shepherds see "the Christmas star?" Where were the "Three Kings" of orient are? We will discuss these issues further down in this chapter.

As discussed above, Mary was pondering all of this in her heart. Continue to keep in mind. Mary just gave birth to her first baby from a divine immaculate conception. She just gave birth in a barn without the likely assistance of a mid-wife, and now she was a new mother of a divine son. This is a lot to ponder for a young, engaged, teenage mother from Nazareth far away from her home in Bethlehem.

Because Joseph, Mary, and Jesus were Jewish, there were birth customs which had to be abided by. After eight days, Jesus was circumcised, and named Jesus, as was the direction from the angel Gabriel. "Jesus" is our English translation of the Greek Ἰησους (Iesous). In the Hebrew/Aramaic, He would have been known as "Joshua" יהושע or "Jeshua" ישוע in his native Israel.

Circumcision was the circular surgery of removing the foreskin of the penis as per the law laid out in Genesis 17. It is possible that a priest, or Joseph himself would have performed the circumcision on the eighth day as per the third book of Moses, Leviticus 12:2-8. Mary had to fulfill her days of purification. It was forty days before Mary could be in public after the birth of a male child. Eighty days would be required for the birth of a female child. The law goes into a lot of details. Having a woman abstain from sex, and have her and the baby out of the public eye for at least forty days would allow the woman to physically heal, and protect both of them from possible disease of being in public. Besides all of this, this would be a good time of bonding between mother and child. Doves or pigeons would be sacrificed to God at the Temple.

While at the Temple, the holy family met the two interesting people of Simeon and Anna. They were both waiting on the birth of the Christ. It was promised to Simeon by the Holy Spirit that he would not die until he saw the birth of the Messiah or the Consolation of Israel as the Scripture calls it. Anna was a prophetess who had been in the Temple for over eighty-four years. According to the Luke account, the family returned to Nazareth after this temple visit.

THE MATTHEW ACCOUNT

"Now after Jesus was born in Bethlehem of Judea in the days of Herod the king, behold wise men from the East came to Jerusalem," is how the Matthew account records the Christmas story in the second chapter. The first chapter of Matthew presents the genealogy of Jesus beginning with Abraham through Jacob to Joseph the husband of Mary. After the genealogy is the Joseph dream sequence in which Joseph agrees to take Mary as his wife.

MAGI, WISE MEN & KINGS

The wise men, we three kings of orient are, the magi, are some of the descriptions of these mysterious gift bearing men who came from the East to visit the young Christ child. Who were they? Where did they come from? Even more strange; why did they risk hundreds or even thousands of miles of treacherous terrain and travel to even come at all? How many of them were they? What? There were three of course! Were there three? What does the scripture say? The scripture does not say how many wise men there were. The scripture simply states wise men came from the east. Through deduction and tradition, we say that there were three kings because there were three different types of gifts presented to the small child Jesus in the house: gold, frankincense, and myrrh. It is quite possible that there were as few as two wise men bringing the three different types of gifts. Or by contrast, there could have been several wise men. The Eastern Orthodox tradition states there may have been as many as twelve magi. This twelve number would have been in symbolic tradition with the twelve sons of Jacob or thus, the twelve tribes of Israel which are often complementary with the New Testament twelve disciples of Christ. In classic and contemporary art and theater, we see three stately men navigating across the high dunes of the desert following a yonder star. It is quite likely that men of their presumed state would have been traveling in a large entourage for their protection and convenience, contrary to Christmas art with the three lonesome travelers who were astride their camel mounts following their yonder star.

"When Herod the king heard this, he was troubled and all of Jerusalem with him." If the multiple wise men came with a large entourage, these international ambassadors would have come with a lot of high maintenance and "baggage," especially since they came uninvited and unannounced to the court of King Herod with the unsettling news of a new king being born in Israel. Some tradition gives them the names of Caspar, Melchior, and Balthasar. Sadly, nothing in scripture substantiates these names.

Most older and traditional English text translations use the term "wise men." However, the NIV and the Catholic New American Bible use the also familiar Greek term of Magi or Μαγοι. It is highly thought these men from the orient were astronomers/astrologist among other sciences of the day. Due to the Jews being in the Babylonian captivity, it is possible that the wise men in this region would have been familiar with the Jewish prophecies of the coming Messiah. The concept of "kings" may come from several sources such as Isaiah 60, "…the Gentiles shall come to your light and kings to the brightness of your rising …" and Psalms 68, "Kings will bring presents to you." So where did the Magi come from? Verse one straightly states they came from the East. This is what the scripture says in two different verses in chapter two of Matthew's gospel. Matthew 2:2 says the following, "For we have seen His star in the East and have come to worship Him." While again in Matthew 2:9 we read the following: "... and behold, the star which they had seen in the East went before them, till it came and stood over where the young Child was." Based on what the scripture says, in combination with traditional thought, and interpretation the magi came *from* the east. Likely locations of tradition are Mesopotamia, or maybe Babylon, or perhaps Persia proper. The interpretation of the text would be understood as "we saw the star *while* we were in the east" as opposed to "we saw the star in the east while in the west looking east." If the later were the case, then perhaps the wise men could have come from Turkey or Greece or perhaps the Island of Cyprus or even the far reaches of Egypt or Libya. However, verse one says they were from the East.

What did these wise men-magi-kings look like? In traditional Italian Christmas Nativity art, they are dressed in long luxurious robes with some sort of royal looking crown on their heads with a box, or flask, containing their precious gifts for the Christ Child. One wise man is usually presented as looking like a white European Teutonic, or Scandinavian Viking king, another magi usually looks like an Arab, or North African, with a dark complexion, whereas a third king is usually portrayed as being an Ethiopian from the horn of Africa, or perhaps a most melanistic looking man from the far east regions of the Indian sub-continent or perhaps Pakistan. When looking at Isaiah 60, several different countries are mentioned: Tarshish, which may have been in Spain. Camels with gold and incense came from Midian, Ephah which is the lower Sinai Peninsula region and Sheba is thought to be Ethiopia. Sheep were said to have come from Kedar or thus, Chebar which was a river in Mespotamia, and Nebaioth which would have been the shepherd tribe from Ishmael. Outside of the blanket scripture statement of saying the wise men came from the East; Who is to say that they all came from the same place? Perhaps the Italian nativity figurine makers were on to something.

All of this is artist license is conjecture at best. Despite imaginary artist and Christmas play directors, with wishful wardrobe, and costume designers, we have no way of knowing with any certainty what the magi looked like. It is for sure, if they were traveling across the desert mounted on a camel, they most certainly would have had more than their share of sand, grit, dust, and dirt on them, regardless of how well they were arrayed in grandiose and opulent regalia.

CAMELS

Traditional and contemporary art and theater most always portrays the traversing trio as being mounted on camels. Camels are mentioned in Isaiah 60 along with kings bringing gifts of gold and incense. If the magi came from the fertile crescent region or beyond, camel transportation would have been the norm of the day, as it still is by nomads, and other traditionalist in the region. Camels come in two primary types. Dromedary camels are the one humpers which are common in the Sahara of north Africa, and most of the Arabian Peninsula, as well as, some other surrounding regions. This variety is long legged and are normally short-haired. They are generally in the light brown to tawny yellow-cream in color. Bactrian camels are shorter and stockier. They tend to be somewhat shaggy in appearance, with their hair having more range in color with the two very distinct humps. These two humpers are mostly found in the southern and central Asia region. Dromedaries are more suited for riding whereas Bactrian types are better suited for carrying heavy loads. Contrary to popular belief, the humps carry fat for fuel instead of water. These furry, humped, spitting, snorting, and often contrary in disposition ships of the desert, often find their way into the tradition and art of Christmas. However, the wise men could have walked there.

GIFTS

The wise men brought three different types of gifts to the young Christ Child. Once to the house, where the young Child was living with His family, the magi presented their gifts of: gold, frankincense, and myrrh. Gold has been a well known and much sought after precious metal since the very beginning, first mentioned in scripture in Genesis 2:11. Of all the words in the Bible, perhaps frankincense and myrrh are some of the most interesting. Even though George Bailey, from the Christmas movie, *It's a*

Wonderful Life, could not spell the exotic perfume, the wise men were still able to present it as one of the first three Christmas gifts. Frankincense which is white to yellow in color, was a perfume extracted from a type of Balsam tree in the Middle East. Sometimes this perfume was even used in food. It is mentioned in the Scripture seventeen times, but only once in the Revelation of John and at the kingly presentation.

The magi presented myrrh as the third gift to the Christ Child. Myrrh for sure wins the award for the most mysterious and oddly spelled word in all the Bible. This spice, like Frankincense, is also oddly listed seventeen times in the scripture, mostly in the Song of Solomon. Myrrh starts out a yellow gum when it comes out of the shrub, but eventually becomes crimson-to-black as it hardens. As with frankincense, myrrh was also used as a spice or medicine. It is unknown as to why these particular gifts were given to a young child. The gold would always come in handy for the family from Nazareth. But why two types of incense? Was this a precursor of Jesus death and burial preparation? The Pharisee, Nicodemus, would wrap Jesus' dead body in cloth similar to swaddling cloths and anointed Jesus' body in about one hundred pounds of myrrh and other spices as recorded by John 19. Here again: dig, discover and discuss.

THE CHRISTMAS STAR

What was the Christmas Star? This is a much debated subject. Many have speculated that the Christmas star was a naturally occurring comet or other heavenly obiting object which was making a trek across the sky during this time. This is a possible hypothesis. Some Christians and scientist alike have asserted that the Christmas star was a celestial confluence of several stars and/or planets lining up to create this "Superstar" for Jesus Christ birth. There are as many star-theories as there are stars in the sky. Like the first theory, this second theory too is possible. Like the great fish in the Jonah saga, is it possible that the Christmas star was a special creation that God created for this special event which is and was the apex crossroads of all human history? Regardless of what it was, God created the Christmas star either in the original creation or as a special creation. The star was a celestial and majestic sign for the magi to come and find the Lord of Lord and King of Kings.

"Then Herod when he had secretly called the wise men determined from them what time the star appeared." When did the star appear? When looking at Matthew 2:16, the star had appeared for two years. "...from two years old and under, according to the time which he had determined from the wise men." We can conclude a few different things. Joseph, Mary, and Jesus had moved out of the humble abode of the barn and were now living in a house according to Matthew 2:11. Additionally, Jesus is referred to as a "young Child" παιδιον instead of a baby, or infant βρεφος as in the Luke account. Based upon the wise men and King Herod conversation; King Herod wanted to kill all male children from two years old and younger. It is possible to conclude that the young Child Jesus may have been about two years old at the house visit of the magi and their presentation of the first Christmas gifts. The following conundrum questions must be asked. Was the Christmas star shining bright for two years? Was the star shining at the birth of Jesus? Is it possible that the Shepherds also saw this Christmas Star while they were entertained by the angelic heavenly host? How did the wise men know to follow this unusual star? Why did they come from a far? Why did they bring their particular gifts? When did the magi begin their trek? How long did it take? What was the genesis of this magi journey? Dig, discover, discuss.

This is what we can know. In the Matthew nativity narrative, the Christmas star is mentioned four times, all of which are in chapter two. "For we have seen His star in the East and have come to worship him." There are some references in the Old Testament which elude to the Christmas star. A brief mention is in Numbers 24:17, "A Star shall come out of Jacob; A Scepter shall rise out of Israel." Another verse is the aforementioned in Isaiah 60:3. "The Gentiles shall come to your light and kings to the brightness of your rising." A similar verse appears in Psalms 72:10-11, "The kings of Tarshish and of the isles will bring presents; The kings of Sheba and Seba will offer gifts. Yes, all kings shall fall down before Him; All nations shall serve Him." Wise men and women still seek him. "Go looking for Jesus before He comes looking for you."

THE EGYPTIAN FLIGHT

In the Luke account, after the visit to the temple to see Simeon and Anna, the scripture tells us the following: "So when they had performed all the things according to the law of the Lord, they returned to Galilee, to their own city, Nazareth." So how do we harmonize this with the Egyptian flight in the Matthew narrative? Here are some options. It is *not* likely that the family left Bethlehem for Nazareth after their Temple visit and *then* returned again to Bethlehem for the magi visit two years later when the family was living in the house. Here again, this is not likely, but an option for you as the reader. Here is what is likely. After the birth in the barn, the family is likely to have stayed in Bethlehem for another two years for unknown reasons. If the Roman occupying and local Jewish governments worked like modern government does now, who is to say how long this registration and taxing procedure took? It is likely that during this time that Joseph would have taken up his carpentry trade in the city of David.

After the presentation of gifts by the wise men, the scripture tells us the following in Matthew 2:12, "Then being divinely warned in a dream that they should not return to Herod, they departed for their own country another way." The scripture goes on to tell us, "Now when they had departed, behold, an angel of the Lord appeared to Joseph in a dream, saying, Arise, take the young Child and His mother, flee to Egypt, and stay there until I bring you word; for Herod will seek the young Child to destroy Him." Following on in Matthew 2:22, "And being warned by God in a dream, he turned aside into the region of Galilee. And he came and dwelt in a city called Nazareth that it might be fulfilled which was spoken by the prophets, He shall be called a Nazarene." A way to harmonize these two narratives is this: Luke simply omits the Egyptian flight and takes the family directly from Bethlehem back to Nazareth. The Matthew narrative adds in the Egyptian flight before ultimately taking the family from Bethlehem back to Nazareth.

How long was the family in Egypt? The only thing we can know is, it was long enough for Herod to die and for his son, Archelaus to be the new King in the Bethlehem region. According to scholar, John C. H. McLaughlin, Archelaus was replaced by another procurator in 6 AD. In the Matthew account, the story jumps straight to John the Baptist and his ministry and ultimately the beginning of Jesus' ministry when He was about thirty years old according to the Luke genealogy. The Luke account gives us the story of Jesus and the family being in Jerusalem for the Passover Feast when Jesus was twelve years old. Based on what the scripture tells us, Jesus was likely to have been about two years old when the family left for Egypt. Jesus was younger than twelve years old before they returned to Nazareth. In Nazareth, Jesus likely continued as a carpenter until he was about thirty. Somewhere in the mix of time, Joseph would have died at an unknown age as Mary appears to be a single widow during Jesus' ministry, death, burial and resurrection.

Sadly, for all our traditional and contemporary art, and theater, it is unlikely singing angels, and shepherds with their sheep in tow, were in the simultaneous company with the camel riding, gift bearing, kings of orient are, with the Christmas star, were at the Bethlehem barn. However, there is no reason for us not to combine and enjoy both narratives together to celebrate the birth of our Lord and Savior Jesus Christ in both the church and public square, on or about the twenty-fifth of December.

In taking a step back, what if we only had the Gospel of Mark or the Gospel of John? Would we have a Christmas celebration? In like turn, what if we only had the Matthew account with the magi or only the Luke account with the shepherds? How different would it be than what we have today? However, in God's divine providence, God gave us all four gospels for the fuller narrative we have today in our Bible. A further review of Christmas will be addressed later in this work in the Appendix of American Christian Holidays.

In short, here is the time line of Jesus' earthly life:

Born in Bethlehem and lived there until He was about 2 years old and then the Flight to Eygpt. Some calculations have Jesus being born about 5-6 BC.

At about 12 years old, we have the account of Jesus in the Temple in Luke 2:42. Jesus begins his ministry at about 30 years old according to Luke 3:23.

There is about an 18-year gap between boyhood Jesus visit to the temple in Luke 3 and the beginning of His ministry in Luke 3. It is speculated that Jesus' earthly ministry lasted anywhere from as short as about 1 year to about 3 years.

{Editorial note: Editor Kellie Cyrus asserts that Jesus certainly did not carry the physical genetics of Joseph; and quite possibly, Jesus may not have carried the physical genetics of Mary either. But rather, Mary may have only have been the physical human surrogant, with Jesus only having Divine genes with a physical human body}.

{Editorial note: Pastor James Gifford echoes traditional thought that Jesus' earthly ministry may have been as long as three and half years based on the three Passovers listed in John 2:13, John 6:4 and John 11:55. Jesus may have started his earthly ministry around 26 AD based on Luke 3:1, "Now in the fifteenth year of the reign of Tiberius Caesar..."}

Author notes: (1) With regards to sheep being in the field during the winter; common and traditional scholarship states that sheep may have been "folded" or thus in a pin or barn. However true this may be, livestock are commonly in the "field" regardless of time of year as structures may not be available.

(2) In reference to the length of Jesus' earthly ministry, about three years is the traditional thought which is based on the three Passovers in John. However, the John 2:13 Passover which is listed first of the three John Passover events is likely 1) not in chronological order since this cleansing of the temple likely only happened once and 2) likely happen last since such a tumultuous event would not have been tolerated more than once by the ruling Jewish officials.

Questions and Discussion for
Chapter Eleven – Merry Christmas
Dig – Discover – Discuss

1. Was Jesus born on the 25th of December in the year 0 or 1 A.D.? Explain.

2. Along with the visitation of the heavenly host, did the shepherds also see "The Christmas star?"

3. Did the shepherds and the wise men show up at the nativity stable at the same time?

4. Why did the angels appear to the lowly shepherds? Likewise, why did the magi come looking for Jesus?

5. Was the Christmas star a natural confluence of existing celestial bodies? Or was the Christmas star a special creation for such a time as this?

6. Based upon scripture, how many wise men, magi, or "kings" were in the Matthew account?

7. The Scripture states the magi came from the "east." What possible countries could this have beee? Explain and discuss.

8. Based on Matthew 2, what was the likely amount of time from Jesus' birth until the wise men arrived in Bethlehem?

9. The magi brought gold, frankincense, and myrrh to the young child Jesus. What are frankincense and myrrh and why were they brought to the house in Bethlehem?

10. Why were King Herod and all of Jerusalem so troubled?

11. How does the Bible reader correlate the flight to Egypt in Matthew with the absence of this story in the Luke account?

12. Discuss if we would have the Christmas celebration and exchange of gifts if we only had the Gospsel of Mark or perhaps John.

13. Discuss the conundrum of why there is little of the childhood and young adult life of Jesus mentioned in the Bible.

Chapter Twelve

INRI

When looking at middle ages and some modern art work of the crucifixion, one will often see a sign placed above the thorn-riddled head of Jesus Christ our Lord and Savior. This is Biblical. When using the cross as a symbol, the Greek Orthodox Church includes this sign as a prominent part of the silhouette and shape of the cross.

In much of this art, a four-letter inscription is often printed: INRI. What is INRI? This is a Latin abbreviation for Jesus of Nazareth, King of the Jews as we would write it in English. All four gospels have a record of this sign placed at the request of Pontus Pilate. The John account states that Pilate himself places the sign above Jesus' head on the cross.

> The Gospel of Levi Matthew states it this way:
> And they put up over His head the accusation written against Him:
> > THIS IS JESUS THE KING OF THE JEWS

> The Gospel of John Mark, states it this way:
> And the inscription of His accusation was written above:
> > THE KING OF THE JEWS

> The Gospel of Doctor Luke states it this way:
> And an inscription also was written over Him in letters of Greek, Latin and Hebrew:
> > THIS IS THE KING OF THE JEWS

The Gospel of John Zebedee states it this way:
Now Pilate wrote a title and put it on the cross. And the writing was:
JESUS OF NAZARETH THE KING OF THE JEWS

In the Authorized 1611 King James Version Bible, it appears this way in the text:
IESVS OF NAZARETH, THE KING OF THE IEWES

John 19:20 continues with: "Then many of the Jews read this title, for the place where Jesus was crucified was near the city; and it was written in Hebrew, Greek, and Latin. Therefore the chief priest of the Jews said to Pilate, "Do not write, 'The King of the Jews,' but He said, 'I am the King of the Jews.'" Pilate answered, "What I have written, I have written."

It is from this Gospel of John quote that we get the INRI abbreviation.
"I" would be for "IESVS" which is Latin for Jesus.
"N" would be for "NAZARENVS" in Latin.
"R" would be for "REX" the Latin for "KING."
"I" would be for "IVDAEORVM" the Latin for (of the) Jews."

(remember: I=J and V=U)

The sign was likely just a scrap of wood with the words crudely and hastily jotted down on it. This was likely done by one of the soldiers participating in this most common, yet gruesome military detail with whatever available ink or paint, which may have been on hand at the time, or even blood. Although, on the converse, assuming the direct involvement of the heavy hand of Pontius Pilate; this could have been a most meticulously crafted sign, done with the utmost care.

The Gospels of Luke and John both mention the three different languages that were placed on the sign. Luke lists the languages in this order Greek-Latin-Hebrew, whereas John orders his list in this manner: Hebrew-Greek-Latin. What was the significance of the three different Languages? The native tongue of Jesus, and the other Jews of the time, was Hebrew and/or the very closely related variant/dialect of Aramaic. The international business language of the Mediterranean Sea region was

Greek, as the Hellenistic Empire under Alexander the Great, controlled the better part of the region previously to the coming of the Roman Empire raging from the west. The Romans, and their ever-encroaching empire spoke the Latin tongue. Most any literate person in Jerusalem at the time of Christ crucifixion, would have been able to read the sign in their native language, if not all three.

The graphics on this INRI sign which was done either in cheap ink, paint, blood or gilded with royal precision, may have looked something like this:

ישוע מן־נאזרת מלך היהודים

Ιησους ο Ναζωραιος ο βασιλευς των Ιουδαιν

IESVS NAZARENVS REX IVDAEORVM

However, this is not the end of the story. In the Old Testament, blood sacrifice was the atonement for sin. Jesus was to be the ultimate blood sacrifice for all sin, for all people for all time. Shouldn't this death of Jesus be enough for our salvation? It may have been, however, the divinity of the Trinity would not permit this to be the end of the story. After Jesus was crucified on what we Christians call "Good Friday," Jesus raised from the dead, on Sunday which we Christians call "Easter," or Resurrection Day.

The ultimate Biblical conundrum is: Where was Jesus between His death on the cross on Friday afternoon until His resurrection early on Sunday morning? For some Christians, this is not an issue. However, for other Christians, this is an issue of grave concern.

Since Jesus was to absorb all sin, from time, and eternity, then it is quite impossible that His Spirit and soul ascended back into Heaven during this interim of time. God and Heaven could not look upon this ultimate amount of sin, and certainly could not allow it into the pearly gates of Heaven.

The early church developed what has become known to us as the Apostle's Creed, which now has various forms depending on which denomination one hails allegiance. Some versions of the Apostle's Creed say, "He descended to the dead," while others say, "He descended into

Hell." What does the Scripture say? In I Peter 3:18,19 and 4:6 we find the following Scripture. "For Christ also suffered once for sins, the just for the unjust, that He might bring us to God, being put to death in the flesh but made alive by the Spirit, by whom also He went and preached to the spirits in prison... For this reason the gospel was preached also to those who are dead, that they might be judged according to men in the flesh, but live according to God in the spirit." This above verse can be linked to Ephesians 4:7-10 which says, "But to each one of us grace was given according to the measure of Christ's gift. Therefore He says: When He ascended on high, He led captivity captive, And gave gifts to men. (Now this, "He ascended" - what does it mean but that He also first decended into the lower parts of the earth.)"

If one wants to say that Jesus went to Hell after He died on the cross while taking all of humankind's collective sins with Him; one would have to equate the above scripture terms of 'prison' and 'the lower parts of the earth' to Hell. This seems to be the orthodox view of most Christians. The former Southern Baptist Theological Seminary professor, Doctor William L. Hendricks, produced a play in 1977 called *The Harrowing of Hell*, depicting Jesus going to Hell, being on trial by the seven deadly sins before personally defeating the Devil before resurrecting. Dr. Hendricks would be in theological step with his Catholic brothers and early church fathers which esposed the same. However, there are many Christians which cannot grasp this concept of Jesus going to Hell. Perhaps His soul just stayed in the tomb with His dead body? This is most unlikely. Most all Christians of various views, believe that Jesus decended to Hell to bury all our sins before raising from the grave and ultimately asending to Heaven as recorded in the gospels of Mark and Luke.
HE IS RISEN – HE IS ALIVE!

Questions and Discussion for
Chapter Twelve – INRI
Dig – Discover – Discuss

1. Share with the group where you have seen "INRI." Did you know it was a Latin abbreviation?

2. What three languages were written on the sign? And why were these three languages used?

3. In John 19, who had the sign placed on the cross and why?

4. In John 19, who disagreed with what the sign said and what did they want the sign to say?

5. At the time of the crucifixion, what might the local ethnic groups: Jews, Greeks, Romans, Arabs and others, have thought about the sign of Jesus proclaiming that He was the King of the Jews? What do you think about the sign considering Jesus died for all?

6. Could the Roman authority have meant for the sign to be a political warning to all who wanted to usurp Roman occupation?

7. Discuss where Jesus was in the time after His death before His resurrection.

8. Discuss how Jesus' death and resurrection atones for our sins and allows for us to become saved.

Chapter Thirteen

"That's in the Bible Somewhere – I Think?"

"That's in the Bible somewhere" or "I think that's in the Scripture someplace," are some of the hopeful and wishful assertions that have been made many countless times since there have been Bibles. Sadly, these verbal miscues and inaccurate misstatements have even been said by numerous well read, and well intended Christians, as well as some pastors, priest and preachers.

The Holy Bible is full of common sayings, stories and words of wisdom, which may fall into the general category of the public domain. These longheld concepts are somewhat ingrained into our western culture. Sadly though, with the speedy secularization of western society, this may not always be the case. However, the Bible is not the only source of such public domain common knowledge. Out of a combination of sincere conviction and/or awkward ignorance, the Bible has been credited and/or discredited for containing quotes, stories, or sayings that just aren't there. Below are a few examples.

"I think that's in Revelations," is perhaps one of the most overused escape hatches in Biblical discussions. If everything that was said to be in the Book of Revelation, were actually in the text, the book of The Revelation would be twice the size as it is now. There is no book of *Revelations*. However, there is the book of The Revelation. There is no "s." The book is also known as the Revelation of Jesus Christ or sometimes as "The Revelation of Saint Iohn the Diuine," as it was labeled in the 1611 version of the King James Bible. In the Greek, it was simply called

Apocalypse Αποκαλυψις, or the revealing or uncovering. This may be considered by some as "nit-picking" or "hair-splitting," but this is about trying to be accurate about the Word of God.

"All men are created equal." In concept, this is a Biblical idea when looking at Scripture such as: Galatians 3:28 or I Corinthians 12:13. We all are equal in the sight of God. It does not matter to God whether we are male or female, rich or poor, or what country we come from. We all are made in the image of God and need to be saved by the grace of Jesus Christ through the Holy Spirit because of the original sin of Adam and Eve. As awesome as a concept as this is, this statement is not in the Bible. This is in the opening lines of The Declaration of Independence written by Thomas Jefferson and signed by John Hancock on July 4, 1776 in Philadelphia, Pennsylvania, in bold letters so large that King George III could see it all the way across the Atlantic Ocean in England. Fifty-five others of the Continental Congress also signed the document. With this thought, we all are created by God, in the image of God. From this perspective, we are created equal. However, due to the stain of sin, none of us are equal at birth. Because of economic and physical differences, none of us have an equal start. Some are born to poverty, whereas others are begotten into the opulence of plenty. Some are born with physical disabilities and/or poor genetics, which will give them a life full of built in hurdles. Likewise, some are born to have the sun shine golden upon their cheeks with physical strengths and gifts. And in this same vein, some are born with the traits of intelligence and ingenuity, whereas others are born to be simple and common. Even brothers and sisters born within the same family with the same genes, and same opportunities, will somehow not be equal. Even with identical twins, life is often not equal. The original intent of Thomas Jefferson and the rest of the founding fathers was, that in spite of individual circumstances, in the United States, one does have the opportunity to rise above the misfortune of their birth and circumstances with hard work and determination under the rights and freedoms accorded in America. We as humanity are indeed equally sinful before God. The up stroke to all of this is that we all can come into the saving grace of Jesus Christ.

"We are gathered here today." As blessed, revered, and many times repeated as the traditional and common wedding ceremony is, it is not in the Holy Scripture. There are as many different wedding ceremonies as there are weddings. However, "We are gathered here today in the presence of God to join in holy matrimony ... Who gives this woman? ... for richer for poorer ... in sickness and in health..." and so forth, are not in the Bible. In spite of many movies portraying priest in grand cathedrals or frontier preachers performing marriage ceremonies while reading from a little black book which appears to be the Bible, it is not in the Bible. Sadly, the traditional wedding ceremony is not in the Bible. However, much of the traditional wedding ceremony is in part inspired, or influenced by the Bible. Then what is in the Bible about weddings? "Therefore a man shall leave his father and mother and be joined to his wife, and they shall become one flesh," is the first wedding in the Bible as recorded in Genesis 2:23. Genesis 24:67 gives to us the following about Biblical weddings, "Then Isaac brought her into his mother Sarah's tent; and he took Rebekah and she became his wife, and he loved her." Genesis chapter 29 tells us of another Biblical wedding. "So Jacob served seven years for Rachel, and they seemed only a few days to him because of the love he had for her. Then Jacob said to Laban, Give me my wife, for my days are fulfilled, that I may go in to her .... And Laban gave his maid Bilhah to his daughter Rachel as a maid. Then Jacob also went in to Rachel, and he also loved Rachel more than Leah. And he served with Laban still another seven years." Ruth 3 and 4 gives us another in depth Biblical model of marriage. "So Boaz took Ruth and she became his wife, and when he went in to her, the Lord gave her conception, and she bore a son." King David had his own version of getting a wife in II Samuel 3:13. "And David said, Good, I will make a covenant with you. But one thing I require of you: you shall not see my face unless you first bring Michal, Saul's daughter, when you come to see my face. So David sent messengers to Ishbosheth, Saul's son, saying, Give me my wife Michal, whom I betrothed to myself for a hundred foreskins of the Philistines. And Ishbosheth sent and took her from her husband, from Paltiel the son of Laish. Then her husband went along with her to Bahurim, weeping behind her." For more interesting Bibical reading on weddings, sex and marriage, read Leviticus 18. Finally, in the New Testament, Jesus makes the water into wine at the wedding at Cana.

"Spare the rod, spoil the child." How many parents have chased their children around the back yard after the children have misbehaved, with a paddle or other like item of corporal punishment in hand? Perhaps the parent is proudly spouting Scripture or what they think is Scripture as they said, *"Spare the rod, spoil the child!"* Sadly, this exact phrase is not to be found in the Bible much to the chagrin of many discipline instilling parents. What is in the scripture is, "He that spareth his rod hateth his sonne: but he that loueth him chastenth him betimes" as is says it in Proverbs 13:24 in the traditional King James Version. Here again, this is not hair splitting, but rather being true to the scriptures. What does the scripture say? What does the scripture not say?

"Cleanliness is next to Godliness." Actually, Godliness is next to "godling" and "godmother" in the dictionary. Cleanliness is between "clean-limbed" and "cleanse." This exact phrase is unfortunately not in the Bible. However, Psalms 19:9 says, "The fear of the LORD is clean, enduring forever." There are well over two hundred verses in scripture about being clean or clean before God in both physical and/or spiritual concepts.

"God helps those who helps themselves." Fortunately, this indignant phase of self righteousness and poor theology is not found anywhere in the Bible. The whole book of Proverbs, is filled to the brim with the concepts of hard work, being frugal, and wise thinking in business dealings, as well as, marriage.

"Ashes to Ashes and dust to dust." This phrase is often heard at funerals, but once again, this phrase is not in the Bible. The creation of Adam, is recorded in the beginning chapters of Genesis, as well as, the forecast by God in Genesis 3:19, state that humanity shall return to dust in death, but once again, this actual phrase is nowhere to be found in Scripture.

Questions and Discussion for
Chapter Thirteen – "That's in the Bible Somewhere – I Think?"
Dig – Discover – Discuss

1. What have you heard others mistakenly quote as being in the Bible? Discuss.

2. How does this affect Christianity and the supremacy of Scripture?

3. How should we confront someone who mischaracterizes scripture for personal gain?

Chapter Fourteen

List

Genealogies

Genesis Chapter Four

The following is the genealogy of Cain, the first son of Adam and Eve. Cain killed Able, the second son of Adam and Eve.

GOD
Adam and Eve – Age unknown at birth of Cain and Abel. Cain killed Abel. Adam lived 930 years
Cain and his wife – Cain's age unknown at birth of Enoch. Cain's age at death is unknown.
Enoch – Enoch's age unknown at birth of Irad. Enoch's age at death unknown.
Irad – No records.
Methujael – No records.
Methushael – No records.
Lamech and Adah - 1
Lamech and Zillah - 2
-1 **Jabel**
-2 **Jubal and Tubal-Cain**

No further records of the family tree of Cain.

Genesis Chapter Five

The following is the Genealogy of **Seth**, the third named son of Adam and Eve.

GOD
Adam and Eve – Adam and Eve are 130 years old at the birth of Seth. Adam lived 930 years.
Seth - Seth is 105 years old at the birth of Enosh. Seth lived 912 years. *
Enosh – Enosh is 90 years old at the birth of Cainan. Enosh lived 905 years.
Cainan – Cainan is 70 years old at the birth of Mahalalel. Cainan lived 910 years.
Mahalalel – Mahalalel is 65 years old at the birth of Jared. Mahalalel lived 895 years.
Jared – Jared is 162 years old at the birth of Enoch. Jared lived 962 years.
Enoch – Enoch is 65 years old at the birth of Methuselah. Enoch lived 365 years and "walked with God."
Methuselah – Methuselah is 187 years old at the birth of Lamech. Methuselah lived 969 years.
Lamech – Lamech is 182 years old at the birth of Noah. Lamech lived 777 years.
Noah – Noah is 500 years old at the birth of: Shem, Ham, and Japheth. Noah lived 950 years.

*Able left no heirs and supposedly all of Cain's heirs died in the flood ... or did they?

Genesis Chapter Ten

A full accounting of the genealogies of Shem, Ham, and Japheth are listed in the Tower of Babel Chapter. Due to the significance of Shem, the Shem genealogy will be listed below

Genesis Chapter Eleven

Noah
Shem – Shem is 100 years old at the birth of Arphaxad, 2 years after the Flood. Shem lived 600 years. **Arphaxad** – Arphaxad is 35 years old at the birth of Selah. Arphaxad lived 403 years.
Saleh – Saleh is 30 years old at the birth of Eber. Saleh lived 433 years.
Eber – Eber is 34 years old at the birth of Peleg. Eber lived 464 years.
Peleg – Peleg is 30 years old at the birth of Reu. Peleg lived 239 years.
Reu – Reu is 32 years old at the birth of Serug. Reu lived 239 years.
Serug – Serug is 30 years old at the birth of Nahor. Serug lived 230 years.
Nahor – Nahor is 29 years old at the birth of Terah. Nahor lived 148 years.
Terah – Terah is 70 years old at the birth of Abram. Terah lived 205 years.

It is important to note the following: To understand the family tree of Abraham (Abram), one must first understand that the phrase, "keeping it in the family," was certainly in full force. In current western culture, the concept of marrying your aunt, your uncle, your cousin, or even your half sibling is most always considered anathema, but that is what they did.

Terah and his unnamed wife or wives gave birth to **Abram** and his two brothers **Nahor** and **Haran** whom may have been either full blood brothers or otherwise half brothers of different mothers.

This **Nahor** brother of Abram is not to be confused with his grandfather of the same name. It is also possible that **Terah** and his unnamed wife or wives may have had some unlisted daughters. This is verified by **Sarai** not being listed in the family tree.

Nahor married his niece, **Milcah,** the daughter of **Nahor's** brother, **Haran.** There is no further mention of the sister, **Iscah,** beyond chapter eleven. **Lot** is the son of **Haran. Lot's two virgin daughters,** get their father Lot drunk and then preceded to get pregnant by their own father. These ill-fated unions, gave rise to the nations of **Moab** and **Ammon** (Genesis 19) This is important to note as later, **Ruth,** a Moabites, is in the family tree of **King David,** and our Lord and Savior **Jesus,** the Christ, as we will see later in this chapter.

Abram marries his half sister **Sarai** which would have been a daughter from a different mother who is not listed in the genealogies. (Genesis

20:12). God changes **Abram's** name to **Abraham** as well as his sister/wife from **Sarai** to **Sarah**. At age 86, **Abraham** has his first son **Ishmael** by **Sarah's** Egyptian slave woman, **Hagar** (Genesis 16). At age 100, **Abraham** and **Sarah** gave birth to **Isaac.**

Isaac the son of **Abram and Sarai,** marries his cousin **Rebekah**, the daughter of **Bethuel**, the son of **Nahor.** Isaac and Rebekah's son, **Jacob** goes on to marry his two cousins **Leah** and **Rachel** who were the daughters of **Laban, Jacob's** uncle, brother of his mother, **Rebekah.** Jacob also takes on as concubines, **Leah** and **Rachel's** two slave girls, **Zilpah** and **Bilah.** **Jacob's** brother, **Esau** goes to his Uncle **Ishmael's** house to marry his cousin **Mahalath.**

Abraham and Sarah – Abraham is 100 years old at the birth of Isaac.
Sarah is about 90 years old.
Abraham lives 175 years (Genesis 25). Sarah lives 127 years. (Genesis 23).
Isaac and Rebekah – Isaac marries his cousin Rebeeca at age 40. Rebecca is the grand daughter of
Nahor and Milcah.
Isaac is 60 years old at the birth of **Esau and Jacob.**
Isaac lived 180 years.

Abraham's wife Keturah, gives birth to Midian. Moses would eventually marry back into this family.

FAMILY TREE OF ABRAHAM

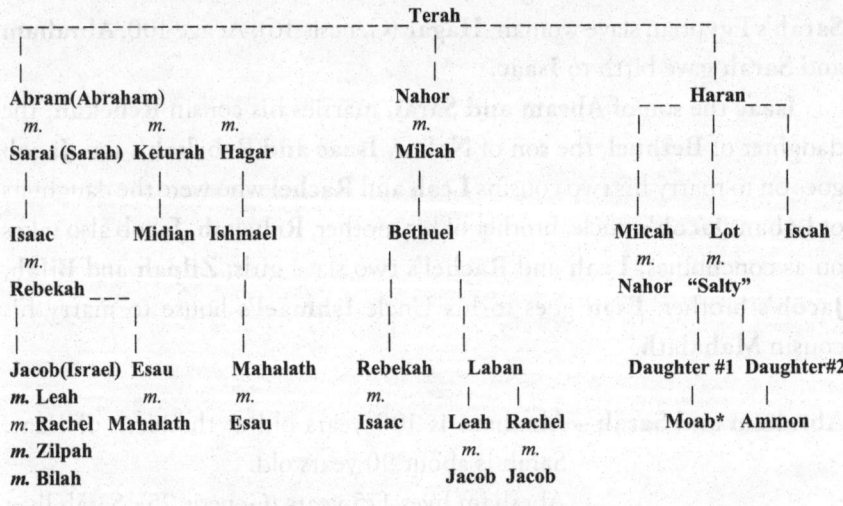

The Twelve Tribes of Israel (Jacob's sons)

Leah	Rachel	Zilpah	Bilah
Reuben	Joseph	Gad	Dan
Simeon	Benjamin	Asher	Naphtali
Levi			
Judah			
Issachar			
Zebulan			

Diana (daughter) (Genesis 29 & 30)

The Twelve Princes of Ishmael
Nebajoth
Kedar
Adbeel
Mibsam
Dumah
Massa
Hadar
Tema
Jetur
Naphish
Kedemah
(Genesis 25)

Sons of Keturah
Zimran
Jokshan
Medan
Midian
Ishbak
Shuah
(Genesis 25)

Sons of Nahor and Milcah
Huz
Buz
Kemuel
Chesed
Hazo
Pildash
Jidlaph
Betheul
(Genesis 22)

Sons of Nahor and Ruemah
Tebah
Gaham
Thahash
Maachah
(Genesis 22)

(Moses marries Zipporah,
a daughter of Jethro
of the line of Midian).
(Exodus 18)

*Ruth was of the line of Moab. Great Grandmother of David.
David was in the line of Jesus through both Mary and Joseph.
However, Joseph was Jesus' legal but not biological father.

Note: *m.* = *married*

GENEOLOGIES

Genesis 5	Genesis 11	Matthew 1	(Matt 1 cont.)	Luke 3	(Luke 3 cont.)	(Luke 3 cont.)	(Luke 3 cont.)
God		**Abraham**	Jotham	God	**Abraham**	Judah	Maath
Adam		Isaac	Ahaz	Adam	Isaac	Simeon	Naggai
Seth		Jacob	Hezikiah	Seth	Jacob	Levi	Esli
Enosh		Judah	Manasseh	Enosh	Judah	Matthat	Nahum
Cainan		Perez	Amon	Cainan	Perez	Jorim	Amos
Mahalalel		Hezron	Josiah	Mahalalel	Hezron	Eliezar	Mattathiah
Jared		Ram	Jeconiah	Jared	Ram	Jose	Joseph
Enoch		Amminadab	Shealtiel	Enoch	Amminadab	Er	Janna
Methuselah		Nashon	Zerubbabel	Methuselah	Nashon	Elm Odan	Melchi
Lamech		Salmon & Rahab	Abiud	Lamech	Salmon	Cosam	Levi
Noah		Boaz & Ruth	Eliakim	Noah	Boaz	Addi	Matthat
Shem	**Shem**	Obed	Azor	**Shem**	Obed	Melchi	Heli
	Arphaxad	Jesse	Zadok	Arphaxad	Jesse	Neri	Joseph
	Salah	David	Achim	Cainan*	David	Shealtiel	Jesus
	Eber	Solomon**	Eliud	Shelah	Nathan**	Zerubbabel	
	Peleg	Rehoboam	Eleazar	Eber	Mattathah	Rhesa	
	Reu	Abijah	Matthan	Peleg	Menan	Joannas	
	Serug	Asa	Jacob	Reu	Melea	Judah	
	Nahor	Jehoshaphat	Joseph & Mary	Serug	Eliakim	Joseph	
	Terah	Joram	Jesus	Nahor	Jonan	Semei	
	Abram(Abraham)	Uzziah		Terah	Joseph	Mattathiah	

*Cainan is listed in the Luke 3 account but is omitted from the Genesis 11 account.

**Solomon the son of King David is listed as a branch of Jesus' family tree, while Nathan the son of King David is listed as a branch of Jesus' family tree.

The Luke genealogy account is in reverse order in the scripture. The order presented in this table is listed in chronological order.

The Matthew account is considered the line of Joseph while the Luke account is considered the line of Mary. However, one must always remember that Joseph was only the legal but *not* the biological father of Jesus.

{Editorial note: Editor Harrison Cyrus theorizes that possible in-breeding could have reduced life spans in the antediluvian world.}

The Ten Commandments

I Am The Lord Your God
Who Brought You Out Of
The Land Of Eygpt Out Of
The House Of Bondage

א

You shall have no other gods before me.

ב

You shall not make for yourself a carved image — any likeness of anything that is in heaven above, or that is in the earth beneath, or that is in the water under the earth; you shall not bow down to them nor serve them. For I, the LORD your God, am a jealous God, visiting the iniquity of the fathers upon the children to the third and fourth generations of those who hate Me, but showing mercy to thousands, to those who love Me and keep My commandments.

ג

You shall not take the name of the LORD your God in vain, for the LORD will not hold him guiltless who takes His name in vain.

ד

Remember the Sabbath day, to keep it holy. Six days you shall labor and do all your work, but the seventh day is the Sabbath of the LORD your God. In it you shall do no work: you, nor your son, nor your daughter, nor your male servant, nor female servant, nor your cattle, nor your stranger who is within your gates. For in six days the LORD made the heavens and the earth, the sea, and all that is in them, and rested the seventh day. Therefore the LORD blessed the Sabbath day and hallowed it.

ה

Honor your father and your mother, that your days may be long upon the land which the LORD your God is giving you.

ו

You shall not murder.

ז

You shall not commit adultery.

ח

You shall not steal.

ט

You shall not bear false witness against your neighbor.

י

You shall not covet your neighbor's house; you shall not covet your neighbor's wife, nor his male servant, nor his female servant, nor his ox, nor his donkey, nor anything that is your neighbor's.

The Ten Commandments are found in Exodus 20:2-17 and again in Deuteronomy 5:6-21.

Comparison Of Old Testament Book Orders

Hebrew/Jewish	Roman Catholic	General Protestant
Genesis	Genesis	Genesis
Exodus	Exodus	Exodus
Leviticus	Leviticus	Leviticus
Numbers	Numbers	Numbers
Deuteronomy	Deuteronomy	Deuteronomy
Joshua	Joshua	Joshua
Judges	Judges	Judges
Samuel*	Ruth	Ruth
Kings*	I Samuel	I Samuel
Isaiah	II Samuel	II Samuel
Jeremiah	I Kings	I Kings
Ezekiel	II Kings	II Kings
Hosea	I Chronicles	I Chronicles
Joel	II Chronicles	II Chronicles
Amos	Ezra	Ezra
Obadiah	Nehemiah	Nehemiah
Jonah	Tobit*	Esther
Micah	Judith*	Job
Nahum	Esther	Psalms
Habakkuk	I Maccabees*	Proverbs
Zephaniah	II Maccabees*	Ecclesiastes

Haggai	Job	Song of Solomon
Zechariah	Psalms	Isaiah
Malachi	Proverbs	Jeremiah
Psalms	Ecclesiastes	Lamentations
Job	Song of Songs (Song of Solomon)	Ezekiel
Proverbs	Wisdom of Solomon*	Daniel
Ruth	Sirach*(Ecclesiasticus)	Hosea
Song of Solomon	Isaiah	Joel
Ecclesiastes	Jeremiah	Amos
Lamentations	Lamentations	Obadiah
Esther	Baruch*	Jonah
Daniel	Ezekiel	Micah
Ezra	Daniel	Nahum
Nehemiah	Hosea	Habakkuk
Chronicles*	Joel	Zephaniah
	Amos	Haggai
	Obadiah	Zechariah
	Jonah	Malachi
	Micah	
	Nahum	1611 King James Apocrypha
	Habakkuk	
	Zephaniah	I Esdras #
	Haggai	II Esdras #
	Zechariah	Tobit
	Malachi	Judeth
		The rest of Esther
		Wisdom of Solomon
		Ecclesiasticus (Wisdom of Jesus, the son of Sirach)
		Baruch

		The song of the three holy children **
		Susanna**
		Bel and the Dragon**
		Manasses
		I Maccabees
		II Maccabees

*The books of Samuel, Kings, and Chronicles are combined into three books, instead of six, in the Jewish text. The Apocrypha books in the Roman Catholic text are intermingled with those of the rest of the Old Testament. Whereas the Apocrypha books in the 1611 Kings James Version are segregated between the Old and New Testament and are not exactly the same books as in the Roman Catholic Apocrypha.

** The 1611 King James Apocrypha books of the Three holy children, Susanna, and Bel and the Dragon are considered parts of Daniel. In the Catholic Bible, these books are intermingled in the Daniel text.

- I & II Esdras do not appear in the Roman Catholic Apocrypha.

{Editor Pamela McIntosh points out that Old Testament and Apocrpha spellings, orders, and actual book appearance, may vary widely depending on what and who one reads.}

A Comparison List Of The Twelve Sons And Twelve Tribes Of Israel

12 Sons in Genesis 29 & 30	12 Tribes in Numbers 1	12 Tribes in Revelation 7
Reuben, *Hated*, by Leah	Reuben	Judah
Simeon, *Heard*, by Leah	Simeon	Reuben
Levi, *Attached*, by Leah	Judah	Gad
Judah, *Praise*, by Leah	Issachar	Asher
	Zebulun	Naphtali
Dan, *Judge*, by Bilhah	Ephraim (Joseph)	Manasseh
Naphtali, *Wrestling*, by Bilhah	Manasseh (Joseph)	Simeon
	Benjamin	Levi
Gad, *Troop, by*, Zilpah	Dan	Issachar
Asher, *Happy, by* Zilpah	Asher	Zebulun
	Gad	Joseph
Issachar, *Wages*, by Leah	Naphtali	Benjamin
Zebulun, *Dwelling*, by Leah		
(Dinah, *Judgment*, the daughter of Leah)		

Joseph, *He will Add*, by
Rachel

Benjamin, *Son of my
right hand*, by Rachel
(Genesis 35:18)

God changed Jacob's name to Israel after God wrestled with Jacob. The actual twelve tribes of Israel differ from the actual twelve sons of Israel in this point. The "tribe of Joseph" was divided into two with the two sons of Joseph, Ephraim, and Manasseh becoming two distinct tribes. This is because the "tribe of Levi" was not given a tribal area due to the Levites being the priestly tribe for Israel (see Numbers 1:47-54). It is interesting to note in the Revelation list of the tribes that Levi, the priestly tribe, is restored in Heaven, whereas they were not given a land grant in Canaan. Oddly, Joseph is once again recognized as full tribe as well as his son Manasseh. However, Joseph's other son, Ephraim is deleted from the heavenly tribe list.

Eventually the tribe of Judah would become one of the more prominent tribes. Perhaps is this why Judah is listed first in the Revelation list. This is especially a point of focus after the nation of Israel split into two after the kingship of Solomon with the northern kingdom known specifically as Israel and the southern kingdom as Judah. The terms Jew and Jewish eventually derived as a corruption of the name Judah. The province around Jerusalem during the time of Christ was called "Judea," a corruption of the tribal area of Judah. The term "Jew" is extensively used in the book of Esther. On a similar note, during the time of Abraham, Isaac, Jacob, up through the time of Moses, the people of God were known as Hebrews. The Hebrew term was first used in Genesis 14 with Abram (Abraham). "Hebrew" or (H)abiru can mean something like "beyond the river" or perhaps "wanderer." Abram, the Hebrew and Sarai came from the land of Ur of the Chaldeans, which is the area of the Persian Gulf near the confluence of the Tigris and Euphrates rivers. The term "Israelite" was first used in Exodus 9, when the Pharaoh referred to the Hebrew people with this name, during the time of the plagues leading up to the Exodus. This Israelite term is not to be confused with the very similar modern term of "Israeli." The current Israelis are the modern Jewish people who live in the nation of Israel which was establish after World War II by the United Nations in 1948. The modern Jew or Israeli in today's Israel may be an ethnic, religious, or political Jew, or some combination of all the above.

This area, previously to the 1948 resurrection of the nation of Israel by the United Nations, was called Palestine. In the scripture, the term Palestine or Palestina is only used in Exodus 15, Isaiah 14, and Joel 3. This is a related term to the Philistines, the people who occupied the southwestern area of Israel along the Mediterranean Sea, or Gaza, or the Gaza Strip, as it is known today. During the time of the Old and New Testaments and even today, this has been a most contested land between the Jews and other people. At first, this land was named Canaan after the grandson of Noah, through Ham. This land retained this name up through the time of Abraham and Moses. The Greek Phoenicians renamed this coastal area Phoenicia. During the time of the Romans, this land was known as Palestine.

Today, in political terms, those who are pro-Israel call this region Israel, whereas those who are anti-Israel, refer to this area as Palestine. A series of short term wars which have been overshadowed by constant conflict, have resulted in the nation of Israel expanding their boarders beyond their 1948 bounds at the expense of their invading Muslim neighbors. This is a constant political tender box. A disputed area west of the Jordan River is called "the West Bank." Before being forfeited in military action, this area was a part of the nation of Jordan. Other areas of dispute are the above mentioned, Gaza Strip, which with the greater Sinai Peninsula, were a part of Egypt. Egypt has since taken back political and military control of the peninsula via treaty, while the Gaza Strip is at times in control of various groups. The Golan Heights in northeastern Israel was formally controlled by the embattled country of Syria. Oddly enough, all these lands have a rich Biblical history with the nation Israel. What was controlled by King David, is roughly the same as what Israel controls today with exception of the "Moab and Edom" regions. Now, as then, the Gaza area was contested, but the southern Negev region is nearly identical to the times of David, as well as, the northern border shared with the nation of Lebanon. Since 1948, the United States has been a political partner with the nation of Israel.

Hopefully, this will remain intact as God made this promise to Abram in Genesis 12, "I will bless those who bless you and I will curse him who curses you." Who knew this Biblical history would stem from Abraham and his wife Sarah. The other side of this coin is Hagar, the Egyptian handmaid of Sarah who gave birth to Abraham's first son, Ishmael. In Genesis 16, Ishmael would be called a "wild man" and everyman's hand would be against him. No truer words would be spoken in all the Bible. This Ishmael issue, along with the very similar Esau event, would be the genesis of the above discussion involving the nation of Israel in both Biblical and present time. To understand what is going on in our world today, one needs to understand what the Scripture says.

A Comparison List Of The Twelve Disciples In The Gospels And Acts Matthew 10 Mark 3 Luke 6 Acts 1

Simon Peter	Simon Peter	Simon Peter	Peter
Andrew	James	Andrew	James
James	John	James	John
John	Andrew	John	Andrew
Philip	Philip	Philip	Philip
Bartholomew	Bartholomew	Bartholomew	Thomas
Thomas	Matthew	Matthew	Bartholomew
Matthew	Thomas	Thomas	Matthew
James, son of Alpaeus	James, son of Alphaeus	James son of Alphaesus	James son of Alphaeus
Lebbaeus Thaddaeus	Thaddaeus	Simon the Zealot	Simon the Zealot
Simon the Cannanite	Simon the Cananite	Judas, son of James	Judas son of James
Judas Iscariot	Judas Iscariot	Judas Iscariot	Matthias for Judas Iscariot

Here are the four lists of the twelve disciples as they are presented in the New King James Version. In Matthew 4, Simon is the first of the disciples to be called by Jesus when Jesus tells the Galilaean fisherman

247

that He would turn Simon and others into "fisherman of men." Simon Peter is always listed first as he is often thought to be the leader of the disciples with Jesus renaming him as Peter or Petros Πετρος in the Greek, or "the Rock" when Jesus said He would build His church upon this rock in Matthew 16. It is thought Jesus renamed Simon, the Rock, because he was a solid individual. On a more humorous thought, Jesus may have renamed him Rock because sometimes he was somewhat on the dense side when perceiving situations. Perhaps it was an insightful dichotomy of both on the part of Jesus. The Apostle Paul sometimes calls Peter "Cephas," Κηφας which means "Stone." Peter is thought by most to have authored the two books which bear his name. Non-Biblical Roman Catholic tradition says all the disciples except John, died a martyr's death. Peter is thought to have been crucified up-side-down. As the tradition goes, Peter did not think himself worthy to be crucified in the same manner as Jesus.

Peter's brother was Andrew. Andrew is listed second in two of the lists, but always in the top four. Andrew is often grouped with Philip and Bartholomew in Biblical thought and content. Andrew and Peter were fishermen by trade as were their business partners, James and John (Luke 5). In tradition, Andrew is thought to have been crucified in Greece in the configuration of an "X," or thus, a Saint Andrew's Cross. Andrew is the patron saint of Scotland. A white Saint Andrew's Cross over lays a blue field on the Scottish flag.

The "Inner Circle" of the disciples is usually thought to be Peter, James, John and sometimes Andrew. James and John are always listed in the top four and James is always listed before John. James and John are known as the sons of Zebedee, or the "sons of Thunder" in Mark 3. Some scholars believe the woman of the cross known as Salome, may be the mother of James and John, and possibly the aunt of Jesus, being the sister of Mary, the mother of Jesus. John the brother of James, is not to be confused with John the Baptist, the prophet, fore-runner, near kinsman of Jesus, who is described in Matthew 3 as eating locust and wild honey while wearing leather clothes in the wilderness, as he baptized Jesus in the Jordan River. John the Baptist was beheaded by King Herod Antipas in Mark 6. John the disciple, the brother of James, is often referred to as the "Beloved Disciple." This John is usually thought to have penned the gospel which carries his name. John is the only disciple not to die a martyr's death, as he died on the Isle of Patmos, sometime after penning the Revelation. John is also mostly given credit for the three smaller letters which bear his name as per our earlier discussion.

James, the disciple fisherman brother of John, may or may not have written the book of James. However, James, the half brother of Jesus, is often thought to have written this letter. This inner circle of Jesus all lived and fished in the northern area of Israel by the Sea of Galilee. In the Greek New Testament, the name James appears as Jacob Ἰακωβος. Apparently, early English translators wanted to avoid confusion with the Old Testament figure of Jacob, the son of Isaac. Tradionally, James the brother of John, is thought to have been beheaded in Jerusalem. As a historical side-note, the supporters of the house of Stewart, in 1715 and 1745, during political and social battles between Scotland and England were called "Jacobites." King James (James VI of Scotland = James I of England = same James) had just put together his Bible translation in 1611. This is important to know if you think King James was important in Bible translation and history.

Philip was from Bethsaida, which is the same home town of Andrew and Peter on the Sea of Galilee. Philip is always listed fifth in all four lists. He is exclusively mentioned in the Gospel of John. Philip recruited Nathanael (Bartholmew?) to be a disciple and was primarily involved with Andrew in the feeding of the five thousand at the Sea of Galilee. Again, with Andrew, Philip introduces Greeks to Jesus at Jerusalem. Philip the disciple appears to be a different Philip from the book of Acts Philip, who is called the evangelist. Tradition has Philip being martyred in Turkey or perhaps somewhere in North Africa.

Bartholomew is one of the disciples who may be referred to as a "silent disciple," as he is only mentioned in the four lists of disciples. He is always listed sixth or seventh. It is possible that he and "Nathanael of Cana," in John 1 and 21 may be one and the same, with two different names just as Peter is called Cephas by Paul. Nathanael is listed with the other disciples on the beach after the Easter event as if he were actually one of the disciples. Nathanael is specifically in mentioned in John 1 where Philip finds him and tells Nathanael that he, with Peter, and Andrew had "found Jesus" and that Jesus was from Nazareth, the son of Joseph. Nathanael quickly and sharply replies, "Can anything good come out of Nazareth?" Philip offers the invitation of, "Come and see." This is what disciples of today still do; invite others to "Find Jesus." Nathanael, is not mentioned in the four lists, particularly by this name. Or perhaps Bartholomew and Nathanael are two different people. Bartholomew is thought to have been martyred somewhere in central Asia.

Thomas is found anywhere between sixth through eigth in the four lists. He is called Didymus or the Twin in John 11, 20, and 21, and is sadly known in common legend as "Doubting Thomas." Thomas said, "Lord, we do not know where You are going and how can we know the way?" But even more so; "Unless I see in His hands the prints of the nails and put my finger into the print of the nails and put my hand into His side, I will not believe." Shorty thereafter, Jesus appears to Thomas and the others and Thomas said without touching, "My Lord and my God." Although, to the Twin's credit, the Gospel of John records Thomas' courage when Thomas said, "Let us also go, that we may die with Him." This was reference to Jesus telling the disciples that He was going back to Judea where the Jewish leadership wanted to kill Him in John 11. Thomas eventually gets his wish to get to die for Christ by dying for Him perhaps in India by a spear, so says tradition.

Matthew appears in the seventh and eighth positions in the four lists of disciples. He is named the "tax collector" in the Matthew list and is called by Jesus to be a disciple in Matthew 9. Matthew is also identified as Levi the tax collector. The names Matthew and Levi do not appear together in the text. However, the stories of Jesus calling the tax collector Matthew and the calling of Levi the tax collector parallel each other. One can conclude or dangerously assume, that Matthew and Levi were the same person with two different names based on the "calling of a tax collector" stories. The name Levi was one of the sons of Israel and one of the twelve tribes of Israel. Perhaps they were two different tax collectors. Mark 2:14 calls Levi the "son of Alpheaus." Even though Matthew was one of the actual twelve disciples and is given credit for writing the Gospel bearing his name, he oddly appears very little in the text. In tradition, Matthew is martyred in Ethiopia by the sword.

James, the son of Alphaeus, is another of the so-called "silent disciples" He is only mentioned in the four disciple lists and is always listed ninth.

This may, or may, not be the same "James the Less" or "the Little" or "the Younger," depending on the particular translation, mentioned in Mark 15:40. This diminutive moniker may have been added because this disciple was either diminutive in physical size or to avoid confusion with James, the brother of John, the son of Zebedee, or James the half-brother of Jesus. This Mark 15:40 reference mentions a "Mary" at the empty tomb of Jesus with Mary Magdalene. This particular Mary is said to be the mother of James the Less and Joses. Is this Mary the mother of Jesus, since Jesus' four half brothers listed in Mark 6:3 are: James, Joses, Judas and Simon? This is another can of worms which is discussed in the Mary Chapter. Since Matthew Levi was called a son of Alphaeus, were Matthew and this particular James brothers? The only time "Father Alphaeus" is mentioned, is in reference to his sons, Matthew and James, thus little is known of Alphaeus. Here are two questions to sort out. Were Matthew the son of Alphaeus, and James the son of Alphaeus brothers? Was the Mary in Mark 15, the mother of Jesus? Jerusalem is where James the Less is thought by tradition to have been beaten to death for the cause of Christ.

Lebbaeus Thaddaeus comes in at number ten on the Matthew disciple list as this is the only list that uses the Lebbaeus first name. The Mark disciple list only calls him Thaddaeus. He too would be listed as a "silent disciple" as this is the only time in scripture he is mentioned. The question is, is this the same disciple as Judas the son of James, listed in the Luke and Acts disciple list? And if so, which James is he the son of? In John 14:22, John is careful to not misidentify this Judas as Judas Iscariot, as this Judas asked Jesus a question. Another tough question is: is this a half brother of Jesus? Not likely since he is called the son of James. Is this the writer of the book of Jude? This Jude book author is often thought to be the half-brother of Jesus or the brother of James as is described in the book. More who-is-who issues to determine. Tradition has this Jude being martyred perhaps in Persia by being shot by a bow and arrow.

Simon the Canaanite, is called such in the Matthew and Mark disciple lists at number eleven, whereas the Luke and Acts disciple lists name a Simon, the Zealot, who is number ten in both these lists. The "Canaanite" and the "Zealot" are thought to be the same disciple. This is all that is said of this silent disciple. It is thought that this Simon is given the secondary name to distinguish him from Simon Peter. Oddly, Jesus had four half brothers named: James, Joses, Judas, and Simon. Strangely, Jesus had two disciples named James, and two named Judas, as well as, two named Simon, none of which appear to be His half brothers. This Simon is thought, by tradition, to have been martyred in Persia.

Judas Iscariot is the last of the original twelve disciples. He is always listed last and is omitted in the Acts list. He is the most notorious of the disciples, as he betrayed Jesus which led to Jesus' capture, mock trials, scourging, crucifixion, and death on Good Friday. This in turn, led to the Easter Sunday morning event, or Resurrection Day! Judas was the treasurer for the band of disciples. He was the man with the money. In John 12, he is said to be a son of Simon. O.K. which Simon? Would this be Simon Peter? Possible, but not likely. How about Simon, the Zealot, or Simon the Cananite, or Simon, the tanner? This is possible, but unknown. Could it have been Simon, the Pharisee, who was a leper, in whose house he was during the anointing in Bethany. This is thought to be the case. During this anointing at Bethany, in the house of Simon, this Judas Iscariot and other disciples are said to be "indignant" because the ointment could have been sold for three hundred denari, or about a year's wages as some count things. After the Maundy Thursday "Last Supper," Judas Iscariot meets Jesus and the rest of the disciples in the Garden of Gethsemane, where Judas betrays Jesus with his infamous "Judas kiss" in Mark 14. From here, the Jewish temple officials capture Jesus and begin His various trials and beatings. In Matthew 26, before the "Last Supper," Judas had met with the Jewish temple officials, and had agreed to turn Jesus over to them for thirty pieces of silver. Judas would soon regret this choice and attempted to return the coins. The sixty-four-thousand-dollar question about the thirty pieces of silver is this; Judas *regretted* his choice to betray Jesus, but did he *repent* to Jesus about this poor choice? We may never be able to know on this side of Heaven. We can only hope that Judas did repent before he took his own life. Although, Jesus says in Matthew 26:24, "The Son of Man indeed goes just as it was written of Him, but woe to that man by whom the Son of Man is betrayed! It would have been good for that man if he had not been born." Now this is another vexing question; how did Judas kill himself? Matthew chapter 27 says that Judas hung himself. The Chief priest then took the thirty pieces of silver and bought a piece of land from a potter in which to bury strangers which would be called, "The Field of Blood." Acts 1 says that Judas "falling headlong, he burst open in the middle and all his entrails gushed out." One could conclude that Judas guts burst out when he hung himself. Either way, Judas took his own life after he betrayed Jesus for thirty pieces of silver, which he regretted. Did Judas take part in the Last Supper with the other disciples and Jesus? According to Matthew, as well as, the Mark and Luke accounts, Judas was present at the Last Supper. The John account is not quite as focused on this detail. Finally, in Acts 1, Judas Iscariot is replaced by Matthias over Joseph Justus by the casting of lots, or dice.

Another man mentioned in Luke, in the Road to Emmaus story was called Cleopas. Here the text infers that this Cleopas was a follower if not an actual disciple Christ. This may, or may not, be the same Clopas husband of Mary, one of the women at the cross of Jesus.

In a final re-cap, this is what we can say about the twelve disciples:

One was a tax collector who wrote a gospel.

Two wrote gospels, two were named Simon, two were named James, and two were named Judas.

Three sets of brothers were in the group, if one counts the sons of Alphaeus as brothers.

Four were fishermen.

Six had at least two or more names. Some could have, or did have, what today we would call "nicknames" such as Thaddaeus, who was also known as Jude. This is much in the same manner as someone today being named William going by Billy, or Bobby for Robert, or even Jack for John. Some had regional recognition such as Simon the Cananite. Others may have had surnames, once again such as Nathanael Bartholomew, Matthew Levi, or Labbaeus Thaddaeus, even though surnames, as we know them today in the western world, did not come into vogue until about four to five hundred years ago. Simon was even given the new name Peter from Christ.

As a printed Biblical note, Robert Barker, the London printer to King James had an artist plate placed at the front of the New Testament of the 1611 King James Bible, which had an icon of the twelve sons of Jacob shown on the left side of the art work. Here it is interesting to note that Joseph and Benjamin are shown in the art instead of

Ephraim and Manasseh. The twelve disciples are displayed on the right side of the plate with the replacement "casting of lots," disciple Matthias, listed instead of Judas Iscariot. A similar artist rendering is shown at the beginning of the Old Testament with various robe and cloak clad figures with at least one being somewhat identifiable as Moses with what may safely be assumed to be the two tablets of the Ten Commandments.

The Women Of The Cross

MATTHEW CHAPTER 27
Mary Magdalene, Mary the mother of James and Joses, and the mother of Zebedee's sons

MARK CHAPTER 15 & 16
Mary Magdalene, Mary the mother of James the Less and of Joses, and Salome

LUKE CHAPTER 24
Mary Magdalene, Joanna, Mary the mother of James, and the other women

JOHN CHAPTER 19
His mother, and His mother's sister, Mary, the wife of Clopas, and Mary Magdalene

It is for sure that Jesus had His twelve disciples whom He had hand picked, and whom were all men. Certainly, Jesus also had women followers who are often seen in conjunction with the twelve disciples. Among them were Mary and Martha, the sisters of Lazarus. There was the group of women whom are often referred to as the Women of the Cross.

Mary Magdalene appears first in three of the four accounts and last in the John account. She was the only woman listed at the tomb in the John account. However, in the John account, she was listed with Peter and the "other disciple," "the beloved disciple," who is thought to be John, and she also spoke with two angels at the tomb after the two disciples left the tomb. She was called Magdalene because she was thought to be from the town or region of Magdala which was on the western coast of the Sea of Galilee.

The "other" Mary was listed as the mother of James (the Less) and Joses in both Matthew and Mark and only the mother of James in the Luke list. Which Mary was this? Was this Mary the mother of Jesus, since Jesus did have brothers who were named James and Joses, as Mary, the mother of Jesus was simply mentioned as Jesus' mother in the John account, or was this other Mary, perhaps Mary of Bethany, the sister of Martha and Lazarus? Could this have been the wife of Clopas? The various Marys are discussed with further treatment in the Mary Chapter.

Who was Salome? She was only mentioned twice in the book of Mark. Was this the same as the mother of Zebedee's sons? Some would suggest that Salome was indeed the wife of Zebedee and the mother of James and John. This may indeed be true, but it is a thin assumption. The Matthew and Mark accounts only list three women. The first two are in agreement; however, Salome and the mother of Zebedee's sons parallel each other in these two accounts.

Joanna was listed twice in the Luke account as a female follower of Christ. She was first listed in chapter eight as the wife of Chuza, a steward of Herod. Joanna was grouped with Mary Magdalene, of who Jesus had healed of seven evil spirits, as well as, a woman named Susanna and many others. The above text could suggest that all these women could have had evil spirits. This was the only notation of Susanna.

Who was Mary the wife of Clopas? Clopas may or may not be the same Cleopas which was the named person who was one of the fellow travelers with the risen Jesus on the road to Emmaus who ask Jesus if he was the only stranger in town not knowing of Jesus, his death and consequent resurrection.

This Luke 8:3 uses the phrase, "and many others," which could be coupled with the Luke 24 passage of "and the other women." Apparently, there was a whole host of followers, or "disciples" who followed Jesus to include women.

Below is a composite list of the possible women who are recorded to be at the cross of Jesus:

Mary, the Mother of Jesus = John account,
Mary's sister (Jesus' Aunt) = John account
Mary Magdalene = all four accounts

Mary, the mother of James (the Less) and Joses = Matthew, Mark and Luke accounts
The mother of Zebedee's sons = Matthew account
Salome = Mark account
Joanna = Luke account
Mary, the wife of Clopas = John account
The "other women," = Luke account

"His mother's sister," the sister of Mary, the mother of Jesus, or thus Jesus' Aunt, as listed in the John account could have been one of several of these other women. This has led some to speculate that the mother of James and John, the son of Zebedee or perhaps Salome, could have been all the same person, thus making James and John the first cousins of Jesus. This is thin speculation at best, but quite possible.

"The mother of James and Joses" could, in fact, be Mary, the mother of Jesus, since Jesus did have two brothers by this name. The John account is the only account to specifically list the mother of Jesus to have been at the cross. It would have been odd for Mary, the mother of Jesus, not to have been at the cross, but of course, the John account does list her as being present for this most horrifying, yet crucial event.

Name Changers

Throughout the Scriptures, God changed the names of particular people for His divine purposes. In Biblical times, one's name often had an actual meaning which often led the direction of their life following God.

<u>Old Testament</u>
Abram = Abraham
Sarai = Sarah
Jacob = Israel
Jethro = Reuel
Daniel = Beltshazzar
Hananiah = Shadrach
Mishael = Meshach
Azariah = Abed-Nego
Hadasseh = Esther

<u>New Testament</u>
Saul = Paul
Simon = Peter = Cephas
Jacob = James
Joseph
John

Genesis records the early genealogies of both Cain and Seth, the sons of Adam and Eve. Both of these genealogies list an Enoch and a Lamech. These were two different people.

In Genesis 17, God begins to call people and change their names. "No longer shall your name be called Abram אברם (Exalted Father), but your name shall be Abraham אברהם (Father of a Multitude); for I have made you a father of many nations."

Further on down in Genesis 17:15, we find his wife getting her name changed. "Then God said to Abraham, As for Sarai שרי (exert/preserve/persist???) to Sarah שרה (Princess) shall be her name."

Jacob יעקב who was known as the Deceitful Supplanter, had his name changed to Israel which means "Prince of God," or "Struggles with God," when Jacob wrestled with God on the banks of the Jabbok River.

When Moses fled into the desert of Midian, he met the Prince of Midian. The Midianites were distant cousins of the Israelites through Abraham's son, Midian, from Abraham's wife, Keturah. Moses married Zipporah and was a shepherd for forty years before God called him to free the children of Israel from their bondage in Egypt. Moses' father-in-law is first mentioned in Exodus 2 where he was identified as Reuel רעואל (which could mean something like "Aiming for or Purpose of God"), but hereafter, he was simply known as Jethro יתרו (which could mean something like "Superior").

During the American Civil War, Confederate General Thomas "Stonewall" Jackson was quoted as saying the following to one of his staff officers, "Captain, my religious belief teaches me to feel as safe in battle as in bed. God has fixed the time of my death. I do not concern myself about that, but to be always ready not matter when it may overtake me. That is the way all men should live and then all would be equally brave." Apparently these same "religious beliefs" were also held by Daniel דניאל (God is my judge), when he was thrown into the lion's den, as well as, when King Nebuchadnezzar saw Shadrach, Meshach, and Abed-Nego untarnished with the "son of God" in the fiery furnace. Daniel was most always known by his Jewish name instead of his Babylonian name of Belteshazzar בלטשאצר (Lady protect the king). Oddly, the other three were mostly known by their Babylonian names. Hananiah חנניה (God has been gracious) was known as Shadrach שדרך (I am fearful of a god or the gods), Mishael מישאל (Who is what God is?) as Meshach מישך (I am of little account) and Azariah זריה[(The Lord has helped) as Abed-Nego

עבד־נגו (Servent of Nebo). One can see that the Babylonians gave the Hebrew young men demeaning names to remind them of their subservient status as captives in the court of Babylon.

SAME - NAMES

In the New Testament, Saul Σαυλος has his name changed to Paul Παυλος in a blinding episode on the road to Damascus. This Saul is not to be confused with the Old Testament Saul, who was the first king of Israel. The Apostle Paul went on to write thirteen of the twenty-seven New Testament books.

Simon was the chief of Jesus' Disciples. Jesus changed his name to Rock or Peter Πετρος in John 1:42. The Apostle Paul, formerly known as Saul, liked to call Peter, Cephas, Κηφας which meant Stone in the Hebrew/Aramaic language. Simon Peter is not to be confused with Simon the Leper which was also a Pharisee or Simon the Tanner. Nor should Simon Peter be confused with Simon, the Cananite or Simon, the Zealot, the other disciple, or Simon of Cyrene, the cross bearer, or Simon the Scorcerer, or Simon, the half-brother of Jesus.

Abraham's great grandson via Isaac and Jacob was Joseph יוסף (He will add). He was the eleventh son of Jacob/Israel who was sold to his Midianite cousins into slavery into Egypt. This Old Testament Joseph is not to be confused with his New Testament counterpart of Joseph, the carpenter of Nazareth, wife of Mary, whom God entrusted to be the non-biological father of Jesus Christ our Lord and Savior.

The book of James in the New Testament is actually spelled "Jacob" Ιακωβος in the Greek. This was likely changed in English translation Bibles to avoid confusion with the Old Testament figure of the Jacob/Israel. In 1715 and 1745, Scottish rebels called themselves Jacobites as they were in support of James II of Scotland as they were seeking independence from England. James VI of Scotland (James I of England) was the 1611 King James.

The Last Old Testament style prophet was actually found in the New Testament. He was a near kinsmen of Jesus and baptized Jesus in the Jordan River. He was called John the Baptist or John the Baptizer Ιωαννης ο βαπτιστης. This John the Baptist is not to be confused with

John the brother of James, the Fishermen-Disciple and writer of the Gospel of John and other New Testament books to include The Revelation.

Jesus strangely had brothers named James, Joses, Simon and Judas. Jesus also had disciples with many of these same names, however, none of Jesus' half brothers were of a part of his band of disciples.

Noah's father was known as Lamech. He is not to be confused with the Lamech in the line of Cain. Likewise, Enoch which was "taken up," is not to be confused with the Enoch, the son of Cain.

Questions and Discussion for Chapter Fourteen – List
Dig – Discover – Discuss

1. Why are genealogies important in the Bible? Discuss.

2. According to Scripture, taking in to consideration that Noah is a direct descendant of Adam and Eve, are all humans descendant from Adam and Eve?

3. Luke and Matthew both give genealogies of Jesus. Keeping in mind, Joseph was not the physical father of Jesus, which genealogy belongs to Mary and Joseph respectively?

4. Do you believe that God actually gave the Ten Commandments directly Moses?

5. The Ten Commandments are the basis of our Judeo-Christian Law. Discuss the Ten Commandments' significance to modern western law.

6. Jews, Roman Catholics, and Protestants have different amounts of Old Testament books in different orders, why? Explain and discuss.

7. God changed Jacob's name, (The Deceitful Supplanter) to Israel, (one who struggles with God). Discuss the significance of the twelve sons of Jacob had and their impact on Jewish and world history.

8. Discuss who the twelve disciples were.
Were there more than twelve different disciples since the lists are different? Or, were they the same men with different names?

9. Discuss who the women of the cross were listed in the four gospels. What were the relationships between them?

10. Many people in the Bible had their names changed by God. Who were they, and why did God change their names? Explain, discuss.

11. Many different people in the Bible had the same, or similar names. Can you discern who is who?

Appendix: of American Christian Holidays

Christian holidays and American popular culture have been interwoven since the beginning of the nation. Beginning slowly in the mid-twentieth century, this once, tightly woven web of Christian-American culture, is now becoming unraveled in many different directions. Secular and left-leaning culture is pulling at this fabric in the name of inclusiveness, diversity, and political correctness. The liberal leaning agenda is attempting, with current great success, to expel any, and all, references to any kind of faith, most especially Christianity, from the public square, display, and discourse. This is all done under the guise of "separation of Church and State." Since this phrase does not appear anywhere in the United States Constitution, this is more of an implied false concept rather than, an actual reality, based upon the Bill of Rights of the Constitution. As an additional note, The United States form of government is *not* a democracy. The form of government we have in the United States is a Constitutional Republic. The words "democrat" or "democracy" do not appear anywhere in the document. So now, most American holidays, either official like Independence Day, or unofficial like Groundhog Day, Christian based or otherwise, are all now celebrated in much the same basic manner by many. American holidays, regardless of basis or tradition, are now merely seen as a time to be off work, and to spend time with family and friends. Granted, being off work and being with family and friends is a grand, and wonderful thing to always be celebrated! Regardless of the season, or celebration, many Americans celebrate all these built in, calendar scheduled-occasions, much in the same way, by doing such things as going to the beach or the lake, for a cook out or a barbecue, and perhaps drinking too much. Once again, there is nothing wrong with having a picnic and spending time with your family. However, many times with holidays, Christian or otherwise, we have lost the bubble of original intent, reason, or purpose. In short, we celebrate most every holiday the same way. We simply put up different colored decorations. When beginning with American Christian Holidays, we should start at the beginning with New Year's Day. Since the New Year's Holiday is so closely combined and related with the Christmas holiday, here we will combine them in this discourse.

As with the broad intent of this *Cain's Wife* book, I will challenge the reader to dig, discover, and discuss. I will many times be using broad strokes to stoke the reader's interest of investigation in exploring these holidays. As with most things in life, "attention to detail" is often in engaged in a neverending battle with its opposite counterpart of "the bigger picture."

MERRY CHRISTMAS & HAPPY NEW YEAR

Neither Christmas nor the New Year's holidays are exclusively American events. What is unique, is how Americans celebrate them. First thing out of the box, is the word "Holiday" which is simply a corruption of the phrase "Holy Day." For those who want to expel Christ from Christmas or Holy from the day, they are only fooling themselves by using this term. This is a firm foundation for the following folly which we will be discussing here in this appendix venue. Those who like to use the expression of "Xmas," let us discuss what this really means. Some may simply use this short hand term as a handy abbreviation while scrawling *xmas decorations* on a cardboard box with a Sharpie before shoving the box back into its dank tomb of the dusty attic, garage, or basement before digging it back out again the following Thanksgiving. Some left leaning individuals do it with the express purpose of attempting to exclude Christ from Christmas, however, they have missed the mark. The "X" is not an "x" but rather a Greek "Chi" χ as in Chi-Rho Χρ which is an ancient church symbol for Christ. In essence, what this short hand is really representing is: CHR-mas, or Christmas. In the end, Christ remains in Christmas.

When looking at our calendar, which is in widespread use throughout America and most of the modern civilized world, we find that the first day of winter is usually recognized on or about the 21st of December, which is only four days before the day we have set aside to celebrate as Christmas, the recognized day to celebrate the physical birth of Jesus Christ. The 21st day of December is the shortest day of the year, as it only has about nine hours of daylight. This is the winter solstice. It is also just ten days before when we celebrate the so-called New Year. When thinking about this, should not the 21st or 22nd of December be the beginning of the New Year?

Based on ancient New Year celebrations and calculations, we are currently a week off the old calendar. What is most odd about people celebrating the New Year, is that nothing is really new. For years we watched the the crystal ball drop in the Big Apple of downtown Manhattan in New York City. Confetti is dropped along with so many inhibitions, as many may be tipping the goblet too much. On New Year's Day we can watch a few college football bowl games, which now actually produce a real national champion, but in our real lives, what is really new? Unless we have gotten married, had a baby, had an untimely death, or divorce, gotten hired, or fired from a new job; what has changed? You only have to remember to write the New Year correctly when writing your checks for those still using paper bank checks. Many will make New Year's resolutions. Unfortunately, many of these unrealistic resolutions are defaulted on, or conveniently forgotten, within a few fleeting days, or weeks of their hopeful, and wishful pronouncement.

In short, when looking at ancient cultures, the winter solstice is exactly when the New Year was. On a related note, younger school children and early morning drive time radio hosts still participate in ironic short stories and fibs in honor of the so-called "April Fool's Day, the first day of April. For some ancient cultures, the first day of April or the beginning of spring, was the beginning of the New year.

With the growth and consolidation of the early Roman Catholic

Church, there was concern with swaying the newly converted pagans of northern Europe to forsake their long-held pagan ways, and high holydays or holidays. One of these Teutonic Norseman holydays was The Yule, or the Yule Tide with the Yule Log for bon-fires, as we still remember in Bing Crosby's *White Christmas* Christmas Carol. The main figure in this Norseman holiday was the long white bearded Odin, who brought gifts while riding his horse across the Borealis sky.

Since we really don't know what time of year Jesus was born in Bethlehem, what better excuse to celebrate "The Son," the light of the world instead of "The Sun," a light in the world. Speaking here in broad historical strokes, the early Roman Catholic Church decided on the 25th of December to be the officially recognized birthday of Jesus Christ, in an attempt, to overshadow the pagan holiday of the Yule Tide, or the New Year celebration."

As with so many old traditions, they die hard. Many remnants of the old winter pagan holiday still persist in the modern western celebration of Christ's birth on the 25th of December. What is Christmas without Santa Claus? Sometimes Santa gets a hard knock from ultra conservatives as they say the jolly ol' elf is trying to replace Jesus who is the reason for the season. Let us dig a little deeper here before we black list the red clad Norseman. As a starting point, "Santa" is a word for saint, in some Latin-based languages. There really was a Saint Nicholas. In broad strokes, Saint Nick was a priest-bishop type figure in what we now call Turkey, who gave gifts to poor children in the 1300's. Saint Nicholas is often portrayed as being arrayed in a long red robe, which may be best described by some as being "popish" in appearance. "Claus" is simply a corruption of the name Nicholas. Over time, the name Santa Claus has come down to us. In the lowlands of Belgium and Holland, the jolly, red clad gift giver was known as Sinterklaas. In merry old England, they celebrated with Father Christmas. What about the red suit and the funny hat? If you take the funny Santa hat, stand it up straight, and make it rigid, then you have a Pope-like hat to go along with his red suit. Over the years, the long Pope-like robe morphed into a shorter, fur-lined coat, better for navigating the Christmas Eve skies, and negotiating soot filled fire places and chimneys. Two things propelled this transition. The *Night Before Christmas* poem which was originally known as *A Visit From Saint Nicholas,* when it was originally penned in 1832 by Clement Clarke Moore. Pressing forward about one hundred years, the 1930's Coca-Cola advertising campaign, solidified the final form of Saint Nick; the red arrayed elf from the North Pole. What about the whole North Pole thing, the flying reindeer, with Christmas trees, and holly? Once again, this all goes back to the pagan traditions of the Teutonic pagan tribes of north central Europe. Between the three gifts of the magi, and the gift giving of Saint Nick, we now have spawned the American indulgence of giving away too many gifts at Christmas, often over-shadowing the birth of Jesus Christ, who was the best gift ever given to mankind, who may, or may not, have been born on the 25th of December on, or about Anno Domini year one or zero.

"Merry Christmas" is the greeting we begin hearing sometime around the "Black Friday" shopping madness, the day after the American civil-religious holiday of Thanksgiving. Hopefully, in the future, we all will continue to be able to say and hear this most wonderful phrase of Merry Christmas in the public square. Many of the liberal ilk, now want to replace the "Merry Christmas" greeting with the generic "Happy Holidays," or the even more benign "Seasons Greetings." The question that begs to be asked in response to both of these alternative greetings is which holiday or holyday are you celebrating? Season? For what season are you offering greetings? In this same train of thought, public school children have traditionally been given a week or so off from school for Christmas and New Years which was called "Christmas break or Christmas vacation." Due to secular and liberal forces controlling many local public school boards; this Christmas vacation time is now bluntly termed as "winter break."

Many Americans celebrate Christmas in some form with, or without, Christ as a centerpiece to their various celebrations. Many Americans will have a Christmas light display on their house exterior and a decorated tree on the interior of the house, which may have a myriad of diverse themes and schemes.

Currently, many Americans, Christian or otherwise, celebrate Christmas in various ways. As just mentioned, many will put up simple to elaborate decorations and Christmas light displays. Some of them will be Christ-birth centered, while many are winter-pagan based with Santa Claus, reindeer, snowmen, red and white candy canes, polar bears, penguins and so forth. As a special note, there are no penguins at the North Pole. All seventeen to eighteen varieties of penguins live in the southern hemisphere mostly in and around Antarctica and the South Pole. Likewise, there are no polar bears at the South Pole. Candy canes on the other hand, are a very Christian symbol. Instead of being a mere cane, they are actually a "J" for Jesus. The red on the striped candy represents the blood of Jesus, while the white is for purity. Other decorations may be of a countless myriad of various themes, and non-traditional sorts. A large fraction of Americans will do elaborate and expensive shopping, mostly for family members and friends, while piling up credit card bills that they will pay for with high interest rates for the lion's share of the coming year. Gifts are often exchanged on Christmas eve and/or Christmas day. "It is for the Children," is a horrid term used by some. No! Christmas is for everybody, as Jesus came to save us all from our sins. Christmas is not just an expensive excuse to give spoiled children gifts. Many will celebrate Christmas in their own American way, whether it is Christian or not. Giving and getting presents to celebrate Christmas does not make you a Christian any more than putting on a costume and eating candy at Halloween makes you a devil-worshipping pagan. Enjoy!

Alongside Christmas is the Jewish Holiday of Chanukah, or Hanukah, or the Festival of Lights. Chanukah is an eight-day festival where one gift is exchanged each night as one candle is lighted on the candle holder called a Menorah. This is to commemorate the victory of the Maccabees over the Syrians. Sadly, to the chagrin of many Jews and Christians alike, this is often ignorantly referred to as the "Jewish Christmas."

DOCTOR MARTIN LUTHER KING JUNIOR DAY

The Christian significance of the Doctor Martin Luther King Junior Day is that Dr. King was a Christian minister who was the paramount civil rights leader of the mid twentieth century in the United States. His positive influence still reaches down to us today. Additionally, Dr. King was named after Martin Luther, one of the great leaders of the Protestant Reformation. Sadly, some today on both sides of the political spectrum attempt to undo his work. Even more sad is that some of those trying to undo his civil rights efforts are the very ones Doctor King sought to uplift.

We all should be judged by the content of our character, and not by the color of our skin… for any reason.

SUPER BOWL

The Super Bowl is currently *not* a federally recognized holiday in America. However, the Super Bowl is one of the most celebrated days on the American calendar, by both ardent fans and fake fans alike. The fake fans are the ones who ask which two teams are playing, and want to know how many home runs have been shot, while they brag about their asparagus dip which they brought to the party. Many intense pigskin prognosticators will bet on how many points will be scored by the gridiron gladiators with a myriad and multiplicity of cyber metrics, and other mathematical statistical analytics. In recent years, the ultra expensive ridiculous TV commercials, and often outrageous halftime entertainment shows have overshadowed the game itself. For the last four to five decades, pastors, ministerial staffs, and deacon boards have debated, fought, and sought, on how, and if, to have Sunday night services. Although, many of these same deacons seldom-to-never showed up on Sunday nights anyway. Some churches have even decided to have Super Bowl Parties at the Church itself, often to the dismay to many staunch conservatives and traditional old-timers. As well as being a retired Southern Baptist minister and Navy/Marine Chaplain, I outwardly admit to being a big sports fan to include the NFL. Sadly, in today's culture, it is often difficult to discern what is more important on Sundays, honoring the Sabbath, or the National Football League. Pass the Doritos.

GROUNDHOG DAY

There is no real Christian or national significance to Groundhog Day. However, there is always much foolish interest in whether a Pennsylvania woodchuck, Punxsutawney Phil, will see his shadow in early February, to see if we will have six more weeks of winter. Of course, we will, and maybe more if you live up north. Most Americans should be more interested in Easter when Christians celebrate Jesus, the Son of God, rising out of the tomb, instead of a rodent rising out of his burrow. Just a thought.

PRESIDENT'S DAY

President George Washington and the founding fathers found it fit to have freedom of religion in America by writing it into the First Amendment of the Bill of Rights of the United States Constitution. Christians should consider President's Day a significant holiday because of this point. Just like any other lot of Americans, some holders of the Executive Oval Office on 1600 Pennsylvania Avenue in the District of Columbia, have been Christians, and supporters of the same, while others have been less so.

MARDI GRAS/ASH WEDNESDAY/LENT

For our Roman Catholic brothers and sisters in Christ, Lent is a significant part of the faith. It is of lesser significance to most non-Catholics. Even though the forty-day event is not actually prescribed in scripture, it is somewhat conceptually based in Scripture. Forty days is a significant time period in the Bible. Abstinence from personal desires, indulgences and/or sin can always be a good thing. Many Americans, Catholic and non-Catholic alike often participate in Mardi Gras, also known as Fat Tuesday. It is a day of opulent indulgence of every kind of sin, desire, and debauchery known to man. It is often celebrated by lavish parades, eating, drinking, and so forth with lots of beads. This carnival, or festival of the flesh, is most commonly celebrated on Bourbon Street in the French Quarter of New Orleans and the Gulf Coast where it originally began in Mobile, Alabama. Fat Tuesday is ironically followed by Ash Wednesday, when practicing Catholics have a cross drawn on their forehead by a priest from the ashes of the burnt palms from the previous Palm Sunday which always proceeds Easter Sunday. This is the beginning of Lent, the forty days of personal sacrifice, leading up to Easter.

SAINT VALENTINE'S DAY

Ah, Saint Valentine's Day. This is the day in which the amorous thoughtfulness and mental metal of men is tested by the women in their lives. Each February 14th, flowers, greeting cards, chocolate covered candies in heart shaped boxes, and even diamond rings, and jewelry of various and diverse sorts, are given to giddy women over elegant dinners, all in the name of love. Some women even give gifts to their male counterparts. School children will even exchange cute and quaint cards to their class mates. The origins of this unofficial holiday are thin. Saint Valentine was an obscure Roman Saint who is thought to have been martyred, and is associated with love.

SAINT PATRICK'S DAY

"Kiss me, I'm Irish," is something you may hear around the middle of March, particularly on the seventeenth. In America, Saint Patrick's Day is the ultimate excuse to take an extra long lunch, or leave work early. Many will go to a so-called Irish pub, put a four-leave clover pin on their collar, and wear green, while getting drunk on a pint of Guinness, some Killian's Irish Red, or some cheap green beer. This is normally done while watching a NCAA March Madness college basketball game as their brackets crumble into oblivion.

Some may enjoy a Chicago drum and bagpipe parade. Strangely, bagpipes are more specifically Scottish rather than Irish, but being Scottish or Irish still falls under the general realm of being Gaelic and/or Celtic.

What is Saint Patrick's Day really all about? Who was Saint Patrick? Straight out of the starting blocks, to the dismay of many, Saint Patrick was *not* Irish. What!? Patrick was born in the 400's in the Roman province of Britannia, or more specifically in what we today call England, to British/Romans parents. In broad historical strokes, as a teenager, Patrick was captured by Celtic Druid invaders and taken prisoner to Ireland to be a slave for several years. Eventually, he escaped from Ireland back to England. In time, he studied to become a priest, and from here he became a missionary and returned to Erie's shore of the emerald isle. Patrick used the three-leafed clover or the shamrock, to represent the three-in-one Trinity of God the Father, Jesus the Son and the Holy Spirit. Four leaf clovers and the luck o' the Irish, have nothing to do with Saint Patrick's Day, as neither do Leprechauns with pots o' gold at the rainbow's end. On a related note, the tri-color of the Irish national flag contains green for Catholics, orange for Protestants, and the white is for the peace which is between them. If you are a non-Catholic Christian, you should really wear orange instead of green on Saint Patrick's Day, but what fun would that be?

Northern Ireland, which was traditionally called Ulster, is politically a part of the United Kingdom with Scotland, Wales, and England. This political petition has been a source of bloody religious and political conflict for centuries as Northern Ireland has been traditionally Protestant, most specifically, the Church of England. Ireland or Northern Ireland, is represented on the current Union Jack British flag by the thin red Saint Patrick's Cross, which overlays the white Saint Andrews Cross of Scotland. Before the current green, white, and orange flag, the Irish flag was white with the red Saint Patrick's "X" cross, thus, looking very much like our Florida and Alabama State flags. Like most South Bend, Indiana, University of Notre Dame Fighting Irish students, and football fans, I prefer the green football jerseys over the blue ones ... Touchdown Jesus!

HOLY WEEK/ EASTER & SPRING BREAK

"Happy Easter" is often a phrase which is uttered in the spring of the year when hazy eyed little boys and little girls awake to candy filled baskets on the front porch, which were left there hours earlier by the Easter Bunny. These woven wooden baskets with high-arching handles, are often filled with plastic green grass, thinly veiling a treasure of pastel colored plastic eggs, Palmer chocolate bunnies, yucky yellow peeps, and sticky-toothed jelly beans, which are eaten except for the black ones – yuck! The ground may be covered with glistening velvet ivory snow, or bounding bright with bouncing sun beams, as the morning sun crest over the distant tree line of the eastern horizon. Later that same morning, these same little boys with chocolate smudged faces don their new bow-ties and suits, and little girls dance with sugar-filled dreams in their, darling dainty dresses, with loosely tied bouncing bonnets, as they head off for church, with either giddy anticipation, or glum anxiety. This spring time Sunday morning ritual of "church" may either be an annual event, or an ardent weekly expectation. From there, it is off to the grand "Easter egg hunt." Children, parents, and reminiscent grandparents alike, drown and dye their white eggs in a potion of pastel colors in coffee cups. The Easter Bunny, in addition to the porch candy laden baskets; laid eggs all about in a nearby high grass field. The so-called Easter Bunny is an old pagan contrived creature, which was celebrated for spring fertility. Of course, everyone knows, rabbits and hares are mammals, which give live birth to their bunnies, with hares having 'hair' when they are born, thus, their name, and rabbits being born hairless. Additionally, everyone knows that rabbits do not lay eggs much in the same vein that cows do not lay eggs. Eggs are *not* a dairy product! As with Christmas and Halloween, we have the scrambled-egg mingling of the pagan and Christian in our holiday celebrations.

Holy Week is the pinnacle of the Christian year, only being rivaled by the Christmas season. Holy Week begins with Palm Sunday. Palm Sunday commemorates Jesus riding triumphantly into Jerusalem on a colt of a donkey, while the people laid their clothes and palm branches in the road while they praised Jesus by singing and saying "Hosanna." Monday, on a lesser note, remembers Jesus cleansing the Temple, by driving the money changers out of the most holy building by overturning their tables. Jesus in normally portrayed doing this cleansing with a whip, in John 2:15. Thursday is known as "Maundy Thursday." This was the evening of the "Last Supper" or the "Lord's Supper," in which Jesus had the Jewish Passover meal with His twelve disciples. It is here that we have the precious elements of the Communion or The Lord's Supper. Jesus used the yeast free bread of the Passover meal to represent His physical body, which would be broken the next day. He also took the cup with the red wine to represent His physical blood, which would pour from his thorn-torn pierced brow, beaten bloody back, spike-hammered hands and feet, and His spear struck side. This red wine was held within a cup, which in history, and mythology, has become known as the "Holy Grail." This cup has been sought after for centuries by kings and common men alike for centuries. What should be sought after is the Potter and not the pot; the Creator and not the creature. Thursday evening morphs into Friday morning, which has been traditionally known as "Good Friday." In the shadows of the dark of night, Jesus was betrayed by Judas' kiss and captured by torch toting, and sword swinging soldiers of the Jewish chief priest and pharisees. From here, Jesus endured a series of mock trials and was beaten nearly to death by Roman Soldiers, before ultimately being crucified, and dying on the cross. Although, this is not the end of the story.

Finally, Resurrection Day, also known as Easter Sunday, is the hinge point on which all of Christianity stands. Jesus, as He foretold, arose from the grave, conquering both Death and Hell. Without this event, there is no true Christian Faith.

The term "Easter" occurs in some text in Acts 12:4 such as the 1611 KJV, whereas the NKJV and other English text refers to this word as "Passover." In the Greek, the word appears as "Passover" πασχα. Why is Easter called "Easter?" Oddly, this is the name of a pagan goddess of spring.

Many will ask the question, "why is Easter sometimes in March and sometimes in April?" In the Eastern Orthodox tradition, Easter is always later in the spring because the Eastern Church uses the Julian calendar instead of a Gregorian or the standard calendar. Easter can be as early as the 22nd of March, or as late as the 25th of April. The date of Christian Easter is somewhat based on when Jewish Passover is since this is when, and why Jesus went to Jerusalem before His crucifixion. The Passover date is based on a lunar calendar instead of a solar calendar, so the date varies. Passover begins on the 14th day of the Jewish month of Nisan. Easter is the first Sunday after the first full moon following the first day of Spring on or about the 21st of March.

Ah, Spring Break!!! Traditionally, many public schools and private businesses alike would have Good Friday off from their work and school schedules. In the process of time, public schools, as well as, colleges began to take the whole week of Holy week off from studies. Now, spring break may, or may not, be on or around Holy Week. Spring Break for some upper-classmen high schoolers, and college students is for going to the satin white beaches of the Gulf Coast, the rough wave beaches of the Carolinas, or the sun-drenched strands of Florida, for a week of uninhibited self-indulgence of riotous living, and debaucherous drinking of various adult beverages in copious amounts. What is the Christian connection of Holy Week and Spring Break? Not much, just the co-incidence of their confluence on the calendar.

MOTHER'S DAY & FATHER'S DAY

Mother's Day and Father's Day along with high school graduation are considered by some churches as a time to focus and celebrate the Christian family. Strangely enough, both Mother's Day and Father's

Day both have their origins in the most obscure of places. Anna Jarvis and Grace Golden Clayton were the driving forces for the Mother's Day and Father's Day celebrations respectively, as they were both from the State of West Virginia.

Both days of parental recognition are mostly celebrated by many by getting Mom or Dad some sort of small gift, coupled with an expensive greeting card. Perhaps going out to eat after church is also a part of the celebration. Easter and Mother's Day are the two most insane Sundays in which to attempt to go out to eat, unless you like standing in line for two hours at your favorite restaurant.

Some churches recognize mothers and fathers at church by merely having them stand during the service. Other congregations may give flowers or token gifts to mothers. Some churches may even give "awards" for the most children born, or present at the church service. In days gone by, some churches may have even given gifts for being the "oldest mother" and/or the "youngest mother." Giving recognition to the oldest mother was and is always a wonderful thing: However, after much embarrassment to everyone present, some churches finally figured out that giving a gift to the youngest mother was not a good idea, as some of these child bearers were still children themselves, who may not yet be out of high school and normally, not yet married – ugh.

For Father's Day, taking Dad out to eat is usually a good option, but as with the option of a cook out on the barbeque, Dad would still end up paying the bill for all present, or doing all the grill work. In many cases, he would have rather went straight home after church, to watch the ballgame or the NASCAR race. Where's the remote?

MEMORIAL DAY/DECORATION DAY

Memorial Day was established to remember fallen Union soldiers of the American Civil War. In the South similar sentiments were celebrated, and it was called Decoration Day, a day to decorate the graves of the fallen with flowers. Strangely over time, for some, Memorial Day has become a day to decorate the graves of everyone, and not just veterans. (On a humorous note, this "decoration day", is the final day you may socially be allowed to have your Christmas decorations still hanging from last Christmas). This three-day holiday weekend, like so many other of our holidays, has lost its bubble of original intent, and is only seen by many as the "unofficial beginning of summer." A time to go to the lake for a barbeque and a beverage. A time to try-out the boat for the first time, just before the kids get out of school for the summer. Where's my fishing hat?

INDEPENDENCE DAY - THE FOURTH OF JULY

Every nation in the world has the Fourth of July, but only the United States has this as Independence Day. On this 1776 hot sultry day in Philadelphia, the Declaration of Independence was signed and the idea of this great nation was birthed into history. One of the main tenants of the concept of American liberty and freedom, is the concept of "Freedom of Religion," and the so-called concept of "separation of church and state." It was so important for the founding fathers to have freedom of religion, that on the 15th of December 1791, they made it the very first amendment to the Bill of Rights of the Constitution. "Congress shall make no law respecting an establishment of religion, or prohibiting the free exercise thereof, ..." This has been a topic of hot debate ever since. As an additional note, The United States form of government is *not* a democracy. The form of government we have in the United States is a Constitutional Republic. However, this is a very fine line of definition. The words "democrat" or "democracy" do not appear anywhere in the document. For the last several decades, the liberal left has attempted to expunge any sort of faith or religion from the public square. The concept of separation of church and state is only an implied idea and does not actually appear in the Constitution. The founding fathers did not want an official state church such as the Church of England, which was supported by all British subjects either willingly, or unwilling, by paying taxes. Nor did the founding fathers want the suppression of any church, or faith, by the government. During colonial times, there were various sorts of faiths and religions in the Americas to include the many of the then existing sub-sets of the Christian faith. Taken as a whole, most Americans were of some sort of Christians as they were known at the time. Modern Christianity in it various forms and the new fledgling

American experiment grew up and grew together in culture, for the last two and a half centuries. With the freedom of religion in America came many religions from throughout the world. As in Europe, there were many conflicts with the Americans between Catholics and Protestants and once again, many conflicts within the Protestant faith groups. Jews and Mormons of various sorts, were both welcomed and tormented over the stretch of American history. Eventually, such faiths as Muslims, Hindus, and the different sorts of Asian philosophies, came to American shores. As with all the other faiths, they faced both acceptance and intolerance. In short, America has traditionally been called a "Christian nation," however, over time, it has become less so, even though this was a strong part of its foundation.

Today, Independence Day or the Fourth of July, as it is more commonly referred to, is often celebrated locally with morning parades down Main Street, with local high school marching bands, veterans often being honored, and many flags being unfurled as the red, white, and blue paint the breeze. During mid-day, many barbeques are set aflame while much beer is drunk while sitting pool side, or out on the boat at our favorite beach or lake. Later that night much "Ooohing & Aaahing" is voiced in cooperate unison as fabulous fireworks explode their rocket's red glare in the dark of the ten o'clock sky.

Some churches participate in "God and Country Day" services around the fourth of July. These patriotic services may be as simple as recognizing past and present service members who may be invited to wear their old uniforms if, in fact, they can still pry themselves into them. Other congregations may have full blown patriotic showcases with color guards, and musical presentations, which are under-pinned by a Biblical sermon.

As of the writing of this page, there are some so-called Americans who no longer desire to stand for the Pledge of Allegiance or for the National Anthem. These individuals are normally of the same ilk who do not want to say, "Merry Christmas." Sadly, little is often discussed of the bloodshed by early American Patriots against their British oppressors. Much blood would continue to be shed by many for the American masses in the centuries to follow. Americans began fighting on the side of the red-coat clad British, starting with the French and Indian War in 1754 -1763, also known worldwide as the Seven Year's War, before declaring our independence. (See Veteran's Day)

LABOR DAY

As with the beginning of the traditional school year, Labor Day marks the unofficial close of summer, even though the calendar summer reaches to about the 21st of September. There is little to no Christian connection to Labor Day, but Labor Day is celebrated in much the same way as are the other American Holidays. A time to cookout on the grill perhaps for the last time for the summer and spend time with family and friends. During this weekend, school children either anticipate, or dread, the beginning of the school year.

PATRIOT DAY

Clouds of gray-brown dust and smoke bellowed down the urban canyons of Manhattan, as the twin Towers of the World Trade Center fell. Islamic terrorist from Saudi Arabia flew two passenger filled planes into the iconic American buildings on the morning of September 11th, 2001. Meanwhile, near by the District of Columbia in northern Virginia, the Military Pentagon Building was also hit by the same ilk. Also, Flight 93 crashed in an obscure field in Shanksville, Pennsylvania, when some of the brave passengers on board attempted to stop the Islamic terrorist suicide pilots as the American heroes called out, "Let's Roll!" to each other. Although, this day is not an official holiday, as in a "day off work," and likewise, it is not "celebrated" as are other holidays. It is a solemn and sad day of remembrance in America. A day that changed America forever ... and not for the best.

I was working for Tracey Hanning's Christian roofing company called, "The Solid Rock Roofing Company," roofing a house in Kettering, Ohio. I bet you also remember exactly where you were, and what you were doing at this awful time. Something we all will never forget. For those not yet born, or too young to remember, know this – this changed America forever, binding and strangling our civil rights to include our freedom of religion. This horrid event has affected how we see our own religious rights, as well as, the religious rights of others, which may be in conflict with our own faith. As of the writing of this text, some sixteen years after the event, American religious liberty for Christians and other faiths are still an unresolved issue. These issues are likely to become even more unresolved as the years go by if that is even possible, or conceivable. God help and bless us, even if we don't deserve it, for the cultural weeds we have let grow.

COLUMBUS DAY

Every October, around the twelfth, the banks are inconveniently closed, there is no mail, and for some strange reason, children in public schools are often out of school for the day. Columbus Day is what I like to affectionately call, "Lost Italian Day." The simple truth is, Christopher Columbus, or Christoforo Columbo, never discovered the mainland of North America. What!? Columbus did, however, discover what today we call the Caribbean Islands, the West Indies, and the north end of South America. After the Christians drove the Muslim Moors off of the Iberian Peninsula back into Morocco of North Africa, most of Hispania, except Portugal, joined together to form the country of Spain under Queen Isabella and King Ferdinand. Shortly thereafter, the Italian entrepreneur, explorer, Christopher Columbus, approached the scepter of the royal Spanish couple to request financial backing, for the purpose of, finding a shorter trade route to Japan, China, India, and Asia as a whole. Columbus had already made several pitches to various other European monarchs for financial support, but was thwarted without any success. He rightfully claimed that the world was in fact round and not flat. However, this "flat world" notion was mostly already debunked by most, as more fiction than fact. With the backing of the Spanish throne, Christopher Columbus set off in search of a shorter route for the spice and gold of the Far East. His flag ship was the Santa Maria, which was accompanied by the Pinta, and finally, the Nina which, which was actually christened, the Santa Clara. Even though he never actually reached the American mainland in any of his four voyages, many others did. Among these were, Juan Ponce de Leon, Hernando De Soto, Francisco Vasquez de Coronado, and others.

Who is "America" named after? Strangely enough, America was named after another Italian explorer, Amerigo Vespucci. The term "America" started to be used for the New World by explorers shortly after 1500. This led to more exploration, and exploitation of both North and South America. Besides the obvious European exploration and land grabs for gold and riches, Catholic missionaries also were a part of these expeditions, thus fulfilling the Great Commission by bringing Christ to the nations. This bringing of Christ to America was slow to be received by the American residents. However, in time, Christianity, in the form of the Roman Catholic Church took root, and eventually spread like wild fire with most of Latin America from Tijuana to Teirra del Fuego. The statue in Rio de Janeiro, "Christ the Redeemer," is the capstone of this 1492 missionary accomplishment. Columbus went to his death bed believing that he had landed in perhaps what we today call Indonesia. This is why we call the Caribbean islands, the West Indies, and why we call the indigenous people in North America, Indians.

At the end of the 1400's, there were many multitudes of different cultures, nations, and tribes of native people living in both North and South America, as well as, the Caribbean Sea, and Central America. At best, the population was widely and thinly dispersed. There was a great deal of diversity among the various tribes in language, religion, social structure, technology, diet, dress, habits, and most every part of their lives.

My ancestor, John Filson, in his 1784 book, *The Discovery, Settlement and present State of Kentucke,* described the Indians of Kentucky in the following manner: Filson speculates that the American Indians were from Asia, and he described them as being from the "Tartars (Tatars) of central Asia and that they likely came to North American shores via a "narrow sea or strait, six leagues wide." Filson also strangely states that some of the tribes in North America already spoke the Welch Language. Filson goes on to state that by the unearthed technology found during contemporary archeology, that apparently, another culture, not akin to the currently present Indian cultures, were formerly present in North America. Most particularly, Filson physically describes the Indians in this manner: "*The Indians are not born white and take a great deal of pains to darken their complexion by anointing themselves with grease, and lying in the sun. --- they also paint their faces, breast and shoulders of various colours, but generally red. --- their features are well formed, especially those of the women, --- in many parts of their bodies prick in gun powder in very pretty figures. --- They shave or pluck the hair off their heads except a patch about their crown which is ornamented with beautiful feathers, beads --- their ears are pared and stretched in a thong down to their shoulders --- and adorned with silver pendants, rings and bells which they likewise wear in their nose. Some of them will have a large feather through the cartilage of their nose. --- wear a collar of wampum, a silver breast plate and bracelets on their arms and wrist. ---a bit of cloth about the middle ---mockasons which are shoes, of a make particular to the Indians --- with a blanket thrown over their shoulders complete their dress --- but when they go to war, they leave their trinkets behind --- There is little difference between the dress of men and women, excepting that a short petticoat --- their hair is exceeding black and long clubbed behind --- execpt the head and eyebrows, they pluck the hair with great diligence from all parts of the body --- the Indians are not ignorant as some suppose them, but are a very understanding people.* John Filson goes on to describe in detail the various tribes found in around the Ohio River Valley and Kentucky with their vast diversity.

Yes, some peaceful trading and interaction occurred between the cultures. However, sadly, brutal warfare often occurred when cultures clashed including barbaric butchery, enslavement, and even human sacrifice. Likewise, in Europe, much of the same activities were occurring concurrently. There was little to no unity between most of the tribes and nations before or after the arrival of Europeans.

The Vikings, with the likes of Erik the Red, actually "discovered" Iceland and Greenland in the 900's, while his son Leif Erikson, and others, were some of the early finders of North America, most particularly "Vineland (possibly Newfoundland, Canada) somewhere around the year 1000, some hundreds of years before the long string of Latin explorers starting in 1492. Some say Brendan the Navigator, from Ireland in the 500's and others, may have made the initial western trans-Atlantic tour of discovery. If you speak to a Mormon, they will also give you an American discovery story. However, if the depths of the sea floor with many ship wrecks resting on its bottom could be conjured up, perhaps we could find many other ships full of souls, who may have found the new world, but were lost to time and history, as the waves of the sea drowned their story. We were all told in school, that Asians crossing the Bering Strait land bridge long ago "discovered" what we now call North America.

"Newfoundland," "Jamestown," "Saint Augustine" the debates continue – you make the call. Some "scientists" say earlier Europeans may have crossed the Atlantic on ice during one of the various Ice Ages. This theory is due to recently found artifacts such as so-called "Clovis points" and so forth. Either way, Christopher Columbus did not actually discover mainland North America, but it does make a good day off work for federal employees to rake leaves.

HALLOWEEN/ALL SAINTS DAY/ REFORMATION DAY

"Trick or Treat" is the phrase that many masked minions and twilight trick-or-treaters tout and shout as they ring their neighbor's door bell. With decorative bags, plastic orange jack-o-lanterns, and pillow cases in hand, extended with the hopes of receiving: Sweet-tarts, Snickers, Blow-pops, Reese's Cups, Bazooka, and bubble gum of pink, and hard various varieties, Jaw Breakers, Candy-corn, Hersey Kisses, M & M's, and Mars Bars of various bites, along with other chocolate delights. These tiny-tot masked minions may be outfitted as superheroes, sports heroes, army men, policemen, firemen, doctors, nurses, fairy-tale princes, hobos, clowns, ghost, witches, vampires, devils, demons, and ghouls of every diverse description.

In the last decade or so, many adults have been taken back to their childhood roots with adult Halloween parties, with costumes as diverse as there are ideas. Halloween is beginning to rival Christmas for decorations, parties, and so forth, but why? What exactly are these fall festival frolickers celebrating? If you were to ask them, they may simply reply, "Well, Halloween of course!" What does that mean? Are they celebrating death? Are they celebrating evil? Are they celebrating the fall harvest? Or are they just celebrating "celebrating?" This is the old American tale, of just having a holiday with the express purpose of having a party with family and friends; a time to just be silly.

Halloween began as a Celtic-pagan holiday of celebrating the dead during ancient times. Because of the darkness of this time of the year, it was thought that the "veil" between the living and the dead, or this world and the afterlife was very thin. It was thought that mask, costumes, and disguises were used to scare away, or fool, evil spirits. The gathering and giving of food was some sort of sacrifice to appease the evil spirits and/or the dead. Pope Gregory IV in 835 instituted All Saints Day or All Hallows Day on November the 1st. This was a sort of Christian "Memorial Day" to remember fallen saints. Like placing Christmas over top of the yule tide, this was an attempt of the early church to cover a pagan celebration with a Christian Holy Day. Over the years, All Hallows Eve was verbally corrupted into Halloween.

In 1517, the German monk, Martin Luther, used this day to nail his 95 Thesis on the church door in Wittenberg, turning the Christian world on its head, by birthing into being the Protestant Reformation. Halloween can also be called "Reformation Day." Just like Christmas, by putting up a Christmas tree and exchanging gifts does not make you a Christian: and likewise, putting on a costume, collecting candy, and going to a party, does not make you a devil worshipper. – Enjoy!

VETERAN'S DAY

World War I was ended on the eleventh hour of the eleventh day of the eleventh month in 1918. This was to be the war to end all wars. Due to poor politics, and acknowledgment of language, culture, religion, history, and being overshadowed by pride, and egos, wars and rumors of wars, have continued down to us one hundred years later. Many of the graves of American warriors in both exotic and domestic cemeteries, are engulfed in grave markers, which are mostly white in color, and mostly Christian crosses in shape. Certainly, not all these fallen heroes were Christians, in the sense that they were believers in Jesus Christ. In the past, Christianity and American culture walked hand-in-hand. It was then common practice to have an American grave marked by a Christian cross. Today, if one were to visit a veteran's cemetery, one would find grave markers of various sorts. Eventually, the Star of David would mark the plots of Jewish Americans. Religious symbols of various and sundry sorts now can be found in these same grave yards. For those who served in the Marine Corps, the Marine Corps Birthday, which is remembered on the 10th of November is often celebrated alongside the November 11th Veterans Day.

The following is a list of bloody sacrifice to guarantee our freedom of religion, as well as, our other unique American liberties and freedoms: Casualties numbers are quoted from Wikipedia article: "United States Military Casualties of War" dated 18 October 2016:

American Revolution against the British Empire (1775-1783) 25,000 casualties

The War of 1812 also against the British Empire (1812-1815) 15,000 casualties

The Mexican War against the Republic of Mexico (1846-1848) 13,283 casualties

The American Civil War (1861-1865) 750,000 combined Union and Confederate casualties

The Indian Wars (1866-1890 – these years vary) *

The Spanish-American War against the Empire of Spain (1898) 2,446 casualties

World War I against Germany (1917-1918) 116,516 casualties

War War II once again against Germany/Axis Powers & Empire of Japan (1941-1945) 405,399 casualties

The Korean War against the Communist Koreans and Red China (1950-1953) 36,516 casualties

The Vietnam War against the Communist Vietnamese (1955-1975 – these year vary) 58,209 casualties

The Persian Gulf War against Iraq (1990-1991) 294 casualties

The never ending two-headed war against Islamic Terrorism in Iraq and Afghanistan beginning in 2001.

As of 18 Oct. 2016, as per the Wikipedia article, there were 4,497 casualties in Iraq and 2,356 in Afghanistan, 14 of which were in under my watch care in 2009 as their Chaplain.

From the American Revolution up to our current on-going conflicts, there have been over

1.4 million service members to give their lives for our American liberties and freedom to include our freedom of religion.

*There were thousands of US service members who were lost in the

so-called "Indian Wars" in the later part of the nineteenth century. Many American service members and civilians alike were also lost during the exploration and colonial period up through the American Civil War. An uncountable amount of American Indians have lost their lives to either "tribe on tribe" conflict, or against the American explorers, and settlers, as well as, American government service members in the last four hundred plus years. Also, thousands of American Services members were lost in a great number of mostly forgotten minor conflicts such as the Black Hawk Wars, The Barbary Coast Pirate Wars, Beirut, Grenada, and the like. Especially in the earlier wars, many service members died of disease such as dysentery and amputations gone bad. Additionally, in the early wars, record keeping in general was poor, including casualty reports. During this time, it was difficult to discern between dying weeks or months later from a combat inflicted wound, instead of dying from dysentery, or in many cases, expiring from both.

THANKSGIVING

March winds bring April showers, and April showers bring May flowers. But what do May flowers bring? Pilgrims of course! Every year on Thanksgiving Day … it's the same thing. After watching the morning's same-ol'-thing of the Macy's marching bands and helium filled balloon parade, many moms, grandmothers, mothers, and sisters of brothers, painstakingly attempt to produce a feast of all feasts to include: orange sweet potatoes, regular white mashed potatoes, with brown gravy, green beans, yellow corn pudding, with bronzed dinner rolls, maroon beets and cranberry sauce, dressing, apple pie, pumpkin pie, and so much more lest we forget the Turkey. The gobbler has been, with much mystery, put into the oven, and covered with shining silver foil, with the hopes of taking it out at the correct estimated time of proper cooking with, or without, the "button-thingy" popping up. Meanwhile out in the living room, or down in the den, the men are watching the Detroit Lions getting beat, which is always closely followed by the Dallas Cowboys, playing some other National Football League team. The men may be bragging, or remembering remorseful, and regretful stories of the previous week's deer hunt. Perhaps the younger cousins are playing out in the yard, and trying not to get too dirty while stepping on the prized potted plants and flowers, while playing some symbolism of football. After about an hour of group gorging resembling something similar to a cackle of Hyenas devouring a Zebra on the plains of the Serengeti, we cease and desist from eating. Finally, our American appetite is fulfilled with Turkey, and the never-ending seconds of side dishes, and the final slice of pie, which is strenuously shoved and pushed into our body. With the men folk lounging around in a semi-slumber state of conscientiousness, while the gridiron gladiators are blurring in vivid colors on the flat screen, suddenly the female of the species, with an unexplained resurrection of energy and enthusiasm, arise from the ashes of a mountain of dirty dishes, and go en-masse to the local mall to participate in the gladiator specter of near hand-to-hand combat with credit cards swiping and slashing at holiday sales which is called Black Friday Shopping. What does all of this have to do with Thanksgiving?

The Pilgrims, as we have come to know them, left merry ol' England because of religious persecution. The pilgrims referred to themselves as Puritans. They did not want to be a part of the Church of England. However, they did not come straight to the shores of America. First, they went to the nearby shores of the low country of Holland. The Pilgrims stayed here for a while, but left as they felt they were losing their English identity. From here, they set sail and went forth to the New World on the Mayflower. It is common knowledge, that in 1620, they landed at the so-called Plymouth Rock in what we now call the State of Massachusetts. Here, they were met by the Wampanoag Indians. However, Plymouth Rock was not the Pilgrim's intended destination. Their intended destination was the Jamestown colony in the Chesapeake Bay region, of what we now call Virginia.

The Pilgrims were not the first English to land in the Cape Cod region, as they were greeted by an Indian man called Squanto of the Pawtuxet Tribe. He already spoke English. In short, this man was captured by the English and taken to England as a slave. While in England, he learned the English language. Eventually he was brought back to America before 1620, where he joined the Wampanoag tribe, as his Pawtuxet tribe had been decimated by disease.

After a rough first year in the New World, many Pilgrims were stricken with disease and died. Others died from other various calamities. In 1621, they, with some of their Indian neighbors, had what we would call our first Thanksgiving meal. This was a time of prayer and of faith in God. This is the Christian connection to Thanksgiving. President George Washington in 1789 declared a holiday for the new nation. There is much debate as to how, who, and when, we actually got Thanksgiving as we know it today. What did they eat at this first meal? Yes, they did have turkey, which would also be joined with goose and ducks. They also had deer, fish, lobster, and shell fish of various sorts. Corn in mush and cake style was eaten, as well as fruits and berries. Pumpkins were stewed, as well as, pumpkin bread, but no pumpkin pie. This would have all been washed down with Pilgrim beer. As you, and your family, and friends sit down at the dinner table at about two o'clock on the fourth Thursday of November, try to remember what the Pilgrims endured in their flight from England because of religious persecution. Envision their rugged sea voyage across an unknown Atlantic. Envision the trials they survived in their first year in a foreign and unforgiving forest. Compare their first Thanksgiving meal to yours as you root on the Lions and Cowboys before you go Black Friday Shopping.

Questions and Discussion for
Appendix: of American Christian Holidays
Dig – Discover – Discuss

1. Discuss the impact of Christianity on the laws and traditions of the United States or your native country.

2. Discuss the impact of American secularism on American Christianity with regards to Christian based holidays.

3. Discuss how your family or friends celebrate various holidays.

4. Did you and your friends learn anything new from reading this book?
   Explain your conclusions.

5. Did this book change your view, or perspective on any issues in the Bible?

6. Did this book strengthen your faith in Jesus Christ? Explain

Post Script

With the rambling and rumbling of Fox News on my nearby TV, often with the concurrent background broadcast of my radio tuned to 700 WLW (often pronounced as *dub-yah el dub-yah)*, the creation of this work began in January of 2015. As life does, life happened, and work on this volume was put aside until writing resumed in January of 2016. The hope was to complete this odyssey that same winter. But as life would once again have it, winter turned to spring, spring turned to summer and likewise summer fell to the fall, and fall to winter, with completion nearly in sight as the discussion topics swelled in both number and depth. Finally, the actual writing phase was mostly completed around Christmas in 2016. I suppose I could have written more, with more variety of topics, with more clarity and depth. Writing a book is akin to eating bacon & Cheetos. At some point you just stop and say "Enough!" Remember, "A good idea is only a good idea, if other people think it is a good idea."

After many dangers, toils, and snares, the bulk of the editing (and re-editing and re-editing) absorbed the better part of 2017, finishing in early October. Also, during 2017, I hired on some interior graphics artist. I met Ariane L. Brown and her husband at Xavier University for an all hands "cattle call" for movie extras. The movie featured such stars as Robert Redford, Casey Affleck, Danny Glover, Sissy Spacek and Keith Carradine, in *The Old Man and the Gun.* I found Mr. Carradine to be a kind man. The movie was filmed partly in the Dayton-Cincinnati area. As luck would have it, I landed a spot as an extra in the movie as "Officer Gordon," a Dallas Policeman. I hope I made the cut. Additionally, Jennifer L. Martin of Centerville, Ohio, was later added to the interior art team. I met her through her mother, Patricia M. Acker, who is also a Dayton area author. In the summer of 2017, I was re-aqquainted with my third artist,

Connie S. Gifford. I was on staff at the Bellbrook Baptist Church where her husband, Jim Gifford, was the senior pastor in 2001-2002, before I got my commission as a Navy/Marine Corps Chaplain. And just for fun, I added in a couple of pencil drawings myself.

I do hope you and your discussion group friends enjoyed reading and discussing the topics displayed in this book as much as I enjoyed writing it. I trust your discussions were all done in the love of Christ, and founded on what the scripture says. Ultimately, I trust this book strengthened your faith in Jesus Christ, and your knowledge of the scripture. As an additional note, hopefully this work displaced any misunderstandings, false ideas, or beliefs you, and your friends may have had about the Bible.

Despite supposed human intelligence, academic pursuits, advancements in technology, religion, politics, culture, language, in any time or place, one thing is always for certain in this fallen uncertain sinful world, "Jesus Christ is the same yesterday, today and forever."

If you were not a Christian, I pray this book was a conduit to you giving your life to Jesus Christ as your eternal savior. This volume would not have been complete without offering a plan of salvation as a capstone. My late great Uncle Eugene Smith told me on several occasions, as a young minister, to always give an invitation at the end of a sermon, because we never know who is listening. We all need to be saved by the grace of Jesus Christ. I believe the following short story entitled as *Heaven's Junk Yard*, is the best part of the book. I believe this small, but true story, will bring a tear to your eye and a smile to your heart as it did mine.

Heaven's Junk Yard

Upon a visit to the Pigeon Forge/Gatlinburg area of Tennessee, I met a young man in May of 2016, who was an employee at our Westgate timeshare. (This same timeshare was severely damaged in the November 2016 forest fire.) His name was Donnie Coleman. He was also a part time youth minister at a local Freewill Baptist Church in Dandridge, Tennessee. If memory serves me correctly, the church was called the Muddy Run Church. Before being at Muddy Run, Pastor Coleman was in a church in Pikeville, Kentucky.

As Donnie began to speak and relay this touching story to me, a tear began its escape from the corner of my eye and made its salty journey down my cheek. Donnie had a young boy in his Pikeville youth group, who would be best described by all accounts as "un-churched," as was his family from which he came. As any good youth minister would discuss over the course of time, Donnie asked his young people the often ask question, "What does Heaven look like?" After the description in the book of Revelation was referenced, typical answers, responses, hopes, and wishful thinking, were expressed by the gathering of youth, before Donnie heard the following tear-jerking description of Heaven. This description might be best described as to what was *outside* the Pearly Gates.

The unchurched young man, with all earnestness of heart and thought, began to speak as the residual conversations and comments from the others, slowly echoed away. "Pastor Donnie, I am not real sure what Heaven looks like on the inside, but I know what it looks like on the outside." Mr. Coleman, being intrigued in his soul at this point, encouraged the young lad to continue as his peers also listened with bated anticipation. "On the outside of Heaven, all the way there from the graveyard, is a giant junkyard." "What?" the others replied in stunned awe. "It is a giant junkyard filled with wheelchairs, walkers, canes, and crutches, with some leg braces, and wooded legs, and fake arms. There's also lots of hospital beds, heart monitors, and breathing machines, with bunches of false teeth, glasses, wigs, and hearing aids. There's piles of pill bottles there too – the kind you can't get the lids off of. And right before you go in, there's tons of broken tombstones, and coffins 'cause in Heaven, we won't need 'em anymore Pastor Donnie. That's what Heaven looks like on the outside."

Did I need to write anything else?
. . . as this was the best page in the book.

Plan of Salvation-My Commitment to Jesus Christ

God loves us:
"For God so loved the world, that He gave His only begotten Son, that whosoever believes in Him should not perish but have everlasting life." -John 3:16

We all are sinners and need God: "For all have sinned and fall short of the glory of God." -Romans 3:23

Our Sin must be paid for: "For the wages of sin is death, but the gift of God is eternal life in Christ Jesus our Lord." —Romans 6:23

Salvation is for all: "For whoever calls on the name of the Lord shall be saved." -Romans 10:13

We can not get to God through our good deeds: "For by grace you have been saved through faith, and not of yourselves: it is the gift of God, not of works, lest anyone should boast. For we are His workmanship, created in Christ Jesus for good works, which God prepared beforehand that we should walk in them." -Ephesians 2:8-10

Do not delay: "Behold now is the accepted time: behold, now is the day of salvation." -II Corinthians 6:2

Believe!
"Believe on the Lord Jesus Christ and you will be saved." -Acts 16:31
Be Baptized!

"See here is some water. What hinders me from being baptized? Then Philip said, If you believe with all your heart, you may. And he answered and said, I believe that Jesus Christ is the Son of God. So he commanded the chariot to stand still. And both Philip and the eunuch went down into the water, and he baptized him." -Acts 8:36-38

I have already made my confession in Jesus Christ as my personal Lord and Savior and was baptized on __/__/_____ (day/month/year).

Dear Jesus, please forgive me of all my sins! Please accept my soul into your eternal heaven as I give my total life to You and want to live for You. Write my name in Your Lambs Book of Life.

Today __/__/_____(day/month/year), I, _____ (your name), make my profession of faith to follow Jesus Christ as my personal Savior and vow to follow Him in full emersion Biblical Baptism.

"Well done good and faithful servant" - Jesus, Matthew 25:23b

Printed in the United States
By Bookmasters